A Pioneer in Perfection

The True Story of Nadia Comanaci

A 90-Minute Biography *for kids*

Steven Matthews

Words Are Swords Publishing

A 90-Minute Biography Written by Steven Matthews

A Pioneer in Perfection: The Nadia Comaneci Biography

Copyright © 2021 by Words Are Swords Publishing. All rights reserved.

Published in the United States of America by Words Are Swords Publishing, Los Angeles, California.

www.WordsAreSwordsPublishing.com

No part of this book may be reproduced, stored in any retrieval system, or transmitted by any means, electronic, scanned, photocopied, or otherwise, without prior written permission of the author or publisher, with the exception of brief passages used for review.

A Pioneer in Perfection: The True Story of Nadia Comaneci A 90-Minute Biography

Written by Steven Matthews

First Edition.

A 90-Minute Biography Written by Steven Matthews

A Pioneer in Perfection: The Nadia Comaneci Biography

Dedication

This book is dedicated to all of the dreamers and doers out there. To all of the kids who want to be something when they grow up – never stop reaching for the stars!

A 90-Minute Biography Written by Steven Matthews

A Pioneer in Perfection: The Nadia Comaneci Biography

Table of Contents

Dedication 5

An Important Message from the Author 8

Chapter 1 Who is Nadia Comaneci? 10

Chapter 2 Nadia as a Kid 15

Chapter 3 1976 Olympics: A Legend is Born 21

Chapter 4 1980 Olympics: A Pioneer in Perfection 25

Chapter 5 Escape to America 30

Chapter 6 Finding Love 34

Chapter 7 Nadia Today: Still Nailing It 39

Chapter 8 Her Immortal Legacy 45

About the Author 50

Recommended Reading 51

A 90-Minute Biography Written by Steven Matthews

An Important Message from the Author

Like many kids all over the world, I grew up watching the Olympics with my family. Even when my parents went to sleep, I would often sneak into the living room and lay on the ground in darkness, illuminated only by the announcer on TV as he revealed the origin story for each of the world's greatest athletes – and no other athlete stood out more than the little Olympian gymnast from Soviet Russia, Nadia Comaneci.

I put my heart and soul into this book, and before we get to that I have one simple request: Please do not forget to leave a review for this book. The value of book reviews – even just a single review consisting of a few words – can have an tremendous positive impact on the trajectory of books, the people who read them, and the authors who write them.

Scan the QR code to leave a review for *A Pioneer in Perfection: The Nadia Comaneci Biography*.

If you spend the next 30 seconds leaving a review for this book within the marketplace you purchased it, it will not only help *me* enormously, but it will also help readers like you who are looking to be inspired by Olympic true stories.

A Pioneer in Perfection: The Nadia Comaneci Biography

Whether you choose to leave a review for this book now or later, by simply sharing one thing you learned or liked about this book in your review you will help support me writing more books like this and more readers around the world who are seeking similar books.

Thank you. I am grateful you have chosen to purchase this book and are taking the time to read it. You can find similar books by scanning the QR code below:

Thank you,

- Steven Matthews

A 90-Minute Biography Written by Steven Matthews

Chapter 1
Who is Nadia Comaneci?

How important are sports to you? Do you enjoy playing sports with your friends at school or in your neighborhood? Do you enjoy watching competitive sports on TV with your friends and family while you all cheer on your favorite athletes? Maybe you choose not to play spots altogether. No one is good at any sport the first few times they try it, but the only difference between an average kid and Olympic gold medalist is practice, practice, practice!

Whether you're watching professional sports on TV or cheering on your favorite team from the stands, there are few things on this earth that can make someone so excited, passionate, and motivated than professional competitive sports. It's that moment when the team that you grew up watching, followed every season and watched every game wins the championship that you can't help but feel like it was a major victory for you, as well.

Have you ever been playing a game of baseball with your friends and, just as you step up to bat, you picture yourself as Babe Ruth or Bryce Harper, ready to knock the ball out of the park? Maybe you play basketball and you like to image that you're Michael Jordan or Stephen Curry when you go in for a slam dunk. If you enjoy tennis, you might like to pretend that your Venus or Serena Williams when you backhand the tennis ball all the way across the court.

A 90-Minute Biography Written by Steven Matthews

No matter than sport you enjoy most, it's important to have an idol. Someone you can look up to and motivates you to train as hard as you possibly can so that, one day, you can beat all of the records that your idol holds. These are the trailblazer athletes that broke records that no one thought was possible before they did it. Only by learning from the most successful people in the world can we become the most successful people in the world.

Professional athletes need fans just as much as fans need professional athletes. When things look rough for athletes and they're in a pinch, it's the enthusiastic cheering from their dedicated fans that gives them the courage to overcome any obstacle. This is the same reason why we look up to professional athletes. Their stories inspire us, their strength empowers us and their skills and commitment to their sport is what motivates us to never give up.

For many aspiring gymnasts and professional gymnasts alike, for boys and girls all around the world, for disabled children and healthy children, from Romania to Oklahoma, Nadia Comăneci is a tremendous source of inspiration in their lives.

Among Nadia Comăneci's numerous achievements, she is most famous for winning three gold medals at the 1976 Summer Olympic games in Montreal, Canada. She also won two gold medals at the 1980 Summer Olympic games in Moscow, Russia. In 2000, the Laureus World

A Pioneer in Perfection: The Nadia Comaneci Biography

Sports Academy named Nadia one of the Athletes of the Century, a very prestigious honor. As the first gymnast ever to score a perfect 10 in *any* Olympic gymnastics events, Nadia is an inspiration to millions around the globe.

Nadia Comăneci believed that the only way to achieve success was by putting in lots and lots of hard work, but Nadia's breakthrough success wasn't just because she trained tirelessly since the age of six. Her outlook on life on and off of the mat is what drove her to continually improve herself as a gymnast and as a human being. Even after winning titles that no other gymnast held, Nadia still looked for different ways for her to improve her gymnastics routine.

But it's much more than her professional victories that make Nadia Comăneci a perfect 10. As we will see in the course of this book, Nadia Comăneci inspired greatness in everyone around her and believed that surrounding herself by positive and productive people was one of the keys to success in life.

Nadia Comăneci is still as relevant today as she was in 1980. Along with her husband, Olympic gold medalist Bart Conner, the two have created dozens of different charities and organizations that help people all over the world. All her life, Nadia Comăneci never stopped improving herself, the people she surrounded herself with and she never stopped improving the community and neighborhood she lived in.

A 90-Minute Biography Written by Steven Matthews

In this book, we will take a look at the story of Nadia Comăneci, from her early childhood, her rise to fame in the Romanian gymnastics community, her famous achievements in the 1976 and 1980 Olympic games, and even the victories that Nadia still achieves today in order to see what made her so successful.

> I worked hard in gymnastics since the time I was six years old until I retired at 23 years of age.
>
> *Nadia Comaneci*

Chapter 2
Nadia as a Kid

"Romanians have a saying, 'Not every dog has a bagel on its tail.' It means that not all streets are paved with gold. When I began my career, I just wanted to do cartwheels."

- Nadia Comaneci, Letters to a Young Gymnast

A 90-Minute Biography Written by Steven Matthews

Whatinfluenced Nadia's indomitable spirit and commitment to her craft that made her into the most well-known gymnast in the world? In this chapter, we will take a look at Nadia's family life growing up in Romania, her first experience with gymnastics at an early age as well as all of the other influences early on in her life which would help her become so successful later on.

Nadia Elena Comăneci was born in Onesti, Romania where she lived with her mother, Ștefania-Alexandrina Comăneci, who was a factory worker, and father, Gheorghe Nadia, who was a car mechanic, and little brother, Adrian Nadia, who was four years younger than Nadia. Nadia's mother named her after the protagonist in a Russian film that she saw when she was pregnant with Nadia. In the film, the main character was named Nadya, or Nadezhda in Russian, which means "hope".

Nadia, it turns out, wasn't a naturally flexible child herself, but she was strong, hugely competitive and very, very determined. As a child she dreamed of flying. Nadia didn't show much interest in playing with dolls and children's toys. Instead, she loved physical activities such as playing outside with her friends in the streets of Onesti, climbing and jumping on things. Nadia even broke four of her parent's couches by running and jumping on them when she was a kid.

A Pioneer in Perfection: The Nadia Comaneci Biography

Looking at Nadia's long career of high achievement, it's no surprise she started gymnastics at a very young age. Nadia started gymnastics when she was still in kindergarten with a local team who called themselves Flacara, which translates to "The Flame". It was "The Flame" that ignited Nadia's fiery passion for gymnastics at a very young age, which would burn bright for the rest of her life.

When Nadia was just 6 years old, she was chosen to attend Béla Károlyi's experimental gymnastics school after Károlyi spotted her and a friend, Viorica, doing cartwheels at school. Béla Károlyi was looking for female gymnasts that she could train from a very young age and when the recess bell rang and all of the kids when back to class, Károlyi started searching each and every classroom looking for Nadia and her friend Viorica. When she finally found the two in class, Károlyi told the girls about her gymnastics class and set up a meeting with their parents.

Nadia's childhood friend, Viorica Dumitru, would later go on to become one of Romania's top ballerinas.

Nadia was ecstatic and couldn't wait to start training at Béla Károlyi's gymnastics school. In 1968, when Nadia turned 7 years old, she began to train with Károlyi at one of the very first gymnastics schools in Onesti, Romania. From the very beginning of Nadia's gymnastic career at the age of 7, she trained tirelessly. She had an edge on the other girls in her gymnastics class because she lived close to the school, while most of the other girls had to commute from far way.

In 1969, when Nadia turned 8, she entered her first Romanian National Championships where she placed 13th. Even though she was only 8 years old, Károlyi was hard on Nadia. Károlyi gave her star pupil a ragged doll as a reminder that she should never place 13th again, as the number 13 would bring her bad luck for her entire gymnastics career. After that, Nadia went on to compete in hundreds of gymnastics competitions and never came in 13th place ever again.

The following year, Nadia began competing with the Onesti gymnastics team and went on to be the youngest gymnast to ever win the Romanian Nationals. Then, in 1971, Nadia competed in her first ever international competition, which was a dual junior meet between Romania and Yugoslavia. She won her first all-around title and contributed to her team winning the gold.

Over the next few years, Nadia continued to compete as a junior in competitions all throughout Romania and was beginning to make a name for herself. She represented Romania in dual meets with countries like Hungary, Italy, Poland and many more, winning most of her competitions. In 1973, when Nadia turned 11, she won the all-around gold

A Pioneer in Perfection: The Nadia Comaneci Biography

in addition to the vault and uneven bars title at the Junior Friendship Tournament.

It wasn't until Nadia was 1 year old that she won her first major international championship during the 1975 European Championships in Skien, Norway. During the international competition, Nadia won the all-around gold as well as gold medals on every single event, with the exception of the floor exercise where Nadia placed second.

That year, Nadia swept nearly every gymnastics competition she entered, winning the all-around gold at the Champions All event as well as placing first in the vault, beam, and bars the Romanian Nation Championships. That same year, Nadia entered the pre-Olympic test competition in Montreal, where she won the all-around and the balance beam golds, as well as silvers in the vault, floor, and bars behind accomplished Soviet gymnast Nellie Kim, who would prove to be one of her greatest rivals over the following years.

In March 1976, Nadia competed in the inaugural edition of the American Cup at Madison Square Garden in New York City where she received an unprecedented perfect score of 10. Her perfect routine without any deductions on the vault in both the preliminary and final rounds of competition won her the all-around gold. Nadia also received 10s in other meets in 1976, including the Chunichi

Cup Competition in Japan, where she posted perfect marks on the vault and uneven bars.

The international gymnastic community as well as the press started to notice Nadia, and she was named the United Press International's "Female Athlete of the Year" for 1975.

A Pioneer in Perfection: The Nadia Comaneci Biography

Nadia became the first Romanian gymnast ever to win the Olympic all-around title as well as holding the record for being the youngest Olympic gymnastics all-around champion ever. She is also the most recent female Olympic all-around champion to have competed at another Olympic Games after her all-around victory, a distinction that held in 2012 when Nastia Liukin, who had been the all-around champion in the 2008 Summer Olympics in Beijing, did not make the American team.

Nadia's victory at the Olympics made her a household name all over the world. The instrumental song from the soundtrack of the 1971 film, *Bless the Beasts and Children*, "Cotton's Dream" became associated with her after Robert Rigerused, a reporter for ABC, used the song in a video of slow-motion montages of Nadia on the television program *ABC's Wide World Of Sports*. The song became a top-ten single in the fall of 1976, and the composers, Barry De Vorzon and Perry Botkin, Jr., renamed it "Nadia's Theme" in Nadia's honor, although Nadia never officially performed any of her routines to the song.

In 1976, Nadia won the BBC Sports Personality of the Year award in the overseas athletes category as well as the Associated Press's 1976 "Female Athlete of the Year". She also retained her title as the UPI Female Athlete of the Year. Back home in Romania, Nadia's success led her to be awarded the "Sickle and Hammer Gold Medal" and named a "Hero of Socialist Labor".

You can still watch the original video from Nadia's Olympic performance and first perfect 10.0 on YouTube here:

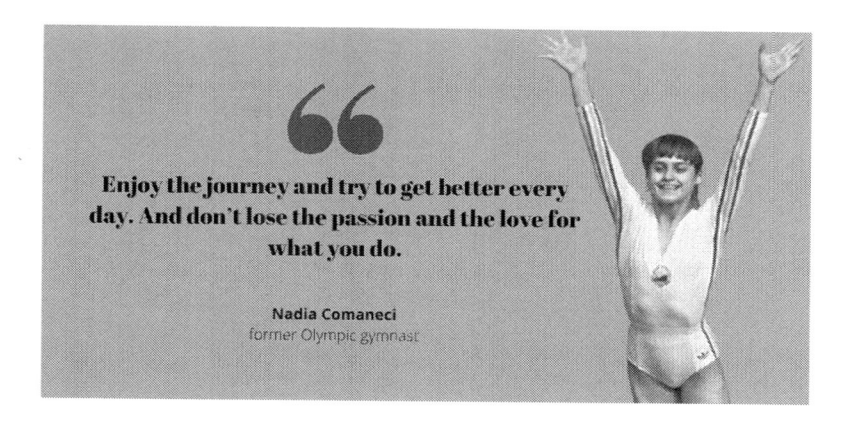

> Enjoy the journey and try to get better every day. And don't lose the passion and the love for what you do.
>
> **Nadia Comaneci**
> former Olympic gymnast

Chapter 4
1980 Olympics: A Pioneer in Perfection

A 90-Minute Biography Written by Steven Matthews

Even though she shattered records at the 1976 Olympics, Nadia never got complacent for a second. She continued to train harder and harder every day, but no amount of gymnastics training could have prepared her for what would happen next.

In 1977, Nadia successfully defended her European all-around title yet again, however, other competitors called the judge's scoring into question. Nadia's team was ordered to return home to Romania, which spurred a huge controversy when the girls had to leave the competition right before the final event.

Immediately after Nadia's team was ordered to leave the 1977 European's, the Romanian Gymnastics Federation separated Nadia from her longtime coach, Károlyis. Nadia was sent to Bucharest to train at an industrial sports complex called "August 23".

Nadia did not take the change very well. Her parents had recently gotten divorced, so the stress of that on top of losing her coach of 10 years while being thrown into a new training environment made her very depressed. As a result, her gymnastics and overall fitness suffered.

Nadia competed in the 1978 World Championships in Strasbourg looking heavier and out of shape; she was also several inches taller than in Montreal. A fall from the uneven bars resulted in a fourth-place finish in the all-around behind Soviets Elena Mukhina, Nellie Kim, and Natalia Shaposhnikova. Nadia did win the world title on beam, and a silver on vault.

After the 1978 "Worlds" competition, Nadia was permitted to return to her former coach, Károlyi. Nadia was overjoyed to be back at the side of her long-time coach and started training harder than ever. Her depression lifted, her health improved, her motivation returned in full force, and in 1979, a brand new and refreshed Nadia won her third consecutive European all-around title. Nadia was the first gymnast ever to achieve a threepete at the European's.

At the World Championships that December, Nadia led the field, however, she was hospitalized before the optional portion of the team competition for blood poisoning because of a cut on her wrist from her metal grip buckle. The doctors ordered Nadia to remain in the hospital overnight, however, she left the hospital and competed on the beam, where she scored a 9.95 which helped give the Romanians their first team gold medal.

After her performance, Nadia spent several days recovering in All Saints Hospital and underwent a minor surgical procedure for the infected hand, which had developed an abscess. Although disregarding the doctor's orders may have caused Nadia to further injure her wrist, the fact that she couldn't sit idly by in a hospital bed while her teammates needed her shows her true indomitable spirit and commitment to teamwork. The fact that, even on an injured wrist, Nadia was still able to score a 9.95 on the beam illustrates her true expertise and skill.

Nadia went on to participate in the 1980 Summer Olympics in Moscow, where she placed second, by a small margin, to Yelena Davydova in the individual all-around event. She successfully defended her Olympic title on the balance beam and tied with Nellie Kim for the gold medal on the floor exercise. Romania finished second in the team competition.

Then, in 1981, Nadia made the decision to retire from competitive gymnastics. Her official retirement ceremony took place in Bucharest in 1984 and was attended by the chairman of the International Olympic Committee as well as thousands of dedicated fans.

Because Nadia would constantly come under fire by the other gymnastics, who often claimed that she was cheating or that the judges were bias in their scoring, retiring from gymnastics competitions was one of the humblest and most gracious things that Nadia could do. The other gymnasts didn't think it was fair for Nadia to win every single competition and thought that she was hogging the limelight. Although she could have continued to win more competitions, one of the reasons influencing Nadia's retirement was to allow the other athletes a chance to win competitions as well. It takes great humility for a

A Pioneer in Perfection: The Nadia Comaneci Biography

Life was looking going great for Nadia after her victory at the 1980 Olympics, but little did she know that things were about to take a turn for the worst. Communist Romina was in a constant state of turmoil and Romanians were restless.

After retiring from competitions, Nadia participated in a gymnastics exhibition tour in the United States. During the tour, her coaches, Béla and Márta Károlyi, along with the Romanian team choreographer Géza Pozsár, all defected to America. After her return to Romania, Nadia's actions were strictly monitored. She was granted leave to attend the 1984 Olympics in Los Angeles but was supervised for the entire trip to make sure that she, too, would not defect. Aside from that journey, and a few select trips to Moscow and Cuba, Nadia was forbidden to leave the country for any reason. She was a prisoner of her own country.

In Romania, between 1984 and 1989, Nadia was a member of the Romanian Gymnastics Federation and helped coach the Romanian junior gymnasts. On the night of November 27, 1989, a few weeks before the Romanian revolution, she defected with a group of other young Romanians.

In an interview with The Daily Mail UK years later, Nadia expresses her true feelings the night she left Romania.

A 90-Minute Biography Written by Steven Matthews

"At that time, just before the revolution, leaving meant you were gone. You couldn't go back. I didn't tell my mum. I thought she'd have a heart attack. I told my brother, Adrian, who was and still is my best friend. I took him and my sister-in-law close to the Hungarian border with me. Then me and the six other gymnasts walked over the border into Hungary and from there to Austria. I went to the United States embassy and they provided me with a flight to New York. I've never talked about it before. It was hard that night. When I think back to that moment it's hard because I thought I was never going to see my family again. I didn't know the revolution was going to happen. If I had, would I have stayed? Yes, probably."

Leaving Romania was the most difficult challenge that Nadia had ever faced in her entire life. But just like all of the challenges that Nadia faced, this was something that she had to conquer in order to get to the next stage in her life.

A Pioneer in Perfection: The Nadia Comaneci Biography

When Nadia arrived in America, one of the Romanians who organized their escape, Constantin Panait, became her business manager and was constantly by her side. He was a married father of four and was very controlling of Nadia. When she arrived in the US, she looked bloated with spiky hair and fishnet stockings, which generated a lot of negative press for her. The news headlines talked more about her make-up and clothing than they did about her escaping Romanian oppression or her gymnastic achievements.

With the help of her long-time coach, Karolyi and his friend, Romanian rugby coach Alexandru Stefu, who lived in Montreal with his family, she was able to break away from Panait after two months and settle with her friends in Montreal, Canada, where she immersed herself back in her sport. Nadia spent most of her time touring and promoting lines of gymnastics apparel, aerobic equipment and modeling.

It wasn't until June 29, 2001, that Nadia became a naturalized citizen of the United States. She also retained her Romanian passport, making her a dual citizen.

A 90-Minute Biography Written by Steven Matthews

**Chapter 6
Finding Love**

A Pioneer in Perfection: The Nadia Comaneci Biography

The story of Nadia and her husband, Bart Conner, is a classic tale of star crossed lovers. For starters, they are both Olympic gold medal winning gymnasts, but that's not where their similarities end. They both showed an interest for gymnastics at a very early age. The two all-star gymnasts would end up meeting each other time and time again before they eventually ended up getting married.

While she was living in Montreal, former American gymnast Bart Conner, whom she had met for the first time in 1976 at the American Cup in New York, contacted her and invited her to live in Norman, Oklahoma. Their first kiss was in 1976 as a photo opportunity. Each had won a silver cup at a Madison Square Garden tune-up for the Montreal Olympics, where she would become a legend, the first perfect princess of gymnastics.

The two seemed fated to fall in love. While Nadia had already shattered more than her fair share of records in Romania and Europe, Bart Conner is the only American male gymnast to win gold medals at every level of national and international competition. Conner's glory is well known. His tireless training allowed him to become an Olympic Champion, USA Champion, NCAA Champion, Pan-American Games Champion, World Champion, and World Cup Champion.

Incidentally, Nadia and Bart Conner were both at the Olympic games in 1976 and 1980. Conner, however, also went on to participate in the 1984 Olympic games in Los Angeles, California. Nadia did not compete in the 1984 Olympic games in Los Angeles, California, therefore, Nadia and Bart missed connections once more. Conner won two gold medals and a perfect 10 on the parallel bars, which he used to get himself jobs, endorsements, the International Gymnast Magazine, a 1,000-student, 32-instructor gymnastics academy back home in Norman, Okla., and a beach house in Venice, Calif.

Not unlike Nadia, Bart Conner's interest in gymnastics began in grade school gym class when he excelled at acrobatic moves. As a child, Bart participated in many sports, but at every opportunity, he would try to stand on his hands for as long as he could. By the time he was a teenager, he had a set of parallel bars in his back yard and a pommel horse in his basement that he used every day.

In 1976, Bart Conner moved to Oklahoma to study journalism at the University of Oklahoma and joined the school's gymnastics team. There, he earned 14 NCAA All-America honors, and led his team to 2 NCAA team titles. That was also the year that Bart and Nadia first met.

Conner watched from afar, concerned for her and for the image of his sport. As a TV commentator, he was able to talk himself onto "The Pat Sajak Show" when she appeared. He sensed her fear of Panait. He offered help. He helped make the connections that eventually led to her escape from that abusive relationship, and a new life in Montreal with a Romanian rugby coach and his family.

The following year, Bart and Nadia spoke on the phone nearly every day. It wasn't long before romance bloomed and the two started working together, making appearances, and in the summer of 1991, in California, romance bloomed. They became engaged in 1994. With Conner, she returned to Romania for the first time since her defection and the couple were married in Bucharest on April 27, 1996. The ceremony was broadcast live in Romania, and the reception was held in the former presidential palace. Fifteen hundred guests have been invited. The train on her dress was 23 feet long.

Together, Nadia, Bart and their business partner, Ziert Today, own the world's premier gymnast magazine, International GYMNAST. They also have a gymnast supply company named GRIPS and produce gymnast grips, supports, tumbling shoes, equipment and gymnast collectibles. Bart and Nadia are also pioneers in pairs gymnastics, a sport-art form they invented, in which they tour around the world and do lyrical routines.

In 1991, Conner was inducted into the US Olympic Hall of Fame, and in 1997, he was inducted into the International Gymnastics Hall of Fame. In 2006, Conner's 1984 Olympic Gold medal-winning team was inducted into the US Olympic Hall of Fame. Conner also now serves as the President and

A 90-Minute Biography Written by Steven Matthews

Chairman of the Board of the International Gymnastics Hall of Fame.

Nadia and Conner welcomed their first child, a son named Dylan Paul Conner, on June 3, 2006, in Oklahoma City, Oklahoma.

Today, Conner, Comaneci, and their five-year-old son, Dylan Paul Conner, enjoy traveling the world and delivering inspirational speeches to young athletes while promoting their own charities, gymnastics, fitness, and healthy lifestyles.

Chapter 7
Nadia Today: Still Nailing It

A 90-Minute Biography Written by Steven Matthews

Nadia and Bart live together with their son, Dylan, in Oklahoma City, Oklahoma. Nadia is active in many charities and international organizations and has a long history of giving back to the community. In 1999, she was the first athlete to be invited to speak at the United Nations to launch the Year 2000 International Year of Volunteers.

In the world of gymnastics, Nadia is the honorary president of the Romanian Gymnastics Federation, the honorary president of Romanian Olympic Committee, sports ambassador of Romania, and a member of the International Gymnastics Federation Foundation. She and her husband own the Bart Conner Gymnastics Academy, the Perfect 10 Production Company, and several sports equipment shops. They are also the editors of International Gymnast magazine.

You can still occasionally see Nadia and Conner on TV providing commentary for many gymnastics meets, most recently the 2005 World Championships in Melbourne, Australia, and the 2008 Olympic Games in Beijing, China. Additionally, several spotswear companies, such as Addidas, will use footage from one of Nadia's performances in their commercials.

At this point in their lives, any retired professional athletes could have chosen to live out the rest of their days in luxury and not let the rest of the world bother them. While

A Pioneer in Perfection: The Nadia Comaneci Biography

Nadia and Bart could have settled down in a big, secluded house with their son and lived out the rest of their lives in comfort, the two proved time and time again that they were never the type of people to simply walk away when there is still room for improvement. The two have dedicated their lives to the betterment of others and are active in a wide variety of charities and support many causes that they passionately believe in.

She has also personally funded the construction and operation of the Nadia Children's Clinic, a clinic in Bucharest that provides low-cost and free medical and social support to Romanian children. In 2003 the Romanian government appointed her as an honorary counsel general of Romania to the United States to deal with bilateral relations between the two nations.

Who would have thought when Nadia fled Romania all those years ago that she would end up being appointed a position by the Romanian government? The home country eagerly welcomed Nadia and her humanitarian efforts back into the country and Nadia was happy to finally return to Romania, although only briefly. Nadia still works tirelessly to build relations between the US and Romania.

Both Nadia and Bart are members of the Board of Directors for the Special Olympics. They have traveled all over the world to support the mission of Special Olympics to give opportunities to those with special needs through sports training and competition.

"I have seen firsthand the transformative power of this important movement to change people's perceptions about the potential for people who face intellectual challenges." Nadia said famously after becoming a member of the Board of Directors of the Special Olympics.

Nadia is the founding member of the Laureus Academy, whose mission is to use sports as a tool for social change by celebrating excellence in all sports. The Laureus Academy currently includes 46 living legends from all over the world and in all different sports.

Both Nadia and Bart are volunteers and supporters of the Muscular Dystrophy Association. The MDA provides research and patient services and, more importantly, provide hope for individuals and families who have been affected by neuromuscular disease.

Nadia also started The Nadia Comaneci Foundation in Bucharest, Romania. When establishing her non-profit foundation, Nadia made sure that it would not be affiliated with any political or government organizations. The purpose of The Nadia Comaneci Foundation is to provide encouragement, support and promotion of exceptional performance in any field of sport, thereby educating and improving the overall lives of the Romanian people.

A Pioneer in Perfection: The Nadia Comaneci Biography

As members themselves, both Bart and Nadia support the mission of the International Gymnastics Hall of Fame in preserving the legacies and inspiring stories of the most accomplished gymnasts in the world.

Bart is proud of the state where he grew up and is constantly working to improve the community any way he can. He is an active member of the Board of Directors of Creative Oklahoma, who endeavors to establish the state of Oklahoma as an epicenter for creativity and innovation in education, commerce and culture.

Bart also owns and operates The Bart Conner Gymnastics Academy in Norman, Oklahoma is one of the largest and most well-equipped gymnastic centers in the world where hundreds of the best gymnasts' train every day.

The two hold their annual multi-sport, health and wellness event, The Bart & Nadia Sports Experience, in Oklahoma to promote good choices when it comes to personal health and wellness by offering free health screening and interactive fitness challenges. Through this event, Bart and Nadia hope to encourage young people to be more proactive about their own fitness and health goals.

The two started their very own TV production company, Perfect 10 Productions, Inc. in 1998 in order to promote televised gymnastics events from all over the world. The TV

A 90-Minute Biography Written by Steven Matthews

station also broadcasts Nadia's own gymnastics competition, The Nadia Comaneci International Invitation.

Today, Nadia is still one of the most influential voices in the world of gymnastics, but as we can see from all of her modern achievements, vault was a piked Tsukahara (a half-turn pre-flight followed by a piked back salto). Later she vaulted a tucked Cuervo (handspring half turn into tucked back salto).

On the uneven bars, Nadia performed her own release move, a kip to immediate straddled front salto to regrasp the high bar. The skill is named after her in the 2013-2016 women's *Code of Points*, where it is currently rated an "E" element (worth 0.5 points). Also named after her is the "Nadia dismount," an under swing half turn into a back salto. According to the Code of Points, this dismount is rated as a "B" element (worth 0.2 points).

Nadia is one of the only gymnasts to leave a legacy outside of the gymnastic world as well. She became a household name by 1980 after impressing audiences around the world at the Olympic games and she is still a relevant pop culture icon who is references in movies, television shows, and in songs.

As we have seen through the course of this book, Nadia Comăneci's life is an inspiration to many, but her perfect gymnastics career was only one part of that. What made Nadia Comăneci so successful was her attitude. No matter what challenge was presented to her or what obstacle she encountered, it was the mentality that she could conquer anything which made her score a perfect time effortlessly. Though Nadia no longer competes in gymnastics, she still applies the same mentality of continual improvement by helping her community in any way that she can.

Everyone needs an idol. Someone to look up to and to motivates you to train just as hard as you possibly can so that, one day, you can beat all of the same records that your idol holds. After all, if someone else was able to break those records, there is no reason that anyone else can't break the same records after enough practice. But, just like Nadia, it's going to take a lot of hard work and training both your mind and your body. Only by learning from the most successful people in the world can we become the most successful people in the world. There will always be records to break and there will always be room to improve – and that is the attitude that Nadia Comăneci which makes her so successful.

A Pioneer in Perfection: The Nadia Comaneci Biography

"Friend, no one ever accomplishes your dreams for you, regardless of tears, fits, or any other means of manipulation. They can give you ideas and direction, but in the end, you have to do it alone. You must figure out your own destination and the best route to get there because no one else knows the way."

— Nadia Comaneci, Letters to a Young Gymnast

A 90-Minute Biography Written by Steven Matthews

About the Author

Bestselling author Steven Matthews has lived a life full of adventure and intrigue. Born into poverty, Steven had to learn a variety of skills to survive. He's worked as an app developer for a while, then opened series of restaurants, then started a cannabis growing operation, built it up, and sold it. He used the money to build and live in a tiny house for a few years while traveling around North America meeting people and doing odd jobs, he wanted to see more. When he realized he couldn't take his house across the ocean, Steven sold it and moved to China for a few years… That's when things got interesting.

Today, Steven lives in the desert outskirts of Las Vegas in a house he built himself. Together with his American Eskimo, Gala (Portuguese for "Lady Killer"), Steven is determined to catalog all of the information he's picked up over the years by writing a new book each week. He hopes to hit 100 published books by next year.

See all of Steven Matthew's published books by scanning the QR code below:

A Pioneer in Perfection: The Nadia Comaneci Biography

Recommended Reading

90-minute biography series

The 90-minute Biography series written by Steven Matthews are fast and fun reads for fans in every walk of life. You can find them at any book retailer.

The Many Faces of John McAfee -
Biography of an American Hustler

The world-renowned computer scientist, activist, business leader and cryptocurrency evangelist made himself a career that spans nearly the entire history of computing.

Jon Stewart

Beloved former host of the Daily Show turned Academy Award winner, how Jon Stewart Went from Making Political Jokes to Changing the World

A Very Stephen Colbert Biography

From The Colbert Report to The Late Show, how Steven Colbert made headlines going from fake news to real comedy.

Learning from Steve Jobs

His Inventions, His Principles, His Life & Finding Innovation in an Age that Needs It Most. These are the immortal lessons that entrepreneurs around the world learned from Steve Jobs.

Other Books by Steven Matthews

Interested in being the best version of yourself you can be? Here are more self-improvement books by Steven Matthews.

Learn to Conquer Any Fear, Phobia, or Anxiety in Under 60-Minutes

This book explains the fundamental strategy that people around the world use to conquer their fears and phobias permanently! Even the most stubborn of irrational phobias can be conquered, thereby lowering your stress levels and dramatically improving your health. All it takes is 60 minutes of your time. What have you got to lose?

YOUR CLOTHES ARE KILLING YOU! The Little -Known Fact About How Some Fabrics Heal & Some Can Kill

This book is a deep dive into the fascinating world of fabrics, and if "fascinating fabrics" sounds like an oxymoron to you, then just try and say that after reading this book! You don't have to be a seamstress, sewing machine junkie, or even a fan of fashion to benefit from this book, and who knows? It may even save your life.

The Laws of Persuasion, Manipulation & Influence

This book will help you to better understand these laws and gives situational examples of how they can be used to influence others. You will also learn the principles of influence in dark persuasion psychology that are proven to work on the human brain.

Homestead Secrets

Homestead Secrets is the perfect book for dreamers who are still weighing the options of starting a homestead and homestead beginners who are just starting out, as well as intermediate homesteaders who just need a few more good ideas on how to make money homesteading or marketing the products and services they currently produce on the homestead.

Everything but the Wood Tiny House Essential Information + Free Tiny House Building Blueprints & Floor Plans

The author understands that building your first Tiny House can be scary! Rest assured that all of the tools in this one book will arm you with the knowledge and confidence you need to build a tiny home that will be an endless source of adventure for generations to come - No experience necessary!

Perfection is a Lie: A Weight-Positive Book of Body Acceptance, Self-Esteem & Confidence

Perferction is a Lie is the body-positive book that understands what teenagers are going through will help walk them through building healthy expectations when it comes to self-acceptance, self-esteem and self-image.

A 90-Minute Biography Written by Steven Matthews

Thank you for reading!

Don't forget to leave a review for the book by scanning the QR code below with any smartphone camera.

See all books written by Steven Matthews.

Made in the USA
Middletown, DE
19 November 2021

AMERICAN RAIN

A NOVEL

by

Jim Stempel

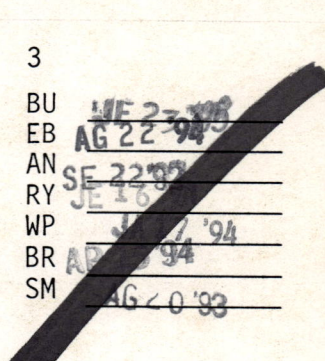

Monacacy River P
9095 Bessie Clemson R
Union Bridge, MD 21

©1992 Jim Stempel. Printed and bound in the United States of America. All rights reserved. No part of this book may be reproduced or transmitted in any form or by any means, electronic or mechanical, including photocopying, recording, or by an information storage and retrieval system—except by a reviewer who may quote brief passages in a review to be printed in a magazine or newspaper—without permission in writing from the publisher. For information, please contact Monacacy River Press, 9095 Bessie Clemson Road, Union Bridge, MD 21791, (301) 898-0300.

ISBN 0-9629340-9-7

LCCN 91-061017

Although the author and publisher have made every effort to ensure the accuracy and completeness of information contained in this book, we assume no responsibility for errors, inaccuracies, omissions, or any inconsistency herein. Any slights of people, places or organizations are unintentional.

ATTENTION CORPORATIONS, COLLEGES, UNIVERSITIES, AND PROFESSIONAL ORGANIZATIONS: Quantity discounts are available on bulk purchases of this book for educational purposes, gifts, or fund raising. Special books or book excerpts can also be created to fit specific needs. For information, please contact our Special Sales Department, Monacacy River Press, 9095 Bessie Clemson Road, Union Bridge, MD 21791, (301) 898-0300.

This book is dedicated to my mother and father.

1

Why stay? Why hang on when all the pretensions you've struggled to hold close for a lifetime suddenly sift through your fingers like ashes? Why cling to routine, merely trading day for night, day after day, when the excuses have all burned out and the embers of self-delusion aren't worth fanning anymore? For when the smoke screens clear, and the sad truths of our lives become self-evident, the beginning and the end merge into a strange vagueness, a hazy series of events that lack distinction. And life without distinction, without a sense of today and tomorrow, up or down, quickly loses momentum. Finally, it just stops. It can be a frightening time.

Such a time came for me. I was leaning against the window casement, waiting for the students to fill my last period class. I was watching a tumble of clouds to the west, the frenzy of cars on the highway—nothing in particular. It was May. Suddenly I was filled with an awful comprehension of futility. At once the world and everything in it seemed absurd. Every smile, every effort, every cry in the night seemed nothing more than foolishness. The sense of this rattled me with such intensity that I almost collapsed. I dismissed the class and went outside.

I felt hollow. I sat on a bench near the practice fields until they were empty and the sunset glowed red. At that moment, I knew I would never again be able to pretend what I was doing, what I had been doing as far back as I could remember, was in any way meaningful or central to my ultimate desires. I realized vividly that time—which had once seemed limitless—was now working against me. I would have to act decisively or forever resign myself to a life of compromise and disillusion. It was a turbulent, dreadful, magnificent moment. In an instant, the thought of simply packing my bags and leaving for anywhere at all seemed no more foolish or irresponsible than staying on in a life that was utterly beside the point.

So why stay?

The next day, I composed and delivered a letter of resignation. It was a strangely simple thing to do. Over the next few weeks, I said goodbye to those who cared and loaded the few belongings that mattered into my car. I packed light. I played out the remaining school days, and when the last bell rang on the last day, I waved so long and headed down the road. I didn't look back.

Like everyone, I suppose, I had always felt destiny held for me some special, immutable distinction. But now I'd come to see it would never be realized by just waiting and pacing. Nothing, it became clear, ever was. Only effort is rewarded, and that only occasionally. Tomorrow is there for everyone, but destinies must be claimed.

I had no idea how to proceed. I only knew a first step had to be taken and this step would, of necessity, have to be away from the past. Other than that, the exact direction didn't matter.

Heart racing, I yanked the tie from my neck on the last day of school and tossed my jacket into the back seat. Like a wolf sniffing the breeze for a scent, I stood at the open door and took a deep breath of the windy afternoon. I laughed with excitement.

The world can be a strange and dangerous place, but I felt no fear at that moment. I felt only the thrill of anticipation and the challenge of the quest. Gripped by a sense of adventure, I started the car and pulled from my parking spot. I was thirty-two years old and starting anew. Yet the faint voice of destiny that whispers to us all was calling me loudly that June afternoon. I could hear it clearly above the engine's roar. In fact, it was all I could hear. What it wanted of me I could not tell, but I resolved at that moment never to give up the search until my destiny—whatever it was—had been claimed.

I slipped the gear shift into drive. Success owes more to conviction than it does to brains, more to persistence than vision. The choice was simple. I stepped on the gas pedal and turned the wheel toward the open road. It was done.

2

The open highway stretched before me, I imagined, like a magic carpet. I made my way down I-95, crossed the Susquehana River and rumbled into Maryland. The countryside was green and lush. My '79 Ford rattled up the palisades from the river as wind swirled in from the open window. The sun was high. I was free.

My course south had come to me almost providentially, it seemed, just two weeks prior to my departure. It was then my mother had received a telegram from my Uncle Max's rather ornately-named attorney, Henri Goldleaf Lafayette III, informing us of Max's unfortunate and untimely demise. Further, his only worldly possession of any consequence—a dilapidated residence off Charles Street in Baltimore—had been left to none other than me.

That I should benefit so substantially from Max's demise seemed to me profoundly justifiable, for over the years I had been the only member of the family who spoke to him or showed him even the simplest of courtesies. It was no secret Max had been the black sheep of our family. He drank like a fool, ruined three marriages with his constant drunken debauchery, and never worked for an honest day's wage in his life. He ate like a pig, farted like a foghorn, and was considered by even casual acquaintances to be one of the most vile and despicable men on earth.

That he considered me a sporting chap I considered a mixed blessing—for my mother, his sister, had forbidden even the mention of his name in our house since I was thirteen years old. He favored me because once in my young and foolish years, I had displayed the pluck necessary to smuggle a quart of imported escargot, three bottles of champagne, and a dozen chocolate eclairs into his sickroom. At the age of thirty-three, he was suffering from his third serious ulcer condition and had been placed on a strict diet that he could not abide for even an hour. He bribed the newspaper boy to bring him pizza and beer, the mailman Kentucky bourbon.

I can see him still—sitting on the bed with a fat cigar stuck in the corner of his mouth, round belly sticking out of his pajamas like a hairy balloon—as I ever-so-carefully made my way along the outside ledge of his window. When he saw me there, he cackled with glee and bounced from the bed like a child at Christmas. He pulled me carefully through the window then devoured the snails, champagne and eclairs in a display of outrageous gluttony the likes of which I had never before imagined possible. All the while he sat puffing on his cigar, gulping, farting, slurping and burping. I sat there slack-jawed until he emitted a final, thunderclap of a burp, and wiped the goop from his face with the back of his sleeve. For this, I received an IOU for $1.25 and Max's undying admiration. Five minutes later, his wife was frantically dialing an ambulance.

Not long after, we moved to the Garden State and I more or less lost track of him. Occasionally, his name would pop-up in conversation—generally whenever talk ran towards depraved and suicidal lifestyles, diseased minds, or manic infidelity. The last I had heard of him—and that had been at least four years ago—was that he had taken to impersonating the indigent and was successfully begging door-to-door in the more affluent neighborhoods of North Baltimore—a practice which he had evidently developed into a reasonably lucrative profession of sorts.

That he had reportedly died of a heart attack while vigorously rutting between the legs of a harlot, so outraged and offended my entire family they refused to acknowledge him in death anymore than they had in life—although the unofficial reaction to his passing was a sigh of good riddance. My mother didn't even want me to consider accepting the home he had left me, but I had other ideas. As to Uncle Max, I came to know through the good offices of his attorney, Henri Goldleaf Lafayette III, that he had been buried unceremoniously in a meager plot in West Baltimore. The contents of his last will and testament were forwarded to us as his last request.

I arrived in Baltimore about four in the afternoon. The sky was still bright blue, and my spirits were high. I drove down Charles Street through the plush suburbs of Roland Park and found Max's old street. The route came back to me with ease. I pulled-up in front of the house and was immediately struck by the change. I leaped from the car and stood on the sidewalk staring.

The house had originally been built by Max's father who'd had a lucrative position with the B & O Railroad. He'd left it, along with a considerable trust for it's upkeep, in excellent condition to Max. A substantial dwelling of colonial design, upon Max's occupancy it decayed almost immediately into a neighborhood eyesore. Paint chipped, gutters collapsed, and stairwells all but rotted out, as Max, with nary a thought toward work or repairs, chased women around the block and drank himself into a stupor. Over the years, it sagged and cracked into utter disrepair. The last time I saw the grand old place, it was almost uninhabitable, windows out, yard overrun, bugs and mice everywhere.

Thus it was a shock of considerable magnitude when I stood on the sidewalk and surveyed the place now as neat and prim as a gingerbread house. It was like a jewel. The paint was fresh and immaculate, the lawn manicured to perfection. The grounds were lovely, the roof redone. Around the perimeter of the yard ran a white picket fence that ended at the front walk. There a small wooden sign dangled from a golden chain. It read:

> H. Goldleaf Lafayette III, Attorney at Law

And immediately below that:

> The Center for Psychiatric Retribution
> H. Goldleaf Lafayette III, M.D., Ph.D.

I rubbed my chin. I put my hands in my pockets. What was Max's attorney doing in my new house? Was Mr. Lafayette a psychiatrist as well as an attorney, and if so, what in the world was The Center for Psychiatric Retribution? I walked up the front steps to the door where a small gold sign implored me to enter. I did.

The interior of the house was astonishing. Where once rodents had roamed with impunity, the rooms stretched before me all mahogany, leather and good taste. Costly paintings lined the walls. The carpeting was Persian and expensive. An attractive young lady looked up from a desk.

"Can I help you?" she asked with a smile.

"Well, I suppose I'd like to see Mr. Lafayette," I replied.

"Do you have an appointment?"

"No. I just got into town this minute."

"Well," she said, motioning to all the people waiting in what was once the living room, "Dr. Lafayette is a very busy man."

"Yes, I can see that. But I'm not here for professional help. I'm here about the house."

"The house?"

"Yes," I said. "Let me see if I can make this short. My name is Don Mallory and my Uncle Max used to own this house. I believe Dr. Lafayette used to be his lawyer."

She was unimpressed. "Dr. Lafayette has many, many clients and patients."

"Well, anyway," I continued, "my Uncle Max died not too long ago and left this house to me. Dr. Lafayette wrote to my family and sent all the details." I fumbled through my pockets for the letters. "Here," I held them out to her.

She looked them over quickly. "Would you care to have a seat? I'll see what I can do for you."

"Sure," I answered.

She slipped from behind the desk and disappeared down the hall. She was slender, long-legged, and buxom. Dr. Lafayette, I surmised, had fine taste in women.

In a few minutes she returned and approached me directly. Dr. Lafayette, she announced, would labor to squeeze me into his impossibly busy schedule. Would I care for some champagne, caviar, espresso or pastry while I waited? I was impressed. Espresso, I decided, would do nicely.

I sat in the waiting room for about half an hour and watched the crowd slowly dwindle. I sipped the espresso and pretended to examine the paintings but could not help but notice that the entire staff consisted of beautiful young women, each one better looking and more remarkably proportioned than the next. Pleasant scenery but strange, I thought, for a doctor's office. Then I spotted him. He approached through what used to be the library. He was short and extremely rotund, but impeccably attired in a well-fitted gray pin-stripped suit. He walked slowly and, it appeared, with great care. It was a waddle I recognized immediately. I could hardly believe my eyes.

Henri Goldleaf Lafayette III entered the waiting room and stopped a few feet from where I was seated. He made a small bowing motion—clearly, all he could manage—and clapped his hands together. "Monsieur Mallory!" he exclaimed, "I have, of course, been expecting you." He smiled politely."I trust the espresso is to your liking?"

But I was thunderstruck and could not reply. For under the million dollar silk suit, behind the imported Italian tie, and that handlebar mustache, I knew, was none other than my thought-to-be deceased Uncle Max.

He stepped forward slightly. "My young friend," he continued with a look of great sympathy, "the news of your beloved uncle's passing was a great and devastating blow to us all. The entire Free State of Maryland mourns him, I can assure you. I trust your journey to our fair city was a pleasant one?"

"Indeed," I said, starting to fidget.

He motioned back toward the library. "Could you possibly see clear to join me for a spot of tea? We have much to discuss."

"Lead on, Henri."

He lead me quite ceremoniously back through the library to his office and quickly shut the door. He spun abruptly and beamed at me through his mustache. "Donny boy!" he almost shouted, "How the hell ya doing?"

"M-Max," I stammered, "just what in blue blazes is going on?"

He drew himself up and held out both arms to encompass the entire house. "Like it?" he asked. "Your old Uncle Max is doing pretty good for himself, eh Donny?"

I shook my head sternly. "Max," I admonished, "just who the hell you trying to kid here? You can't go around impersonating a doctor. Someone's going to nail you to the wall for this."

"Not just a doctor, Donny," he hastened to clarify, "a psychiatrist. Didn't you see the M.D., Ph.D. out front on the sign? Hmm, maybe I need a bigger sign. And, oh yeah, I'm a lawyer now, too."

"MAX!" I wailed, "you can't do this. Thi-thi-this," I stuttered, "is nothing but an outrageous fraud."

He stepped back as if struck. "Fraud?" he complained. "Donny, I can assure you," he went on, "this is no fraud. I am a well-credentialed and respected professional." He pointed to the diplomas on the wall. "See for yourself."

I walked passed him quickly and stared at the diplomas in disbelief. They were from some of the finest universities in the country. It was impossible. "These are fakes," I said.

He waddled over to his desk and picked up the phone. "See for yourself," he challenged. "Go ahead, give'em a call."

I grabbed the phone and hung up the receiver. "You're serious."

"As serious as I've ever been about anything in my entire life," he replied.

"But that's just the point, Max," I laughed. "You've never been serious about anything in your entire life. Ah," I scoffed, waving the whole thing aside, "it seems to me all the years of booze and debauchery have finally addled your brain."

He pointed a quick finger at my nose. "Watch yourself there, Donny. That sounds dangerously close to slander to me."

I laughed in his face. "Yeah, Max. You're going to sue me, right?"

"I have an itchy trigger finger, boy," he warned. "If I thought you had anything worth taking, I'd name you in a complaint tomorrow." Then he smiled. "But that's not why I got you down here."

I hesitated. "What's that supposed to mean?"

"You'll see."

I laughed again. "Come on, Max," I said, "I'm finding it real hard believing you set all this up by yourself. I think I'm dreaming."

He pointed at me again. "Hey, I'm warning you there, Donny, don't go messing with my reputation like that. I'll get a judgement against you and slap a lien on your earnings for the rest of your life. Or perhaps you're suffering from some kinda neurosis or other. I'll diagnosis your butt off and have you tossed into the nuthouse for keeps."

I was astonished. "Max," I implored, "what in the world has happened to you? Why, the last I heard you were stiffing the rich folks up in Towson, acting like a bum or something. . . . Now this?"

He slumped. "Son, you have one of the most legally deficient minds I have ever encountered. I can see your mother's misguided influence in you, for sure. Why,

15

virtually every other word out of your mouth is actionable nowadays. Looks like I've really got my work cut out for me." He folded his arms across his chest and took a deep breath. "Well," he continued, "let's start with this. The term is not bum. I was not acting like a bum. I was researching the homeless. Got it! I am a professional. I do not *stiff* people. I do research during the course of which I encounter certain, shall we say . . . *expenses*. Bum is a very bad word these days. Very derogatory, very actionable. Big, big bucks suing people for using words like bum nowadays."

I was dumbfounded. "You really are an attorney."

"You bet your butt I am. And a psychiatrist too."

"But Max," I protested, "it takes years and years of schooling to earn just one of those degrees. Here you have several advanced degrees, yet you didn't even finish high school."

He pointed proudly toward the wall. "I assure you, Donny, my degrees are all perfectly legitimate, and from first-rate institutions."

"But they're not in your name, Max. They're all made out to H. Goldleaf Lafayette III."

"I am Henri Goldleaf Lafayette III. Max is no more."

I smiled slowly. "Something smells, Max."

"You mean Henri, don't you?"

"OK, . . . Henri. Now come clean."

"It's nice to see flashes of that spunk I've always admired in you, Donny. It's just a shame you decided to bury it for so many years in that dead-end academic nonsense you were into."

"Hold on, Max," I protested. "I earned two degrees myself. I've studied the history of the world, the history of our nation. I learned a lot."

"You learned a lot, yet you understand exactly nothing. That's why you're stumbling around now. That's why it was so easy to lure you down here."

He walked over to his desk and opened a decanter. "Brandy?"

"Sure," I said.

"Cigar? Sit down, Donny," he said with a wink. "Your real education is about to begin."

3

Max leaned back on his leather chair and puffed thoughtfully on a fat cigar. "It is true," he started off slowly, "that for a period of time I was a self-employed researcher studying the lifestyles of the homeless and the reactions they elicit from the more affluent segment of our population." He stroked his chin carefully. "It was in the course of this residency, as I now like to call it, that certain profound social principles became evident to me." The door jerked open and Max clapped his hands joyously. "Ah, refreshments," he cried. "And just in time. I'm starving."

A uniformed maid wheeled in a giant cart overstocked with delicacies.

"Before dinner, I generally enjoy a little picker-upper just to keep me going, Donny," he said. "Let's just see what looks good this afternoon."

We both stood as she wheeled the cart up to us and gingerly disappeared. "Hmm," drooled Max, "Swedish meatballs, pastas, Waldorf salad, baked salmon, some nice looking New York strips, caviar, oysters, and clams casino. Anything look good to you? For dessert we have some strawberry tarts, banana pie, various assorted puddings and cookies." He looked at me. "What do you say, Donny?"

I could hardly believe my eyes. It smelled delicious. "Well, yeah, I guess. Maybe a little salad, couple oysters, and some steak might do."

He beamed at me. "Dig in."

We both filled our plates and returned to his desk. Max opened a bottle of California chardonay and poured two glasses full. "You see," he continued, talking around enormous mouthfuls, "I must admit that in my initial outings, I did carry on as would your every day trickster or con artist, trying to connive my way into people's wallets with a clever slant or line. Vaudevillian, almost. But what astounded me about it all, Donny, was not that it worked, but how well it worked. It was incredible! I tell you, except for a few tightwads here and there, I was rarely rebuffed at all! Business, or, research rather, wasn't good. It was splendid. Well, kid, I put in some damn long hours, I'll have you know, but all the while this whole thing kept nagging at me, see. Then one night bang! The answer hit me right between the eyes: I was no longer just a simple con running my own nickel-and-dime gig. I had become a merchant of atonement."

I chewed a mouthful of oysters, washed them down with a generous gulp of wine, and laughed out loud. "Bullshit," I said.

He quickly pointed at me. "Don't laugh," he protested. "Think about it, Don. Why the hell do you think all these rich people were so damn happy to throw their money at me? GUILT! That's why! And that's when I realized that I wasn't just a bum or beggar to them, but a means of allaying their sense of guilt. A mechanism. Here all along I had been in the business of guilt reversal, or atonement achievement as I like to call it now, and didn't even know it. But once I realized it . . . oh boy . . . business flourished to say the least. There was absolutely nothing too outrageous to ask for. Money, food, jewels, sex—you name it, I got it. Wanna couple more oysters there, kid?"

"Thanks," I slid a few more onto my plate. "So tell me," I went on, "how does all this fit together, Max?"

"Henri," he corrected. "Max is no more."

"Henri," I said.

He rolled his eyes. "Just follow me, will ya numbskull? Follow me. Business was great, see, but something kept bothering me. Something just wasn't right."

"Wha-da-ya-mean?" I asked. "Like you felt bad about stiffing all those people?"

Max spit a mouthful of wine halfway across the room. "WHAT!" he wailed. "Are you nuts? This was the best thing I ever had going. What bothered me was that I had this feeling I was onto something really big but just couldn't put my finger on it. Like I was nibbling at the edges of a gold mine, Donny. I had this sinking feeling I was using this big time idea of mine—atonement achievement—in a strictly small time scam. Plus, I was just about working myself to death. Out every morning by ten or eleven, then pound the pavement day in and day out for six or seven hours. It was hell. I was bustin' butt like a yankee farmer or something and, although the money was stupendous, I just couldn't help thinking there had to be a better way. Something a bit less strenuous, you know?"

"Something easier than begging rich folks out of big bucks? You can't be serious. You made all this money, untaxed, of course, for doing exactly nothing and you were looking for something even easier?"

He took a bite of salmon. "Yeah, right. How's the steak by the way?"

"Perfect."

"So," he continued, "one day I was walking down Charles Street on my way home, feeling glum, when I go by this church, see. Now, you know I'm not much for religion, Donny, but I figured, why not give it a shot. So I sat on the curb in front of this here church and talked up to God. 'God', I says, 'God, your boy Max here knows there's got to be an easier way, but I just can't hit on it right. I'm sick of stiffing all these geeks up in Roland Park. Clue me in, Big Guy. Give me a break'. . . . And that's when I got it."

"What?"

"The first dynamic principle of economic righteousness."

I dropped my plate. "Come off it!"

"You heard it. Divinely inspired, had to have been."

"And just what is this principle?"

"That the righteousness of any transaction increases in inverse proportion to the amount of effort required to bring it off."

I scoffed. "In other words, if I make a million bucks in one afternoon doing absolutely nothing, my righteousness quotient goes right through the roof."

"Well, more like a billion," he corrected, "but you've got the idea."

"Beautiful," I said.

"You got that! It was the most beautiful and moving moment of my life. I got religion, by damn. I understood at that moment that God and me were in cahoots."

I shook my head. "God admires your operation here, does He?"

"Absolutely."

"And, I suppose, he can't stand most of us nine-to-fivers who just schlep our way through life on a shoestring?"

"Now you're cooking! Hey, you're catching on. See, guys like you—teachers, painters, cooks, all you meatheads out there busting your butts for nothing really—drag down the righteousness in the world. It pisses God off."

I didn't know whether to laugh or cry. "Please, please do go on," I said.

"Blueberry tart?"

"Sure."

"Well," continued Henri, "it led directly to my weekly poker game at Diamonds and to the profession of law."

"Go on."

"There I was at Diamonds playing five card stud with the regular crowd and this new chump, a lawyer. The chump lawyer is boozing, see. He's trying to make time with every skirt in the place and he's losing left and right."

"And you're not?"

"Not losing, kid. Boozing and chasing, maybe, but not losing. I was primed and feeling good. Very righteous. Fact is, the more the lawyer takes it on the chin, the better I look. Money just stacking-up, see. Well, sir, turns out the fool is in way over is head and Bruno Diamond asks me if he should break both of his arms and throw him off a bridge and the lawyer, sober as all get out now, is sweating bullets. I say no, give the chump a day. One day."

I grabbed one last tart. "You have a big heart."

"I got no heart at all." said Henri. "What good is a pair of broken arms to me? I wanted my ten grand. Anyway, come the next day, the idiot can't come up with the coin. The usual crap: he wants to pay in installments, will I take an IOU, his wife's wedding ring? You know the tune. He starts whining about his reputation and all. Seems he's not just any old chump attorney, but the dean of the local law school. And that's when it hit me, Donny, right between the eyes. I heard violins, angels, the whole freaking nine yards, and God pipes—up and tells me exactly what to do."

"God again, huh? Seems you guys have quite a thing going. What'd he tell you this time?"

"He tells me to stiff the dean jerk for a degree in law and never look back."

I sat up straight. "So that's how you got it," I said, pointing an accusing finger.

"Of course," he admitted without hesitation. "I said it was genuine—not that I earned it. Anyway, I immediately commence to putting the screws to the dean, see. No way, he says. Can't be done. Absolutely not, and all that crap. So I go over to the phone and start dialing for Bruno. Bruno's not going to like this, I tell him. He starts to whine, he starts to cry. He's on his knees sobbing, see. It was great. He's got all this geeky looking rococo furniture in the living room, so I tell him he'll look great wearing it. That's when he falls apart. I handed him the phone and he starts dialing between the tears. And that, my friend, was the beginning of H. Goldleaf Lafayette III."

"A remarkable story. But why the new name?"

"Would you have believed it if I'd of told you Max Taylor had become an attorney? Would anyone in the whole family have believed it?"

"No."

"'Course not. No one in the whole world would have. So I had to create an entirely new me. Hey, this is America, right, land of the self-created soul, land of opportunity. Then I straightened up the house a bit and hired a few chicks with enormous tits to hang around as secretaries. That's what this country is all about, kid. . . . More wine?"

"Not right now, thanks."

"I got busy right away. I passed the bar in a week, no problem, 'cause Bruno—still thinking he owed me one—promised one of the fruitcakes on the review board he'd introduce his adenoids to the nearest cement mixer. The first few suits I won went to really doing the place up in a splash.

Then I was off and running. Suits here, suits there. Schools, factories, churches—you name it, I sued it. Money, Donny. Money, money, money, MONEY," he yelled, ruffling through the imaginary mountain of currency on his desk. "You don't have to have a good case. You don't have to have any case at all. The money just keeps rolling in."

I shook my head. "Maybe I'm old fashioned, but what about your clients and professional ethics? What about justice?"

". . . What?"

"Justice?"

". . . What?"

"Never mind," I said. "Just tell me about the psychology thing."

"Oh, well, that was a stroke of genius and a bit of good fortune that miraculously coincided," he explained. "You see, it didn't take me long lawyering to realize no one, absolutely no one, considers themselves responsible for anything that goes wrong or gets out of whack these days. Now, for a lawyer that's great because you've got a virtual never ending supply of clients and defendants. Don't get me wrong, I wasn't complaining. It's just that it seemed to me there had to be a better way of taking advantage of the whole thing. See, this was big, a phenomena or something I discovered. In America, no one is responsible for anything anymore. The courts were ruling on it, teachers were teaching it, and the press was preaching it every day. It has brought about the biggest redistribution of wealth since taxes. I was just nibbling at the edges."

"Wait a second here," I protested. "Explain this: If nobody is responsible for anything, then how can you ever prove someone is at fault? How do you ever win a case if the same argument works for everyone?"

Henri rolled his eyes. "Where you been, Donny? What country you living in, anyway? I don't sue people. I sue institutions. Groups, societies, professions, departments, governments. Get the picture? Now the people in these various institutions might fail, but the failure isn't their fault, it's the institutions. They're off the hook completely. Once negligence is discovered these days, it's collectivized. Then, bingo, it's gone altogether." He snapped his fingers. "Just like that."

"Just like that," I repeated. "So no one loses. You make money and no one gets hurt."

"Exactly."

"And what about all the folks whose lives get dragged through court, whose careers get ruined?"

"Grant it, there's a little inconvenience here and there, but it's all for the best."

"So that's the way you see it, huh? A little inconvenience and nothing else?"

"Nothing else except big, big bucks, sonny boy. The pot at the end of the rainbow, the payday extraordinaire. And now with my psychiatry thing in high gear, I'm working it from both ends."

"How's that?"

"Well, like I was saying, I knew I had to ride this cash cow I'd uncovered but I couldn't quite figure how to mount up. Then one day, it just happened. I was over at the university library."

"To research a case?" I asked.

Henri grimaced. "No, not to research a case. I never research my cases. I like to have an open and clear perspective on each and every one of them," he explained. "Don't you think I owe my clients that much?"

"Oh, sure" I said.

"I really didn't think it was possible, but it does appear I have underestimated your lack of understanding, Donald. Researching cases is boring and just too time-consuming. Not to mention the fact it takes away from the cash flow aspects of the law. And the law is cash flow. Now, my young friend, repeat after me. The law is cash flow."

"The law is cash flow," I repeated.

"Good," said Henri. "Now, where was I? Oh, yes, at the university library, aisle *D*, table 6, chair #3 to be precise. The same chair I have occupied for much of my adult life because from that precise position, and from that position alone, one is afforded a complete and unobstructed view up the stairwell and directly up the skirts of all the lovely females who happen to avail themselves of the second floor. You'd be amazed, Donny, just how many coeds wear no panties these days. Anyway, on this particular afternoon, and through no action or fault of my own, I was brutally, wantonly, and grievously injured—not to mention emotionally traumatized—when a hopelessly negligent university employee accidentally dropped an eraser on my head."

"An eraser?"

"You have no idea the heft those things have," he said, rubbing the top of his head. "Of course, I immediately notified the Chancellor's Office in order to put them on notice of the heinous act, and a strange thing happened."

"They threw you out on your ear?"

"Not at all," he laughed. "The exact opposite, in fact. They responded immediately, and with grave trepidation, as we lawyers like to say. Which means they were scared shitless."

"Why shouldn't they be?"

"Well, a case of the, shall we say, magnitude of the one I was threatening is not generally met with howls of horror; your average Joe simply doesn't comprehend the trauma a rubber eraser can occasion, and so I knew something was up right away. I bribed one of the secretaries and discovered on the sly that the old chancellor had inadvertently allowed the university's liability insurance policy to lapse because he was switching to another company for cost-cutting measures. But the new policy was off by one day. Penny wise and pound foolish it proved to be, kiddo, cause Monsieur Henri Goldleaf Lafayette III was there to catch him the one day he had his pants down."

"What's the big deal?" I asked, "it's still a Mickey Mouse case."

"Anywhere else in the world, yes. But not to a chancellor who was already under fire for being way over budget and generally incompetent. If a word—just one lousy word—got out about how he had allowed the entire university to go unprotected, well, the Board of Regents would have booted his ass right out the window. And he knew it. And then I knew it. So, you see, I had him by the proverbial short hairs, my son."

I understood. "So you busted him for a degree."

"Not right away, Donny. At first I just wanted money, but the creep couldn't come up with enough green for even a decent week or two on the Riviera. That's when the psychiatrist thing came to me and it seemed like a natural. So I just kept putting the screws to him, you see, twisting and twisting, until I had him just about to the breaking point. That's when I popped the degree gig on him, and he jumped all over it. Two weeks later, I was a doctor of medicine and a psychiatrist to boot. Proud of me?"

"Incredible," I said, looking around. "So what is it you do here in The Center for Psychiatric Retribution?"

"Well, I try hard not to *do* anything. Like I said, doing things cuts down on your cash flow and violates the First Dynamic Principle of Economic Righteousness. What I do is dance, talk, drink a lot and file suits."

"No, I mean on the psychiatrist end."

"Yeah, that's what I mean," he replied. "I have a little talk therapy, maybe some dance therapy—the Rumba is big again right now—or maybe some aerobics. Sometimes we taste a little wine, sometimes we go to the track. Whatever sounds good. That's what's really neat about psychiatry," he went on, "you just make it up as you go. Put an 'osis' at the end of anything you want and you're kicking ass in the psychiatry game."

"Sounds to me like you're going in opposite directions with the law and this psychiatry crap. What's the point?"

"Read my lips, shit-for-brains: Concept. It's a concept that works as a whole. It's art is what it is, fer Christ sake. And you can't see it. Look, if a body comes schlepping on in here with some kind of disorder or other to be treated, I can always find a cause or culprit after a few sessions. You know, the job, the pastor, the city water—whatever. Then, while I'm treating their maladies with champagne, Mozart and cheese balls, I sue the villains who caused their disorders for all they're worth. I concoct some psychological hocus pocus about permanent impairments, diminished capacities, and so forth, and before you know it, voila, big bucks. Now if they come in here with a legal problem,

I just work it in reverse. See, they're angry, frustrated with the world around them—clearly in need of psychological counseling throughout their period of trauma. Then I spin the counseling into more legal actions. It's like a perpetual motion money machine."

I shook my head violently. "That can't possibly work. People aren't that gullible or that grubby. At least, most people."

"Wanna check my bank account, kiddo? Business is booming. Why, if I wanted to, I could have a line of suckers, pardon me, clients clear around the block."

"But Max," I protested, "you're doing nothing for these people. You're a complete fraud."

"Henri, if you please, and that's nonsense. The law is simple cash flow, the redistribution of cash from them to you. Once you've learned that, you've learned everything of substance you need to know about lawyering. Psychiatry, on the other hand, is just plain silliness and everyone knows it. So what's the harm in a little fun, especially when it pays so well? The fact is, all my clients love the therapies I offer here, and I've actually had some rather remarkable results."

"Come off it."

"No, really. Take old Mrs. Driscoll, for instance. They wheeled her in here diagnosed as incurably schizophrenic, a real basket case. Well, sir, I treated her aggressively with cha-cha classes, mai tai's, Buster Keaton movies, and a spicy diet, and in two weeks she was up doing Mick Jagger imitations in the parlor. She's a trip, I tell ya. Everybody loves her. She's lost twenty-five pounds; taken to slinky, European fashions; and says she wants to be a model."

"You're crazy," I said. "You're absolutely nuts. This will never work. The cops are going to come in here some day and drag you off to jail."

He smiled. "We'll see. Until then, would you care for some eggs Benedict?"

"No, I'm stuffed. But I would like to know all about my new house."

He laughed out loud. You're kidding, right? The house was just bait to get you down here. I have plans for you, kid. I felt sorry for you in that dead-end, no pay teacher's job of yours. Yech! So I threw the house in 'cause I figured it would be just enough to pry you loose. Besides, I owed you one for the snails.

"It was honest, important work," I heard myself protest. "And as far as the house is concerned, I have the papers right here. "The house is mine, Max, not yours."

He snickered as he wiped the residue of eggs Benedict from his chin with a napkin. "I can tie that will and title up for years with some high- stepping legal razzmatazz." He pointed to my pocket with his fork. "You got enough in there to hire a good lawyer to fight me?"

"No," I admitted.

"'Course not. My guess is you got about enough to live comfortably for a month or so. Right?"

"Yeah."

"Sure," he said, winking. "So play it smart, Donny. Look around. Life here ain't so bad. The best food in the world, more pussy than you can handle, and money, money, money. I need some help, kid. The thing is getting too big for me. So I thought of you. What is that saying, 'if you can't beat'em, join'em?' Wha-da-ya-say?"

"It's not for me, Max. Look, try and understand this. I didn't leave for money. I didn't leave for French cooking or because I wasn't getting any. I left because it just seemed like there had to be more to it than putting in eight hours every day. I just felt in my heart that life had something big in store for me and I had to go out and find it."

He burped the most enormous burp I'd ever heard. "You make me wanna puke, kid," he said, as if I had given him indigestion. "Here I offer you the deal of a lifetime and you hand me goop like that. I ought to have you fucking arrested."

"Sorry," I said, "but I'll be checking out in the A.M."

"Where you gonna go?"

"I don't know. Richmond maybe"

"Guess again," he said, pointing at me. "I'll slap a lien on that piece of junk of yours and have the police stop you on the beltway. You won't get six miles from here. They'll impound your car and you'll be hoofing it back here."

"You wouldn't."

"Try me."

"You don't have the authority."

"Shit," he said, "who do you suppose just happens to be the biggest contributor to the Policeman's Benevolent Association in the whole frigging state of Maryland."

I lowered my head. "Just what exactly do you want of me?"

He smiled again. "That's better. Be reasonable, that's all. Give me a couple weeks. Work as my assistant. I'll teach you the ropes. It'll be great. If it doesn't work out, it doesn't work out. Just give it a shot. That's all I'm asking. Are you with me?"

I slowly reached for the bottle of wine and filled my glass to the top. "Pass the oysters," I said.

4

The next morning I was awakened early by the sound of squirrels on the roof and robins in the trees. My window was open to a fresh southern breeze. I slipped from between silk sheets and went to the open window. The sky was blue and motionless. Alvon the butler came with hot coffee and placed it beside the bed; this would be easy to get used to.

I dressed quickly and decided to have a look around. In the upstairs hallway, I heard the sound of Henri's morning bubble bath being drawn by Alvon. Downstairs, the cooks (there were several) were busy preparing breakfast. The delicious aroma of cheese, eggs, bacon, and pastries danced enticingly through the house. Outside, the chauffeur was spit-shining Max's Silver Cloud and the gardener was busy edging the flower beds. I sat on the patio and sipped my coffee until a maid came and took my breakfast order. At Henri's, you didn't just have breakfast. You ordered. Anything.

When I'd finished my coffee, I ambled back into the dining room for breakfast. I had ham and eggs, and they were delicious. As I was finishing, Henri came waddling into the room. Alvon uncorked a bottle of French champagne as Henri sat down to an enormous meal of steak, eggs, fruit, clams, sausage and cheese. When the champagne was gone, he washed it all down with an additional magnum or so of burgundy.

It was more than simply amazing. It was awe inspiring. It was as if he were trying to devour the world, consume in a mad hour every delicacy that had ever been invented. When he had ceased feeding, he bid me join him with a cup of espresso in his office across the hall. I complied.

We settled into comfortable leather chairs with our drinks. "Cigar?" offered Henri. "Brandy?"

I declined both. I was all business. "Let's get on with this. I'm anxious to move along. I didn't quit my job and chuck it all just to get shanghaied."

He smiled. "That spunk will serve you well. You'll need it. Now, let's see. Our first case is a legal action I am undertaking on behalf of the sorely victimized youth, Wilbur Rollins." He leaned back and opened a file. "Ah, yes," he cooed, "this case has the happy look of money all over it."

"What sort of action?"

"Well, it seems our young client has been the victim of a most inept, inadequate, and just downright incompetent educational system. Through the absence of professional planning, care, and even the most remedial of teacher-related services, the poor lad has been grievously injured—his heart, soul, and skill proficiency woefully stunted. The child has been permanently scarred as a result of this heinous ineptitude, and he requires that we now ride forth on his behalf and pluck a sizeable judgement from the villainous educators and stumbling bureaucrats who have allowed this travesty to transpire."

"Educational malpractice," I said, "what a dead end. These things have been tried before, and no one has ever succeeded to the best of my knowledge. You're beating a dead horse here."

"Persistence, persistence," he admonished. "The fools who tried these things before went after the wrong source. You can't sue a teacher. No jury will ever convict a teacher. They're entirely too sympathetic a figure. No, you go after systems, functions. You sue the state for negligent and discriminatory dispersal of funds, you sue the school board for unprofessional systems management, and you sue the teachers union for inadequate training and sensitivity awareness. You don't sue people. You sue the operation as a whole for it's faults in the aggregate."

"It's been tried," I repeated.

"Yes, but not enough, and certainly not from enough angles. If someone slams the door in your face, you come through the window. If they close the window, you try the chimney. There's always a way in, you just gotta keep trying. Then one day, whamo! Some insurance company executive is cutting you a monstrous check. It's all very gratifying."

"Hmmm," I said, "let me see this case." I took the file from him but there were no papers inside. There were no notes, not even a scribble. . . . There was nothing. I held the empty file up to him.

"Oh that. Well, . . . I very much prefer to maintain a verbal file on my cases as opposed to a written one. It's so much more . . . ah . . . personal, don't you think?"

"Sure, Henri," I said, arching an eyebrow. "Would you mind telling me how you happened by this case?"

"Well, Mrs. Rollins came to me with her son for some sort of psychological work-up or other. Seems the waif had been expelled from school a few hundred times or something and the school counselors had suggested professional help for the lad. I don't know. Anyway, after only a few sessions with the master, I was able to convince her there was nothing at all wrong with her son. Nothing, that is, that could not be remedied with some assertiveness clinics at a few hundred dollars a pop. And there were some serious tortfeasors banging around out there that needed looking into. Needless to say, she jumped at it."

I frowned. "What is wrong with the kid?"

"How the hell do I know? He's a moron, a mutant. Who cares? I don't make money curing people, only treating them. Anyway, we don't have time to debate the stupid bastard's condition. They're all outside in the waiting room. You ready?"

I took a deep breath and let it out slowly. "Why not?"

The Rollins family entered in a wrangle of disarray, Mrs. Rollins first, followed by Carl Townsend, Wilbur's stepfather, an Uncle Lou, and finally, the infamous Wilbur. After being introduced by Henri as his trusted and learned assistant, I sat on a chair in the corner somewhat out of the line of fire. Wilbur took a seat directly across from me. He was spindly, dirty, and he had the look of a very dangerous dog: stupid and unpredictable. I knew instinctively he was the type of person you could feel very sorry for—until he opened his mouth. Then you wanted to strangle him.

Henri walked dramatically to the center of the room and bowed to them all. "Kind, gentle people," he addressed them, "my assistant and I are ever so delighted to see you again. And how are you, Wilbur?"

"Who gives a shit?" snapped Wilbur, drawing back suddenly as if bitten on the calf.

"Ha-ha-ha," Henri chuckled dutifully. "That famous Rollins' sense of humor at work again. Oh, how I love it." He pinched Wilbur on the cheek. "You're a chip off the old block, you are."

Mrs. Rollins beamed proudly. "I really think we're making progress, Dr. Lafayette," she proclaimed. "Wilbur attended school for an entire week without being punched in the face."

"We-l-l-l," said Henri, "that is progress. And how do you feel about that, Wilbur?"

"I feel like puking all over dem fucking leather shoes of yours, is how I feel, shrink beak."

Max clapped his hands happily. "The child is a pure joy," he said to Mrs. Rollins. "You have been truly blessed. And to think they expelled him!"

Carl Townsend spoke up. "Wha-da-fuck kinda progress dis creep making when he talks like dat? I wanna know dat. Dis is all just a bunch-a-crap is what I think."

"Hush, Carl," scolded Mrs. Rollins. "What the hell do you know about anything?"

"Nah, nah, nah," protested Uncle Lou, stepping into the center of the room, "Carl's got a point here. Wilbur don't seem to be improving at all to me, and we spent a lot of dough so far here, Doc."

Henri stood up quickly. "Gentlemen, gentlemen," he said, holding out his hands to them. "I assure you progress is being made. And now, even as I speak, my secretaries are busy at work preparing your suit. Reparations, I guarantee you, are close at hand. Let's not lose our patience, now that we are so near the promised shore."

Lou tapped Wilbur gently on the shoulder. "Now he's talking, hey Willie?"

"Why don't you cram it, Lou?" replied Wilbur.

Lou slapped Wilbur on the back of the head, and Wilbur responded by grabbing a paperweight off Henri's desk and trying to bury it in Lou's cerebellum. The two of them rolled around on the floor for thirty seconds or so before Henri and I could separate them. They got up spitting at one another.

Henri moved quickly to his desk. "I was hoping we would rise above this sort of thing this visit," he said, puffing wildly, "but it appears we have not progressed sufficiently enough to come together without a little moderating influence." With that he pulled a huge revolver from underneath the desk and pointed it directly at Wilbur. He cocked the hammer. "Sit, please."

Everyone quickly grabbed a chair. "That's better," said Henri. He looked slowly across the room and carefully surveyed his desk. "Carl, the solid gold cigarette case that usually occupies my desk right there—he pointed with the pistol—seems to be gone."

Carl's eyes bugged out of his head as he peered down the bore of the immense handgun. "N-n-not me, Dr. Lafayette. I'm clean, I swear."

Henri slowly shifted his attention to Mrs. Rollins. "My dear Mrs. Rollins," he said, "kindly return the cigarette case to my desk within five seconds or I will blow your right arm off at the shoulder."

She pulled up her skirt, yanked it from her undergarments, and tossed it on the desk.

Henri bowed. "Thank you. Now, as I was saying," he continued, "Wilbur's case is most unusual and requires the newest and most sophisticated legal techniques currently available. I have decided to employ my famous 'Las Vegas' strategy in which I sue everyone who, throughout Wilbur's entire life, has ever caused him even so much as a bad night's sleep. We spin the wheel of fortune, so to speak."

"Dis here Las Vegas strategy," queried Uncle Lou, wiping the blood from his nose with a handkerchief, "I betcha it costs a bundle, huh?"

Henri sighed. "My fees, Lou, are hardly the issue here," he replied. "We are, after all, discussing the traumatized history and decreased expectations of this tender and dear child. But, Lou, if you must know, I intend to handle the entire matter on my usual contingency basis."

"Shut yer fat face, Lou," wailed Wilbur. "Ain't none of yer business, enyhow!"

"Oh yeah! How'd you like me to slap that stupid smile of yers right off, Wilbur?"

"Gentlemen, gentlemen," admonished Henri, "I acknowledge the fact that emotions run high in traumatized circumstances such as these, but we are all civilized folk, perfectly capable of conducting ourselves at our decorous best, are we not?" But before anyone could reply, Carl made a quick move and Henri fired, blowing the end table next to him against the back wall into a hail of splinters.

Carl lurched back into the chair and sat like a stone, jaw trembling. Mrs. Rollins wept openly. Wilbur chuckled. "Was that a tissue you were reaching for there, Carl?" asked Henri.

"Yes, Dr. Lafayette, I swear that was all it was. Just a tissue to blow my nose."

The smell of burnt gunpowder hung over the room. Mrs. Rollins peed on her seat. Lou spoke up. "S-so it seems to me you got a mind to screw us for a fat percentage of the take here, Doc."

"Take? What *take*?" demanded Henri. "This is justice, Lou, not five card stud."

Lou looked slowly my way. "Yeah," he said, "what's the jerk in the corner got to say? Who cut him in anyway?"

"Mr. Mallory is here at my invitation. He is an acknowledged expert on educational matters, Lou. I would like him to interview Wilbur in order to form an opinion as to the depth of the child's lack of development. It's central to the case."

I sat upright. All eyes were upon me. To say the least, I felt uncomfortable, gunplay notwithstanding. It was apparent to me that judging Wilbur's lack of educational development was a bit like judging the depth of the Grand Canyon: not so much a matter of degree but method. Was it even possible to measure? How could any court or jury take this kid, this entire family, seriously? I walked slowly to the center of the room and faced the boy. "Wilbur," I said.

"Dorkface," he replied.

I looked sideways at Henri then continued. "Wilbur, tell me about your schooling."

"Fuck off," he snarled, scratching and itching himself in a sudden frenzy.

I stepped back. "Fleas," I said. "Hey, Wilbur's got fleas, Henri."

Lou shouted: "Ain't you never washed yersef, you dumb ass. Hait told you to wash yersef, Wilbur. Shit, we'll all be a-itchin' now."

"Leave the boy alone, Lou," screamed Mrs. Rollins. "Christ knows the poor child's depraved."

"Ahh, . . . I believe you mean deprived," corrected Henri, "but we all understand."

I started over from an additional few feet back. "Did you go to school, Wilbur? Do you recall a place with books and bells?"

"No."

Henri smiled approvingly. "The screw turns. You see, my dear Mr. Mallory, our case is predicated on the fact that Wilbur's attendance record is more or less nonexistent. The thrust of my argument shall be that the school system not only failed to educate him, but failed because he was not there."

"I'm lost," I said.

"Well," continued Henri, "it's really quite simple. It is impossible to educate a child when he is not there to educate. Correct?"

"Certainly," I said.

"Of course. Now, it is rather clear from even the meager testimony given here today, that Wilbur, although a precious child, is utterly incapable of disciplining himself to the task of attendance. True?"

"Probably," I admitted.

"So then, who's responsibility is it? Mine? Of course not. Yours? Hardly. No, Mr. Mallory, the job of tracking Wilbur's attendance, of producing a Wilbur Rollins in a classroom on a daily basis, falls to none other than the highly paid but grossly negligent educational bureaucrats who have failed to achieve a reasonable enrollment of this boy. It has to be someone's fault, right?"

"Wrong!" I yelled. "If it's anyone's fault it's Wilbur's, no matter how stupid he is, and his family's, no matter how ignorant."

"W-H-A-A-A-T!" howled Lou. "Wha'd he say?

Mrs. Rollins hurled a book across the room at my head. I ducked.

"Friends, friends," Henri implored, waving the revolver about for effect. "My assistant, Mr. Mallory, was merely playing the devil's advocate for us, testing our case for holes. A tough assignment, but one that had to be done."

Carl growled rabid-like and eyed my leg menacingly.

"Carl," Henri said, "if you bite Mr. Mallory, I shall shoot you dead. Understand?"

Carl curled up in his chair like a snake coiling to spring. He disappeared from my view, but his growling continued unabated.

"Wonderful, wonderful," cheered Henri. "I think we've all gotten on quite well here this morning. We've made real progress. My assistant, Dr. Mallory, will be handling your case to conclusion—with my constant input and supervision, of course—and I want you to give him your full and undivided cooperation. It won't be long before results will be seen, I assure you. Now, my friends, how about some refreshments? I have a nice California chardonay here, Carl. Eclair, Lou?"

As the Rollins family fell upon the refreshment cart like starved mongrels upon a cat, Henri took me by the elbow and slowly steered me out of the room. In the hallway, he turned to me. "That was some show you put on in there," he said. "Just what in the hell did you think you were doing?"

"I put on!" I stammered. "You pander to those cretins and point a finger at me? You should be ashamed, Max."

"Henri!" he fairly shouted. "Those cretins are my ticket—one of my tickets—to the big time, kid, and I don't need you screwing it up."

"I can't stomach this crap," I said. "How can you sue anyone on behalf of that imbecile?"

He threw his arms up in the air. "This is America, Donny. Look around. It's a gravy train, by God. I just got on board is all. Don't be so pious. Everyone's out their grabbing. The government socks it to the rich, the slow cream the fast, and the dumb sue the shit out of anyone smarter than they are. It don't pay to be rich, fast, or smart anymore, kiddo. Guys like me are after you."

"Well, it stinks," I said, "and what you're doing here ain't got nothing to do with the rich, fast, or smart. It's just pure greed."

"Wait and see, Donny," he said. "We'll have old Wilbur Rollins looking like one of the most sympathetic bastards you've ever seen. You won't believe your eyes."

"I already don't believe my eyes."

"Well, try and calm down some. Have a drink and relax. Our next appointment isn't for awhile. Maybe the psychiatry gig will be more to your liking, what with all these *feelings* you seem to have."

I went into another room and slumped into a chair. I fumed. What absolute fraud. Here was Max, in charge of it all like a cheerleader, orchestrating every phoney detail. And what was that going to make me? I didn't like the thought.

In a few minutes, Henri returned. He was smiling. "Cheer up. Things have got to get better."

"Look," I said, "I've been sitting here stewing about what happened in there. I'm just not cut out for this sort of madness. I feel like a slug just being here."

He pulled up a chair directly in front of me and gently slapped my knee. "It's your first day, kid. Maybe I was too hard on you. The Rollins crew can be a bit testy. Give it a fair shot. You promised."

"There just doesn't seem to be any justice in any of it," I protested. "That Rollins fiasco is a travesty."

"Well," he replied, "I happen to think it quite winnable."

"Sure, it might be winnable—especially nowadays—but that doesn't make it right."

"What's this right and wrong stuff you've got cemented in your head?" he asked. "You're off base. In the law, nothing is wrong if it's winnable. Remember, the

AMERICAN RAIN

law is cash flow, and cash flow cannot distinguish between right and wrong, only money and more money."

I slumped. "This is nuts."

"Stick around," he countered. "This afternoon I have a few juicy cases coming in on the psychology end. Maybe that will be more to your liking."

"I doubt it."

"Yeah, well, wait till you see the paychecks. Now go take a walk, have some lunch—I think it's avocados with prosciutto, beef Wellington with glazed fruit boats, and rum truffles for dessert—and come back around one. You'll see, it's gonna work."

So I took a walk, had some lunch—it was as projected—and met him back in the office that afternoon. When I came through the door, I was shocked to see Henri, half-clothed, dancing around his desk as an enormous boom box blasted rock music. It was deafening. There he was, shirt open to the waist, great belly flouncing this way and that as he attempted some sort of bizarre shimmy.

"Max!" I screamed, but he could not hear me above the din. I cupped my hands around my mouth and yelled as loudly as I could: "MAX!" But it was no use.

Then he started doing this little kick routine, bouncing from one foot to the other, sweat pouring down his face, as he clapped his hands above his head. It was obscene.

"M-A-X!!" Nothing. I'd seen enough. I marched across the floor and pulled the plug on his machine. Silence rushed into the room like a tidal wave, splashing against the walls with an almost audible clap. "What in the world are you doing?" I asked.

He was unfazed. "Rock therapy," he replied. "Elevates the heart rate, increases blood flow to the extremities, and induces electro-nimbo activity in the occipital orbs, among other things. Would you care for some blackberries with cream?"

"No, I ate. Where do we go from here?"

He yanked a towel off the desk top and dabbed his face. "I'm glad you asked, my boy. This afternoon we have two very unique and interesting case studies. First, there's poor Ms. Lawson. She lost her last three jobs because she is hopelessly incompetent and is suffering from a deflated self-image as a result. So far, I have been able to convince her that competence is merely a subjective idealization of certain western cultural and historical myths that are as irrelevant to her existence as is the price of perfume to lake trout. Seems to be working. I've also got her half-talked into providing me with some oral sexual gratification. I think it would be good for her."

"W-W-H-A-T!" I yelled. "You can't do that!"

"Be serious," he said. "Of course I can. Last session I even had her talked into holding the old magic wand. Told her it would have a very positive effect on our combined physiological communication, and that it was a must if we were to resolve her psychological problems. The harder the better, I told her. But she balked when it came to speaking into the microphone."

"You're disgusting. I'm gettin' outa here."

"Oh, come off it, Donny. She's divorced and horny. The old gal could use a good porking, if you ask me."

"Henri, you can't toy with people like that. You could do some serious and irreparable damage or something. Not to mention the fact that it's totally unethical."

"It's what?"

"Unethical."

"What?"

"Never mind," I said.

"Whatever. Anyway, that's only the first case. The second is the real doozy, if you ask me. Pastor Frickenfrayor, what a piece of work."

"What's wrong with him?"

"He's nuts, a complete lunatic."

"So what's he doing here?"

Henri squinted just slightly. "Let's just say he has the vague smell of money about him."

"Of course. What else?"

"Well, the pastor, it seems, is in direct communication with the Big Guy and is working feverishly on a new Bible." He threw his arms wide. "Is that great or what? His family doesn't know what on earth to do with him, so they've been sending him here as a sort of last gasp effort. I've been working with him for a few months now, and I've wormed my way not only into the new Bible—the book of Goldleaf—but into the royalty picture as well, should this thing ever take off. I know it sounds crazy, kid, but you can never be sure about these religious types. Let's just say I've become his patron. If nothing comes of it, I still get the bread for the sessions. And if it ever goes to print, well, I'm in for a fat percentage. You never know where this Bible stuff can lead, you know. Just look what it did for that other guy . . . ah, come on, help me. You know."

"Do you mean Jesus?"

"Yeah, yeah, Jesus, that's it. Put him right on the map, correct? So I'm playing old Frickenfrayor like a fiddle just in case."

Within minutes, Ms. Lawson had arrived for her psychiatric care. She was ushered into Henri's office wearing a pink, red, and white leotard outfit that fit like a glove. She was plump and, I would judge, in her midfifties. She more or less leapt onto the corner of Henri's desk and eyed him playfully. He was pleased. Her schedule for today, he announced, was aerobic therapy followed immediately by a wine cooler group encounter, followed by a private "communications" session with Henri. Ms. Lawson grinned.

Presently we were joined by Sheri, one of Henri's "assistants" who was also in a leotard, and we all lined up to have a go at it. Henri started with a medley of Rolling Stones hits, followed by some generic heavy metal stuff. We formed a conga line and danced slowly around the desk following—but not too closely—Henri's ponderous buttocks, as he wiggled and shook and sang out of tune. Then it was time for free flow expression, each of us working out our deepest troubles and most primitive fears to the tune of "Brown Sugar," one of Henri's favorites. That accomplished, we cooled off to a little jazz whilst, according to Henri, contemplating light and dark and our relationships to it. Ms. Lawson was all but overwhelmed by the experience and fell (quite carefully, I thought) into Henri's arms.

With that it was time for the wine cooler encounter group, and we broke for the library where snack trays were set up along with a bar full of exotic drinks. The room was packed with gregarious clients, none of whom I knew. I did not feel like drinking.

In due course, I turned to Henri. "How much more of this?" I asked, looking quickly at my watch.

"Not much," he answered, arm around Ms. Lawson.

"What next then?"

"For you, Pastor Frickenfrayor. For me, a serious one-on-one encounter with our dear Ms. Lawson."

"Henri, you can't . . ." I started to protest, but he waved it aside.

"Frickenfrayor's down the hall to the right. I'll be in my office."

The room cleared and a wave of depression came over me. I must be insane, I thought. How could I have allowed myself to become embroiled in such abject debauchery? I had not only gone backwards, I'd sunk to the bottom. I wandered down the hall. One more, I said to myself, and that's it. After Frickenfrayor, I'm outa here.

I marched into the office and sat directly behind the desk. I took a deep breath, tried to steady myself, and looked up. Pastor Frickenfrayor sat across from me with a bemused smile on his face. His eyes were blue, radiant, and clear. He was dressed in the traditional garb of a protestant clergyman. I guessed he was in his sixties. He appeared slender, strong, and purposeful. "And you would be? . . ." he asked.

He was not what I'd expected. "Ahhh, . . . Mallory," I responded. "Don Mallory, Dr. Lafayette's assistant."

He smiled. "Wonderful, Don Mallory," he said. "The good doctor has told me he was expecting you. I'm pleased to meet you."

"Likewise."

"And just where is the good doctor today?"

From across the hall the faint but unmistakable sounds of sexual glee rained down upon us. "Well, he's seeing a patient across the way," I said.

The pastor smiled again. "Our Monsieur Lafayette is at it again, is he?" He chuckled. "So I suppose you'll be hearing me today?"

"That's correct," I replied.

"What is it you'd like to hear?"

He caught me by surprise. "I'm not sure," I said.

He looked at me very purposefully. "Would you like to hear what I'm doing."

"Why not?"

"Why not?" he repeated. "Simply put, Mr. Mallory, why not is because everyone, including our dear Monsieur Lafayette, thinks I am as cuckoo as a clock."

"Well," I stumbled, "you're writing a brand new Bible, right? I mean, that does seem a bit . . . well . . . odd."

"Where is it written that the word has ended?"

"I guess nowhere," I said, "but it seems to me the old word is doing OK."

"The old word is not doing OK, Mr. Mallory. Take it from me. I've been a pastor for thirty-seven years, and I know. Oh, some of the devout still attend church and so on, but the Bible is no longer a central part of the community. And there's a reason for that."

"Which is?"

"Things change, Mr. Mallory. Everything changes. People change, continents change, and now the fundamental nature of religion is changing. But you can't tell anyone that. You see, the Bible was written at a time when we humans resided in a world of mysticism. There were mystical answers to every little unknown. If a pot fell in the night, it was the work of some demon, serpent, or divine criticism. We knew nothing of the world in which we lived, and so this was an altogether natural reaction. The Bible, Mr. Mallory, was written from such a perspective. All these angels, miracles, and divine shenanigans were perfectly normal interpretations for their time, but I'm afraid they don't play too well nowadays. Ever wonder why all the miracles stopped?"

"Yes."

"They stopped, my son, because we stopped seeing them as miracles. Our world is a world of scientific definition and law. We know, we investigate, we tear everything apart and reassemble it again, sometimes even for the better. Of course, we have a long way to go, Mr. Mallory, but we have come very far. When a house burns in the night, we no longer consider it an act of Godly retribution but an incident of faulty wiring or workmanship. Yet we have this religion of ours built on the mystical and nothing mystical ever seems to happen. So people drift away. Mr. Mallory, I must admit to you, the only thing in my entire life that even approached the mystical was when I won an extra Big Bongo Burger for scratching the right sequence of numbers off a little card at the local Bongo Burger Corral last week. Not much, huh?"

"I know what you mean." The moaning, thumping, and bumping from the other room became almost deafening. I banged on the wall with my fist. "Hold it down!" I yelled, "consultation in progress!"

"Of course you do," he continued. "Everyone does. We have grown away from our religion as we have grown away from our past. We have become quite different from what we once were."

"You're gonna have a hard time selling that on Main Street," I said.

"Tell me, Mr. Mallory. Why do you suppose I have been consigned to this squalid establishment to listen to the ravings of our Monsieur Lafayette?"

"You're onto him?"

He laughed. "But of course. For the time being, he serves my purposes. And he does have money and some connections. When I'm done with the Bible, I will need those. He also has the rather intriguing idea of suing many of the established religions once my work is completed if they will not accept it as authentic."

"Hmm?"

He sighed. "But the work goes slowly and I am oft times filled with serious doubts as to my direction and inspiration, I must admit. Would you like to hear some of my latest work?"

"Why not," I said.

Happily he grabbed his notes and placed them on the desk. He unfolded one. "This is just a rough draft. It's all on a floppy disc back in the word processor, you understand. Ah, here we are," he continued, "I'll read a bit from The Book of Manipulations, verses six through seventeen:

> Behold, there came upon the exosphere a dark and sinister cloud of exorbitant interest rates of Draconian implication for which the assembled throngs wailed in the night, tore at their eyes, and were sore afraid.
>
> And the Lord came upon the trembling hosts through numerous journals of a financial nature and spake onto them; Fear not the fluctuations of the Dow or the vagaries of the adjustable rate mortgage, for the dollar is still strong, the GNP appears healthy, and deductions remain ample.
>
> For this the people gave mighty thanks, ate less red meat, and exercised regularly.

"Or how about this from First Californians, verses one through eleven?" he asked all in a rush:

> The leader of the assembled hosts came forward and spake onto their ears.
>
> Sue not thine brother if thou whilst need him in a pinch, for blood is thick but litigation is eternal; Be vigorous in body and mind that ye shall surf in the breakers of the Lord, pump iron on the sands of His kingdom, and do drugs in the shadows beneath his gaze; Copulate at will,

ignore thine neighbor, but avoid starches at all cost.

And the Lord looked out across what he had wrought and was momentarily confused.

"Or here, here," he continued, holding up another sheet of paper while knocking several others onto the floor in his excitement. "From the Book of Data:

And the Boston Braves begat the Milwaukee Braves who begat the Atlanta Braves. The Philadelphia Athletics begat the Kansas City Athletics who begat the Oakland Athletics. The Brooklyn Dodg . . ."

"OK," I said, "I get the point."

He looked up at me pensively. "You do?"

"I think so. It's all very good and practical," I continued, "but, and excuse me for saying this, I think it lacks a little something Bible wise."

"He lowered his eyes. "I was afraid of that."

"It's just," I said, "that people look to the Bible for more than just wit, numbers and good advice. It answers certain infinite, unanswerable questions for them. It provides meaning in a world with no discernible or self-evident truth. All religions do that. The Boston Braves? Come on."

"I understand what you're saying," he countered, "but serious truth is no longer in the hands of theologians to dispense. The scientists have cornered the market on that. All we theologians can do is try and keep up and hope the newest finding doesn't blow us out of the water altogether." He put his head down. "I'm a failure. Religion is doomed."

"No, no," I protested, "You're taking it too hard. Look . . ." I continued, but just then Henri burst into the room.

"Gentlemen," he said, smiling from ear to ear, "I trust your session has gone as well as mine."

The pastor and I drew back. "Well," I said, "we seem to be making some progress, yes."

"Pastor Frickenfrayor, can I offer you a libation or two just to cut the dust of the road?" asked Henri, obviously feeling very pleased with himself.

"A double if you would, my good man," replied the pastor. "Seems the young man here feels I'm going nowhere at all. Very depressing."

Henri eyed me warily. "He does, now does he," he replied. "I hope we haven't been dispensing potions of doom and gloom."

"No, no," said the pastor. "Mr. Mallory's points are all well taken. I'm a crazy old fool, is all." I tried to argue the point but Henri was way ahead of me. "Nonsense! Absolute rubbish! I'll have none of that now, Pastor. You're a genius and a great man of religious conviction. A dynamite combination in the Bible biz. You've got a little bit of an internal solvent inversion, is all."

". . . What?" asked the pastor.

"Yeah," continued Henri without a blink. "Oh, didn't I tell you? Sure, no problem at all. Your lab work came back just the other day. The blood work-up shows you're receiving a few too many negative neutrinos on and about the medial syntax"—he pointed to the shoulder area—"and this is producing an ambuscade of the lymph apparatus throughout the area in general." He smiled gently. "I know this all sounds quite technical and scary, but it's nothing at all to worry about. It can be easily treated through dietary intervention."

The pastor didn't know whether to laugh or cry. "Diet?" he asked.

"That's all. Eat a few more steaks and drink at least four bottles of cold beer a day. In a week or two, you'll be ready to take on the world."

The pastor broke into a convulsive howl; he laughed until he could no longer breathe. Then he looked up, saw Henri, and began to howl again. Gradually he gained control of himself and was able to speak. "Dr. Lafayette," he coughed, still riddled with laughter, "I don't know how in the world you do it, but somehow you manage to keep me going. Four cold beers! Gosh that's great. Just great."

Henri stood stiffly and saluted. "All in a day's work, Monsieur. Please check now with Kathy out front for our next appointment. And remember: steak and beer, never fear."

The pastor shook his head in amazement, then looked my way. "Mr. Mallory," he said, "I'm going to keep at this thing. We'll talk again."

"OK," I said.

The pastor left the room still cackling and Henri turned toward me. "You have to get out of this negative pattern," he said. "You're gonna scare off all the business."

"I can't help it," I said. "I really don't know if I can handle much more of this."

"Of what?"

"Of *what!*" I stammered. "The lunacy, deceit, greed, chicanery, and sheer . . . avarice are almost beyond description."

He went to the bar and fixed himself another drink. "I'm not sure I'm following you."

I jumped to my feet. "Not following me. You can't follow me. This place is like another world, a whole other universe. I can't stay, I just can't. The gluttony, the unprincipled fleecing, the unending greed and cupidity is of such noxious proportions that I simply . . ."

At that moment the most beautiful woman I had ever seen walked into the room and approached the desk. My mouth stopped in mid-sentence. I turned to stone. Her hair was black and hung in ringlets about her head. Her skin was as clear and white as I could imagine, her eyes a dazzling blue. She walked elegantly across the room and stopped before Henri. "Your messages," she said sullenly, and dropped a pile of pink slips on the desktop. Then she turned and left the room, all the while my eyes glued to the bounce of her hair, the toss of her hips.

I struggled for breath. I had never been so overwhelmed by a woman before. "W-who i-is s-she," I gasped.

Henri took a long, bored pull on his drink. "Who, her?"

"Yes."

"Forget it," he replied. "I've already tried getting into her pants at least a hundred times. It's impossible. You're wasting your time."

"Who is she?" I persisted.

"Marcy Trimble," he said, "a secretary of sorts. But listen, kid, sounds to me like you've pretty much had it here. You know, all that carrying on you were doing back there really got me thinking. If you've had it, well, you've had it. What do you say, Donny? Ready to hang it up?"

I looked at him as though he had lost his mind. "Hang it up," I repeated, "what in the world, Henri, would make you think for a second that I was ready to leave?"

5

The next morning I was rudely awakened by Henri's overly-perfumed mug one inch from my nose.

"Get up!" he yelled. "We have an important breakfast meeting to attend. You got anything decent to wear?" He ripped open my suitcase. His face drooped. "Is this what teachers wear? My God."

"Never mind," I said, slamming the suitcase lid on his fingers.

"Yhaaaaaaaa!"

"Clothes don't make the man," I continued. "It's what's inside you that counts."

He licked his fingers then turned and spit out the window. "Show's what you know," he said. "Just put on something decent and meet me out back by the limo in five minutes."

"What's this all about?"

"No time to explain now. We'll talk in the car."

I shaved, washed up, put on the only suit I owned—blue pinstripes, frayed collar, and coffee stained—and dashed for the car. Henri was already inside sipping a cup of Java. Alvon was standing next to the open door with a steaming mug for me. I grabbed it and jumped inside. "Off, Jules!" ordered Henri, and the car leaped down the driveway.

I had never been in a Rolls Royce before. It smelled rich and beautiful. It rode like a dream. "So what's up?" I asked, enjoying the deep leather seats and the hot coffee.

"Got a call from Kiddo Kenny this morning. Something big. Something really hot is going down. He wouldn't even talk about it on the phone."

"Who's this guy, Kiddo, Max? What's he do, bust thumbs for the mob or something?"

"Kiddo Kenny London is my broker, you nit. He's nothing short of a financial genius. You'll see."

Something sounded wrong. "What could possibly be so hot that a broker wouldn't talk about it on the phone? Unless it's . . ."

"H-e-y-y," said Henri, you're really catching on aren't you, numb nuts."

We cruised down Charles Street into Baltimore, passed Johns Hopkins University, across North Avenue, and down to the inner harbor. What a place. A city reborn, I thought. Everything gleamed in the early June sunlight. Jules dropped us off at a fancy hotel and we were ushered into the second level dining room for breakfast. Kiddo Kenny was waiting.

"Henri baby," he called from a circular booth off in a corner. He waved for us to join him. Kiddo Kenny was immaculate. His suit was perfect, his hair was perfect. He was maybe fifty-five and thin as a stiletto. Who's this?" he asked suspiciously.

"Donny Mallory," Henri replied. "He's OK, trust me. My new assistant."

"If you say so," said Kiddo Kenny. "How are you, Donny baby? You interested in maybe some stocks or bonds? Futures? Commodities? A good horse?"

"Nah," I said.

"Forget him," said Henri. "What's going on that you had to drag me down here to this tourist trap?"

Kiddo Kenny gave me a wink. "We'll talk, eh kid. Here's my card."

"Sure," I said.

"Henri," said Kiddo Kenny, "I heard this and I couldn't believe my ears. Biggest thing ever. EVER."

Henri fidgeted nervously. "So spit it out."

Kenny looked around the room conspiratorially then spoke barely above a whisper. "I got the inside dope on a pharmaceutical conglomerate that's going to break something new and big in the toothpaste line."

Henri gave me a sideward glance then glared at Kenny. "Yeah, yeah, go on," he said, "there's got to be more to it than that."

"Oh, sure," said Kiddo Kenny. "I also got a tip on a nice little chain of can't miss burger joints out in Fort Wayne, Indiana."

"You're shitting me, right?"

Kiddo Kenny smiled. "And I like the Orioles tonight against the Yanks, even giving up two runs."

Henri smiled knowingly. He reached inside his jacket and pulled out a wad of bills. He laid down five hundred dollars' worth. "Maybe you forgot the big one, huh Kenny?"

Kiddo Kenny looked at the bills. "Something's coming back to me now that you mention it, Henri. But faint, very faint."

Henri kept counting. One thousand, two thousand, three. He laid down the whole wad. Five thousand dollars. Kiddo Kenny picked it up and put it in his pocket, but before he could remove his hand from inside his coat, Henri grabbed a fork and shoved it up his nose. "This better be good, you freaking blood sucker," Henri threatened, twisting the fork for effect.

"It's good, it's good, you lump of lard," exclaimed Kiddo Kenny, trying to push Henri aside as hard as he could. But it was no use. He couldn't budge him.

"Better be," said Henri. "Now spit it out or I'll carve you a new kisser just to celebrate the Fourth of July."

"Mayfair Bank and Trust," exclaimed Kenny, eyes glued to the prongs of the fork. "I have it from very reliable sources that the international drug cartel has selected this little whistle-stop farmers bank to launder their trillions. Word is the whole thing is already packaged and ready to go. If it goes down, the stock in Mayfair is going to go through the damn roof in days. In a year, you'll make one hundred times your investment. It can't miss, and the beautiful thing is it's absolutely clean for outside investors."

Henri smiled and put down the fork. He let Kiddo Kenny go. "Did I tell you this guy was a genius?" he asked me while lightly slapping Kenny on the back of the head. "I love you, Kenny," said Henri, hugging his broker to his side like a rag doll. "LOVE."

"Thanks," said Kenny, gently massaging his nose.

Henri started rubbing his hands together furiously. "How much time I got on this thing, Kenny?"

"You have no time," replied Kiddo Kenny. "It goes down today. You want in, you deliver now."

"Goddamn, Kenny," wailed Henri. "You know I'm tied up in the market. I'm solid; I'm strictly blue chip."

"Sorry, cash and carry only," Kenny said. "No time for credit, no time for squat. It's the green team today, buddy. You in?"

Henri commenced rubbing his face. "Yeah, yeah, I'm in. Just let me think for a second. I'm in. I'm in."

Kiddo Kenny whipped out his ballpoint. "How much action, fat man?"

"Put me down for three. No, make that four."

Kenny arched an eyebrow severely. "Four hundred grand? That's cash by this evening, Doc."

"I know what it is," barked Henri. "Just get me in. How long till the market opens?"

"Twenty minutes," said Kenny. "No sweat, but I hope you know what you're doing, Henri. The big boys won't be happy we don't show up with the green stuff by six tonight."

"You just do your job, Kenny. Me and the kid here"—he said, pointing to me—"will take care of the rest."

"You're in," said Kenny with a wink. "Catch you later." Kiddo Kenny left a fifty on the table to pay the tab and slid out of the booth. "Donny baby," he said.

"Kenny," I replied.

When Kiddo Kenny London had disappeared, Henri clapped and let out an Apache war cry. "I'm rich. I'm rich. I'm rich. Christ, this is a great county, huh kid? The land of opportunity, Donny. This is what America is all about."

"I thought it was all about having secretaries with big jugs?"

"That too. That and this."

"Henri," I said. "This deal, this investment is rotten. Drug money, man. You know how many kids I've seen ruined on that crap? Lives go down the drain every day 'cause of these creeps and their imports. It's like living off death. You ask me, it's like drinking blood."

"Lighten up. Here I'm waving the flag and you got me sounding like Dracula or something. What do you think hog futures are, numbskull? What do you think half the money in your happy little credit union is from?

Half the money in this county is dirty, kid. It never bothered you before who's money was next to yours. Now all of a sudden you're holy. Give me a break already."

"Maybe I just didn't know," I said.

He laughed. "Yeah, ignorance is bliss, huh kid. Now do me a favor and shut your yap 'cause today is going to be some kinda crazy. Listen to me, we've got to raise $400,000 by this evening, and it ain't going to be easy."

I almost jumped out of my seat. "You mean you don't have it?"

"No, I don't. At least not all of it. My money is invested, idiot."

"Well, what are we going to do?"

"I'm going to sell everything I can that's liquid. I'll gut the house. The furnishings, everything, I don't care. Next we'll settle every case we can for pennies on the dollar if the plaintiffs and insurers can get us money in hand today. We'll also call in every patient and client we can get our hands on. Every one in and out. Fifteen minutes then boot them up to the front desk with a bill. We'll do it, sonny. We'll do it. Now let's roll."

We sprinted out of the dining room and whistled for Jules at the curb. When he pulled up, Henri yelled, "Jules, drive one hundred miles an hour home. Be there in three minutes. Kill anyone who gets in the way." Then we piled into the back seat and Henri grabbed the car phone and began calling clients. "Mrs. Pizianni," he cooed into the receiver as we careened around a corner, "Henri Lafayette. It's that time again. Oh yes, yes. I have a special on today, you know, just for you and all the other wonderful psychopathic guys and gals out there. And you know that Cezanne you have always admired so? Yes, the one I caught you with on the driveway. Well, I think it's time we arranged some barter therapy for reality conceptualization, dear. I do indeed. Because you're coming along so well. Great! Make it about two and bring that big check book of yours. Bye now." Then he slammed the phone down. "The witch is good for one hundred *g*'s, mark my words." He looked skyward and grinned. "Thank you, God," he yelled, "I'm your boy."

I came up with an idea. "We're going to need all the help back at the office we can get today," I said.

"You got that right."

"You keep checking your client list," I continued, "and let me ring them up, and I'll have all part-time secretaries called in. It'll save some time."

"Sure," he said. "And make sure they get a hold of Marcy Trimble."

I blushed. "Yeah, I'd thought of that."

"Suit yourself, kid. It's no skin off my nose. Just don't go trying to yank her pants off before six o'clock. We got work to do."

"I hear you," I said.

The Rolls soared up Charles Street like a rocket, made a left turn on two wheels, a right into the driveway barely on one, and slid to a stop three inches in front of the garage in a cloud of smoke, gravel, and dust. Henri pulled himself up from between the seats, where he had become wedged after one particularly violent swerve, and winked. "That's what I hired you for Jules. You're an artist." Then he nudged me. "Ex-fighter pilots," he counseled, "always make the best chauffeurs." We threw open the doors and ran inside.

We stopped at the front desk. "Pull all the cases I have that even approach being legitimate," ordered Henri. "Then call the defense attorneys who are on the other side and advise them I might be willing to settle today—and today only—if the price is right."

"What's going on, Doctor?" inquired Ms. Townsend.

"Fire sale," said Henri. "Then call every client and patient we have and get them in here today."

"But why, Doctor? What shall I tell them it's for?"

"For an oil change and a lube! I don't care what you tell them, Ms. Townsend, just get them in here. What the hell am I paying you for, anyway?"

She grabbed the phone. "Yes, Doctor."

We scurried down the hallway and into Henri's office. "I'll take care of settling all the legal cases, you take care of the cranks. Take the office across the hall. Give each one of them ten, maybe fifteen minutes, then boot them out with a bill in their teeth. Wait! On second thought, use three offices. Run back and forth, assembly line psychiatry. In ten hours, you should be able to see almost three hundred clients and crank out about thirty grand. It ain't much, but it will help. I'll do the rest."

"Three hundred clients!" I said, slapping the side of my face.

The remainder of the day was a whirlwind. I remember only vague faces and names. I said little more then hello and goodbye as I consulted with people diagnosed with strange and exotic diseases—all of which had been created by Max, and were of questionable validity. I met with a young man who was listed as suffering from Environmentally Induced Incompetencia because he had been unable to keep up at three separate universities, in light of a problem with drugs. The folder of an older woman was marked Penile Slumber Syndrome while a younger woman's was marked Penile Arousal Syndrome. A middle-aged accountant was suffering from Induced Fiscal Morbidity, a garage mechanic from a Satanic Wrench Throwing Psychosis. On and on. There was Dumb as a Brick Syndrome; Sexual Nervosa; Monetary Reticencecia Phobiacisis (Latin, according to

Henri, for the fear of turning a buck); Lunar Induced Timidity; and last, but not least, Ugly As A Frog Syndrome. There was a disease for everyone and everything. No one was turned away.

For ten hours, I ran from office to office—grabbing charts and files, smiling at complete strangers, and offering absurd advice. All the while, Henri was across the hall shouting at defense attorneys on the phone, settling cases for pennies on the dollar, and selling the paintings off the walls, suits out of his closet, and shoes off his feet. It was a capitalistic orgy.

By three in the afternoon, I was exhausted. By five, I was hoarse. I heard Henri across the way imploring one of his clients to accept a wretched settlement. "So you lost an arm, Mrs. Davis, it isn't the end of the world. I got people here with real problems, you know. Listen, the money the insurance company is offering today is very, very good. So it won't even cover your expenses. I'm sorry. Your case just isn't so hot, dear. Believe me. *Believe* me. That-a-girl. We'll do better next time, I'm sure." He slammed down the phone. "Ms. Townsend, get hold of Global Casualty and Indemnity and tell them we'll accept the offer on Mrs. Davis if they can express it over here by six. If not, then all bets are off."

He came running into my office with a fist full of paper. "Take a tape," he demanded, pointing to the calculator. "I gotta know where I stand."

I grabbed the machine. "Shoot."

"Art and furniture sales, $53,000."

"Got it."

"Sales of clothing, underwear, footwear and miscellaneous china pieces, $3,075.65."

"Go."

"Total cash on hand from settlement fire sale, $297,000 and some odd change."

"OK."

"Receipts from psychiatry consultations, $29,800."

"Check."

"Well, that's it. How are we looking?"

I hit the total button. "$382,875.65," I said. "You're still $17,124.35 shy."

"That's close enough," he said. "I can cover the rest out of my checking account if I have to and I'm still expecting to collect more on these settlements before the day is out. But I have to get this cash over to Kiddo Kenny right away. Where's Jules?"

"How in the world did you convert all those checks to cash already?"

"I paid Metro Bank to send over a teller. You'd be surprised what they'll do if they think something is in it for them—like a big deposit."

Henri stuffed the cash tightly into a briefcase and headed for the door. "Hold down the fort for me, Donny. If everything goes as planned, we'll be wining and dining out on the town tonight."

He began running toward the door, briefcase in hand, when suddenly the door flew open and Henri collided with Kiddo Kenny London, entering at a sprint. They both went flying backwards onto the floor.

Kenny slowly sat up, rubbing his nose. Then he assisted me with Henri who was flapping around on the carpet like a just-landed trout. "Kiddo," said Henri, "just the man I wanted to see." He held up the briefcase. "I got all 400,000 smackers."

Kiddo Kenny looked at the briefcase as if it were diseased. "Something awful has gone down, Henri baby," he said. "I'm not quite sure how to tell you."

AMERICAN RAIN

Henri leaped—as well as he could ever leap—to his feet. "What? You didn't get me in on time? You snake, you didn't get me in?"

"I got you in, all right. That ain't it."

"What then?"

"The deal was a sting. The Fed's had the whole thing staked out and set up. When the cartel boys walked in this morning with the first couple million for deposit, they nabbed them and all the bank officials who had been in on it, too. Took them off in leg irons. Then they closed down the Mayfair Bank and Trust. Boarded the sucker right up. And as good as I can guess, the bank is done for."

"Belly up?" asked Henri incredulously.

"Belly up."

Henri grabbed Kiddo Kenny by the neck and began shaking him back and forth. "You mean to tell me I paid you $5,000 cash to invest in a bank that collapsed entirely in one freaking day, you rotten sack of shit?"

"I got h-h-here as f-f-fast as I c-c-could," stuttered Kenny.

"Well, get me OUT!" screamed Henri. "Get my money OUT right now! There's still time, isn't there?"

"I can try," said Kiddo, "but getting through at this hour is almost impossible. I'll do my best."

Henri picked Kiddo Kenny London up by the lapels. "Get me out Kenny, or I'll personally take you apart with a chain saw and bury your various body parts in the basement of your stylish harbor town house. Hear me?"

Kiddo Kenny was sweating bullets. "I'll do it, Henri baby. I won't let you down." He reached inside his jacket and pulled out a piece of paper. "Here," he said.

Henri grabbed it. "What's this?"

"House of Cards," said Kiddo. "He's running in the last race today at Pimlico at ten to one."

"House of Cards is a junker," said Henri with a sneer. "I've seen him run."

"Nah, nah," protested Kiddo Kenny. "They been holding him back. Today's the day. The payoff. Get your four hundred grand in and you'll cover Mayfair Bank and Trust and still pull a bundle for yourself." He looked at me "Right, Donny baby?"

"What else you gonna do?" I said. "At least it's a shot."

"OK, OK," said Henri, rubbing his chin. "Donny, you stay here and keep a gun on Kiddo Kenny. If he can't get my money out on time, I want you to lash him to the front lamp post so's I can have Jules run him over at about a hundred and twenty miles an hour on my way back. If he get's my bucks back, let him go. I'll call you from the track. JULES! JULES!"

Henri ran down the hall carrying the briefcase stocked with money as Jules pulled up out front. Kiddo Kenny winked at me. "I'll just go ahead and use the office across the hall," he said. "I can see you're busy, Donny baby. Let's keep our fingers crossed."

"OK," I said.

I sat back down and sighed. What a nut house, I thought. The problem with life at Henri's was there was no time to sit and think, to plot your next move. There was no time for anything. The whole house seemed entirely out of control. Then the door opened and Marcy Trimble came in. I sat stiffly upright. I tried to smile. "Good evening," I said.

She smiled the briefest smile. "Hello."

I had caught glimpses of her on and off throughout the day but had not been able to catch her eye, such was the frenzy of our pace. But she had not been out of my mind since the night before, and her sudden appearance caught me off guard. My mouth felt paralyzed. "H-how's the weather out there today?" I asked, trying hard to warm up the atmosphere.

"In the hallway?" she replied, slowly.

"Well, no. Actually, I meant outside."

She turned casually toward the window. "It appears pleasant enough," she said.

"Oh, yeah."

"Doctor," she continued, "I have your last appointment for the day." She handed me a folder and put her hands on her hips. She was beautiful.

I dropped the folder and slammed my head into the desk top trying to pick it up gracefully. I opened the case file judiciously. "Well, let's see what we have here," I said, trying to appear professional. "Ah-hmm. . . . Hmmm. Ah-hmm. Dr. Myron Wilmer, eh?"

"Yes," she said.

I tossed the file down on the desk top and folded my hands behind my head. I smiled again. "What can you tell me about him?"

She arched an eyebrow. "What can I tell you?"

"W-w-well yeah," I stuttered. "You know, what's he like, for instance?"

"Well," she responded, "you are the psychiatrist, are you not? Why ask me?" There was fire in her eyes.

It was clear I was using the wrong approach. "You're right," I said, looking away. "So, where is he?"

Just for a moment her eyes seemed to soften. "Well, I think he's out back right now. Of course, you'll know when he's arrived." With that she turned abruptly and marched out of the room.

I didn't have time to feel despondent because I immediately heard an enormous ruckus. There was a loud slamming and bashing that started at the back entrance and continued down the hall towards my office. I jumped up to see what was going on and threw open the door.

It was as strange a sight as I had ever seen. Down the hall was a bearded gentleman in a three piece suit, banging his way down the corridor on a pair of cross-country skis. He stumbled and lurched, reeling this way and that as furniture toppled behind him and pictures flew from the walls. I stepped aside as he came at me furiously, bounced off the door jamb and collapsed upon the nearest chair. Then he pulled a handkerchief from his back pocket, wiped his face thoroughly and gave me a smile. "There now," he said, placing his hands on this knees, "that wasn't so difficult after all."

I gazed upon him for what seemed like several minutes, nonplussed. Finally, I sat down. "You must be quite the enthusiast," I offered.

He looked at me noncommittally. "I recently became one," he acknowledged.

"I see." I let out a long, slow breath. "What can I do for you, Doctor?"

"Well, Doctor," he replied, pausing slightly for just the right words, "it seems I've developed a bit of a problem."

My eyes wandered to the shattered lamps, fractured chairs, and harpooned murals that littered the corridor outside. "Oh . . . really?"

"Yes. Specifically, I need your help in order to resolve, or at least better address, certain anxieties with which I am currently struggling."

I thought: this acorn's the king of the squirrel stash. "Go on, Doctor," I said.

"As my file adequately reflects," he continued, "I am a nuclear physicist presently employed at one of the world's largest particle accelerators. For several years,

I have been immersed in the realm of quantum mechanics—quarks, photons, quanta, you know—and as a result of my considerable research have developed certain, shall we say, understandings of the physical universe."

"What sort of understandings are we talking about here, Doctor?"

"The precise nature of these cognitions is neither important nor germane to my visit here today. Suffice it to say that my understandings have generated within me certain feelings of anxiety for which I require your professional judgement in coping. That is all! I am not deranged or otherwise psychologically deficient, I assure you."

Quickly, as if to underscore the statement, he crossed his legs and accidentally swatted the lamp on my desk with the tip of his ski. It fell to the floor with a horrendous crash. I looked at the shattered lamp on the floor and arched an eyebrow. "That might be a matter of opinion," I said.

"I think not," he countered. "I'm really quite well."

"Doctor," I asked, "do you wear those skis all the time?"

"Well . . . yes."

"Everywhere?"

"Ah huh."

"And Doctor," I continued, pressing my fingers together, "would you categorize cross-country skis as the usual and sporting toggery worn by most swashbuckling physicists in Baltimore this spring?"

"Well, no, but . . . ."

"I see," I said emphatically. "So, would you concur that wearing skis on a public conveyance might even be considered somewhat less than normal by an entirely neutral observer?"

"Hmmm, perhaps," he admitted, stroking his beard.

"Maybe even, odd?"

"Well, odd is a relative term," he argued. "I agree it would be odd for most of my colleagues, but not for me."

I was incredulous. "And why is that?"

He sighed. "Because, as I said, I have arrived at certain fundamental understandings regarding the nature of reality that make these skis not only prudent, but virtually required attire. That's why."

"For you but no one else? Not even your colleagues?"

"That's exactly right," he said. "Because I know, and they don't."

"Know what?"

He recrossed his legs anxiously and sent my pen and pencil set flying into the wall. "Sorry."

"You're dangerous."

"I don't quite have the hang of these just yet," he acknowledged. "They're really not made for hallways and sidewalks, you know. Just give me a little time. I'll be all right."

"Well, I'm not going to hold my breath," I said. "Now, you were saying?"

He stared at me for a long while without speaking. "I can't tell you everything. I wish I could, but I can't. Suffice it to say that in the course of my research, I have come to the inevitable conclusion that if one pursues these matters—quarks, neutrinos, photons, quanta, etc.—beyond their differences one discovers a startling commonality."

"I'm no physicist," I said, "but are you talking about some sort of grand unification theory?"

"Precisely."

"And what precisely is this startling commonality?"

"Look, I really should not tell you this. It's very difficult to absorb." He sighed. "Oh well. Listen, if I tell you, please don't overreact."

"I promise," I said.

"What I'm saying is that mountains, atoms, quarks, light, quanta, the whole shebang, are merely temporary representations of the same elementary substance."

"Which is?"

"Nothing."

". . . Say again?"

"Nothing," he repeated. "You see, I shouldn't have told you."

My first inclination was to hit him over the head with something heavy, but I fought it. I'm not sure why. "Nothing?" I repeated.

"Precisely."

I laughed in his face. "But here we are."

"Yes, of course. We are, to a certain extent, because we know no better. We are because we believe we are, because we force the universe into a certain focus. Do you understand? And once we lose that sureness of focus, the universe can crumble beneath our feet. So now I wear cross-country skis because I'm scared that I will crash right through the veneer of this universe and never be heard from again. They are my only support, my lifeline to existence."

"But if the entire universe is nothing at all, why should even the skis hold you up?"

"Because I am not absolutely certain. There is still just a minor, residual doubt in the back of my mind that I cannot shake. I believe it must be innate to our species. Perhaps to every living thing. How else could everything work as it does? So anyway, as long as there is not absolute certainty on my part, the skis seem to be enough of a buffer to keep me afloat."

"Excuse me, Doctor," I said. With that I walked out into the hall and went to the window for some air. I had developed a sudden, brutal headache. As I stood by the window and tried to keep from screaming, it came to me that the office was closing down and that almost everyone had already gone home for the evening. I felt adrift, as though I was about to fall through the floor and disappear forever. I felt lonely and absurd. Then I saw Marcy and out of misery more than anything, I think, decided to take a stab at her one more time. "Long day," I said as she packed her things up behind her desk.

"Yes."

"Listen," I said, "I . . . ah, know we haven't been introduced formally or anything, but I'm kinda the new guy in town here and I was wondering if . . ."

Her eyes flared. "Save your breath," she fairly spat. She folded her arms tightly across her chest. "Get something straight, Doctor," she said, "I work here because I have to, not because I want to. I put up with the constant degradation and humiliation, the pinches and unending sexual innuendo because I have no other choice. But I have no more intention of going to bed with you than I do with Dr. Lafayette, who has demanded that I have sexual intercourse with him every day for the past four months. Do you understand?"

"Yes."

"Good!" she said. "Now you can go straight to hell." With that she whirled and marched off down the hall.

Slowly I walked back down the corridor and into the office. I slumped into my chair. I deserve this, I thought. I deserve it for having joined in this absurd charade. She detests me and she has every right. As long as I stay, I'm no different than Max. The grand

AMERICAN RAIN

dreams of destiny that had filled my head only a day or so before now seemed to me very tiny then.

Dr. Wilmer stirred. "So you see," he said, "I require some serious professional assistance with my state of anxiety. The things I have come to know I shall have to live with forever," he continued, "but it is with this constant fear, this wrenching knot in my stomach, that I need your help in coping. Do you have any ideas?"

I was miserable. I could care less about the lunatic physicist across from me. I was nothing. Less than nothing, I was scum. I was tired and hoarse and desolate. I went to the cabinets and found a bottle of whiskey that was almost empty. I dumped the remainder into a glass and added a few ice cubes and a twist of lemon. It looked wonderful. I came back to the desk and put it down."

"Right!" said Dr. Wilmer, grabbing the drink almost from my hand and tossing it down in three gulps. "Now that's certainly a new and novel approach," he said, licking the last residue of whiskey from his lips with his tongue. "I think I feel better already. Sort of relaxed. By golly, you are a revolutionary, Doctor, a visionary." He leaped from his seat. "Cheerio," he said, saluting. "Until next week, Herr Doctor." He withdrew as he had entered, leaving piles of splintered furniture in his wake.

When the back door slammed shut, I was alone. I sat there between the pieces of broken wood and the pieces of my own fractured dreams, and in the silence of the empty house the howl of my desperation was almost deafening.

6

For what must have been an hour, I sat by the window overlooking the harbor in The Brig and watched thunderheads build to the west. I recalled long ago summer days when I had watched similar swirls gather out that way, over Sykesville or even as far west as Frederick, then come tumbling over Baltimore in a swift and violent burst. Slowly the sunshine gave way to heavy clouds and gusty winds. Then the wind stopped and the first few drops fell, dinging car hoods and awnings as people scurried from the patios and walkways. I motioned to the waitress and ordered another gin and tonic.

I looked back along Pratt Street where traffic was already at a standstill because of the rain. Poor suckers, I thought. Then it hit. In a rush of wind and lightning, the storm exploded over the city in one huge shudder. Trees bent almost to the ground and the harbor became choppy as anchored sailboats strained furiously at their moorings. Rain in a sheet drummed the window in front of me and pooled below on the sidewalks. Deafening peels of thunder ripped overhead but still, above this, above even the piano and the drunken laughter from the bar, I could hear Henri howling as he talked on the phone across the room. Nothing, it seemed, could drown out his good humor. It was depressing.

Somehow the storm reminded me of the futility of my past few days. I'm not sure why. Perhaps it was the simple waste of such enormous energy, the destruction the gale would spawn along the shoreline and down river. It would leave only sunken boats, gutted homes, and broken trees. The very seed of life, rather than nurtured by the rain, would be washed away to die in the muddy bay and sink away from sight out in the open sea. Such energy, such possibilities, squandered.

I ordered still another gin and tonic—they were going down quickly—and listened to the violent din slowly lose force and subside. In fifteen minutes, the whole thing was over and Henri came lumbering happily across the dance floor with a drink in each hand. He sported a wicked grin as he sank into the chair beside me. "I love Kiddo Kenny," he said. "Guy's a genius. I ever tell you that?"

"Yeah, you've told me that."

"Know why I'm smiling? Know why I'm singing 'Zippity Do Dah?'"

"Let me take a stab at it. Your horse posted."

He winked. "Hey, those degrees of yours really did make you smart. You hit the nail on the head."

"So what happened?" I asked.

"Not only did Kiddo Kenny manage to get me out of Mayfair Bank and Trust in time with, I might add, a small profit on active trading before the closing bell, but House of Cards came in at five to one. I ain't RICH, Donny, but for today just plain old rich will do." He tried to cross his legs twice but they were too chunky so he just flung them out in front of him and slumped down in the chair. "That's America, kid, roll those dice.

Every day just roll'em. Some come up winners, some losers."

I laughed humorlessly. "America," I said. "Listen to you, Max. You're making me sick here. You don't know squat."

"Yeah? Who just bagged himself a cool two million and broke the freaking bank at Pimlico? Not you, teacher."

"Money isn't everything," I said, but my words rang hollow to even me. "Look," I pleaded, "this whole deal just isn't working. Today I talked myself hoarse to a few hundred nuts. All I, no, correct that, we, did today was take their money. We accomplished *nothing*."

Henri was astonished. He held up a wad of bills. "*This*," he said, "is nothing?"

"Is that all there is to it?" I asked, obviously rhetorically. "No," I went on quickly, answering my own question. "I left home to find something important in life, to become more than I had ever allowed myself to be before, not to completely lose my self-respect. Which is precisely what I've managed to accomplish."

Henri smiled coyly. "All right, all right," he said, reaching deep into his pocket. He pulled out an enormous roll of cash and started whipping off thousand dollar bills and laying them on the table. "Of course, I was going to pay you, kid. I just wanted to feel the bulk of that roll next to my leg for awhile. Really! Come on, what did you think, I was going to stiff my favorite nephew on his first big pay day?"

"Yes, but that's honestly beside the point. It's not the bucks," I said, waving the money aside. It's the way I've come to feel about myself. What I am."

"What you are is a whole lot better off than you were yesterday."

"That's a matter of opinion. That girl Marcy talked to me tonight as though I were trash. Like I'm slime or something."

He laughed. "I told you not to bother with that slit. She talks the same to everyone. She even talks like that to me. Look," he continued, "you want a piece of ass?" He held up a thousand dollar bill. "Here," he said, "I'll buy you the absolutely best piece in town. One call, no sweat."

I shook my head. "You don't understand. We're just not talking about the same thing here."

Just then the waitress returned with another round of drinks and a bottle of sparkling Italian wine. Henri pulled a smaller bill from his pocket, showed her the face, then rubbed it slowly across her buttocks, over her thigh, and deposited it with a flourish in her undergarment. She smiled, thanked us both, and walked away.

I was stunned. "I can't believe you would do that here," I said. This is a classy restaurant."

He chuckled. "Only difference between high class and low class, kid," he said, "is the face on the bill it takes to toy with the waitress's crotch. You got the right kinda green, kid, then a little tush comes along with the meal just like these jumbo cocktails and fresh bread. It's understood."

"At the risk of sounding overly puritanical," I said disgustedly, "that's just pure bullshit. What you do is dehumanizing."

He waved my protest aside. "It's a transaction, Donny, pure and simple." He picked up his Bloody Mary and downed it in three monstrous swallows, then wiped his mouth with the back of his sleeve. "I'm buying, she's selling. That's all of it. It's jerks like you who try to make more of it than it is." He pointed to his chest. "I should know," he said, "I'm a psychiatrist."

"Is everything just a transaction, Max? Do you really believe that? That nothing goes on out there but mercantile aggrandizement? Twelve-year-old kids die in the streets with needles in their arms. A transaction! Right? Wall Street assholes buy and sell people, ruin lives, crush souls, then go have a martini or two. Just another deal, right? Scum buckets dump contaminated filth down city sewers and don't give a shit who's children they murder because it's just business. Is that the way you see it?"

I was furious. I rolled my cocktail napkin into a ball and tossed it against the window. "Christ, Max, look out there," I demanded. "Even the rain is poison these days, your sweet American rain, just so much toxic sewage! Go smell it." I shook my head. "If you ask me, the whole fucking world is nuts."

"That's just a slew of liberal claptrap," he said. He laughed out of the side of his mouth. "The environment already. Christ, that's priceless. What you need, kid, is a little down home cooking, some solid conservative awareness, and such."

I couldn't believe my ears. "Max," I said, "I *am* a conservative. What, fer God's sake, do you know about *anything*?"

"Calm down, you're embarrassing me. A lot of my friends and acquaintances eat here and I don't want them to hear that kind of tripe. Let's just be civil and have another drink."

"Max . . ." I protested.

"Henri, already."

"Henri," I said, "that's six cocktails. Is there no end to any of this?"

He pointed a mean finger. "Don't lecture me, punk. I just cleared over two mil and I ain't gonna sit here and listen to this puke of yours. I'm just trying to have a good time. I ain't hurting no one, so back off! I have half a mind to slap you with an invasion of privacy suit if you start flapping those fat lips of yours again."

That did it. I stood up, hurled my napkin across the room, and stalked out of the restaurant, face red, heart racing. I had to walk, to move, to get away.

I walked for hours, oblivious of time and place. I don't recall the streets. I remember the breeze whipping at my face, blowing newspapers this way and that. I remember the sound and color of the city at night—the flash, the urgency, the smell of rain on the sidewalks. I walked like a machine, grinding along, burning energy and anxiety with every step until eventually I was alone, tired, and lost.

I thought of Max. Was that all we were . . . transactions, I wondered? Were we all just minor cogs in a mercantile wheel, trading this for that, having value only in utility, in fulfilling our part of the bargain? I looked out across the city. From where I stood, the downtown towers glowed and sparkled in the night, but they seemed hollow to me then, cold, empty memorials to . . . to what? To the bottom line. They were big because bigness generated more revenue. They were beautiful only because beauty attracted clients, big clients, better clients. Max was wrong, I thought. The law is not cash flow. The whole damn world is cash flow.

I stuffed my hands in my pockets and started back. I walked for another hour or so. I marched through Fells Point and Little Italy. I stopped on Baltimore Street for a hot dog and a cup of coffee. It was cool and damp on the street, even for June. I buttoned my coat and looked around.

The Block. All around me pimps hustled their trade, calling to the drunks and conventioneers, selling women, drugs, and death. Colored lights sparkled and blinked everywhere, electric affectation. But it was a carnival without cheer, a circus with no enthusiasm. The actors went about their rolls almost as if in a trance, as if the blood had been sucked from their veins. An old woman fell asleep in the alley across the way covered in newspaper and excrement as a dapper next door put a blow job on his American Express card. America.

I finished my coffee and wondered if the old women would be alive in the morning. It was not fear I sensed, only death. It was there, in the alley, on the faces of the hawkers and the girls as they performed. So close. People did not die on the Block, I suddenly realized, they simply faded deeper into the shadows, forever into the night where death waited patiently to claim them like a hooded scavenger.

A young woman straggled down the street, eyes unfocused, dress torn, obviously consumed by drugs. A young man followed on her heels, screaming this and that, then suddenly knocking her viciously to the ground. Before I could move, he kicked her in the side of the head, then again once more before the police, who were everywhere, managed to drag him away. Few stopped. Less cared.

Drugs, I thought, were everywhere, infesting everything. People were too scared to take the train anymore, to walk the streets, to breathe fresh air. And there seemed no end to it, no sanctuary from the cancerous grip they had on the land. We had become a nation with a needle in it's vein, constantly jazzed and utterly numb to the consequences. I felt like screaming. But at who?

My country had been stolen away, snatched from beneath my feet by a power I couldn't see or confront, taken hostage by the very death I felt so close at hand in the alleys and shadows of night. This enraged me. I felt a sudden and enormous hatred for the pimps and pushers, but it didn't stop there. I hated, as well, the professional apologists who excused it all, who denied every trace of human responsibility. And I hated, too, the fat cats with their buildings and cars who, absolved and above the fray, turned their backs on every honest cry for help. My hate was overwhelming.

I started to walk, then run. I sprinted from the lights, passed the garish placards and hawkers, down Gay Street toward the water. I ran around the harbor until, winded and puffing furiously, I sprawled in the grass near Federal Hill.

There was no one near. Clouds swirled slowly above, the city light playing, shimmering on their flanks. I watched. I laid in the grass and listened to the slap of water on the bulkheads of the boats anchored nearby. It was calming. I was gripped by a sense of vertigo, a profound inability to grasp what I had seen and been through over the past days. Who would bring my county back, I wondered? Where had it gone?

The grass was wet and a chill came upon me. It was very late, I realized. I moved uphill and curled up under a tree. I was too tired to be scared or care. I slept.

I awoke early to the first shafts of red sun that lanced the smoke stacks on Sparrows Point, far to the east. I sat up against the tree trunk and watched the city come slowly to life. As the sun rose steadily and warmed the air, the last few lights blinked off and a few trucks rumbled by below me. Within the hour, the vast industry that was America was up and buzzing about me. I was enthralled.

I walked down to the harbor and found a small eatery that was open. I ordered bacon and eggs and drank several cups of hot coffee. When I finished that, I grabbed a Danish and walked up the street.

On Baltimore Street I was shocked by the alteration. The Block was no more. Oh, the posters and placards were still there—the shops still standing, the lights still in place—but in the clean light of morning the Block seemed to have faded like a chimera into simple mortar and stone. No longer did I feel the presence of death but, to the contrary, the power and reach of the human spirit. Skyward, new buildings were soaring around me as construction crews labored under the new sun. On the sidewalks men and women scurried to work, their faces set, their steps determined.

Then I remembered the old women in the alley and, with a sense of guilt, ambled back that way. She was not there, but further up the street I found her nodding against the street lamp in front of a small hardware store. She was alive. During the night she had seemed an awful sight, a symbol of death, but in the bright morning light, she appeared nothing more than pathetic, almost invisible. As I started to turn to go, a man came out of the store and approached her. He was a black man with gentle features. He stooped over and left a small sandwich and a container—perhaps soup—on the curb next to her. He started back toward his store when he caught my eye. He stopped. "Mr. Harris?" He asked.

"Who . . . me?" I said.

"Yeah, you Mr. Harris from social services?"

"No."

"Oh, oh, sorry. Thought you might be."

"No. My name is Don Mallory. I'm just walking," I said, feeling the need to justify myself.

"Oh. Well, hello to you, Mr. Mallory. I'm David Winthrop. That's my store, Winthrop's Hardware. Need a good hammer?"

"Not right now."

He laughed. "Well, look me up if you do. He looked at the woman on the curb. "Sad thing," he said.

"Yes," I agreed.

He shrugged. "Ain't got nothing, see. Half of 'em are nuts, I think. What can you do?"

"I don't know," I said.

"That makes two of us, Mr. Mallory." He looked up and down the street. "The one's that wind up around here I try to give a little something in the morning, see. If I got enough money, that is. Hate to see anyone hungry, even the nuts."

"That's decent." I said.

"Yeah," he said. "See you around."

"OK," I said. I watched him walk down the street with another sandwich and container in his hand. I lowered my head, ashamed. At that moment I learned something essential from David Winthrop. For all of my self-righteous fury, for all of my finger pointing and hatred, I had accomplished exactly nothing. No one would eat better, sleep warmer, learn more, or be saved from any tortured demon because I, in a fit of moral fragility, had decided to run away from it all. The simplest act far outshines even the grandest of notions. David Winthrop showed me up for what I was: a windy fool.

On Baltimore Street the truth of this came to me with a clarity that could not be denied. If tomorrow was going to be better than today, it would have to come as it had always come, through the small and caring efforts of decent people. Even I could do something. I turned and started back.

By the time I had managed my way back to The Center for Psychiatric Retribution, the sun was high. I was tired, my clothes were dirty, my face and arms were bathed in sweat. I went in the back door and ran into Marcy in the hall. She stood back for a moment or two and appraised my condition. She seemed disturbed. "Dr. Lafayette has been quite concerned about you," she said. She folded her arms. "We . . . he was very worried that he said something to you that was mean and out of line." She looked down. "And so was I."

"What?"

"And so was I," she repeated. "I'm glad you're back. I'm glad you're all right. What I said to you yesterday was uncalled for. I don't even know you. Sorry."

I rolled my shoulders. "It's OK," I said.

With that she turned quickly and disappeared down the hall.

I started upstairs to my room when Henri spotted me and came flying out of his office. "Donny!" he shouted, "Thank God you're home!" He waddled up to me and slapped me on the shoulders. "You had me worried, running off like that."

"I'm OK."

"Well, that's great," he replied. "By the way, I want you to know I gave a lot of thought to some of the things you said last night, and I think you're absolutely right."

"Say what?"

"Yes, absolutely right."

I was astonished. "About what, for instance?"

"About not taking care of myself and always going off half-cocked. It's going to get me in deep shit some day. So I've decided to tone it down considerably."

"That's unbelievable, Henri," I said. "How so?"

"Well, from now on I've instructed Alvon to stop ordering those cheap Italian vintages for the house cellars and to concentrate only on the better Bordeaux and German wines. And I'm going to start working on my tan this very afternoon. That's what you had in mind, isn't it?"

I put my arm around him. "Yes, Henri," I said. "That's exactly what I had in mind."

7

"Well, well, well," intoned Pastor Frickenfrayor, marching smartly into my office with an arm full of papers. "Good to see you again, Dr. Mallory." He sat and smiled sincerely. "Hope you're doing well. I know," he said, gazing slowly around the room, "that these particular surroundings might, shall we say, grate on someone of reasonable—or maybe even of just modest—intelligence."

I laughed.

His eyes glowed. "I've been thinking about our conversation of a few days past. What has it been now?"

"Two weeks, Pastor."

"Has it been that long? My, time certainly flies when you're seriously engaged, doesn't it."

"Indeed."

"Well, I believe I have turned our little talk into a boffo Bible bonanza of sorts. In other words, I hit the bomb, the mother load, the blockbuster of blockbusters."

"Gosh," I said, "you certainly sound up about it."

"Up isn't the term, Monsieur Mallory. I feel positively exultant."

"Pray, tell."

He smiled. "No pun intended, I'm sure," he said. "Well, I just took to heart what you said about my previous efforts and I came to the conclusion that you were absolutely correct. No one would be moved in a religious sense by diet or investment advice. There's already plenty of that afoot. No, I needed more. I needed to blast their eyes right out of their sockets, to grab hold and yank their faces across the room. I needed a Bible with some POW and ZIIINNNG! I wanted to wrestle their attention onto the floor and put it into a full nelson for keeps. I meant business."

"Sounds like it," I said. "So what did you do?"

"So I wrote a Bible with some bite, if you know what I mean. Some goddam, God-fearing PIZZAZZ." He held it up. "This here Bible barks, son. I took the gloves off. Just catch this and see if it don't knock the flock back a pew or two." He thumbed hurriedly through the pages. "Here we go," he said, "The Book of Lamentations, verses six through seventeen":

> And the Lord of Hosts kicked open the door with one big, brawny foot and pointed a mean finger at the defilers of his blessed temple.
>
> "Seek not," he warned them, "the excesses of the dollar and dime, the false pleasures of earthly delight, lest I shalt lay the back of my righteous knuckles onto the nape of thine necks, and knock thou miserable butts ass-over-tea kettle halfway to Toledo."
>
> And when the assembled brethren heard his words, they trembled, sank to their knees and were sore afraid. But still others didn't give a hoot. Some complained, some ignored him, while others went ahead and booked weekend flights to Lake Tahoe.

And when the Lord of David saw this he said, "OK, have it your way, but see how you like this . . ." and he sent forth upon the land of Canaan, the land of Brooklyn, the land of the twenty-five dollar oil change, a host of journalists to hound them into the grave, a phalanx of attorneys to ensnare them, an army of scientists to betray them, and a few lousy psy-chiatrists to addle their brains.

And when the Lord saw the destruction and gnashing of teeth his vengeance had occasioned, he frowned and spake unto them that would listen . . .

"Not such a pretty sight, is it?"

He looked up at me.

"Well," I said, "you've definitely taken off the gloves, haven't you?"

"You bet," he replied, standing suddenly and throwing imaginary punches around the room. "And you ain't heard nothing yet." He stopped and quickly grabbed another paper from his collection. "This I wrote about the ten trillion religions that parade about this earth in various disguises, quarreling, bitching and just generally getting on my nerves. The Book of Impersonations I call it. Here, verses fourteen through thirty-one . . ."

> The pious utterings that spewed forth from the mouths of imperious impostors were so loud and deafening that the simple truths of Jesus could no longer be heard.
>
> Cast out these foolish rantings, sayeth the Lord, lest they piss on my whole parade with this stuff. But no one would stop to listen.

Such was the vanity, conniving, and contempt of these conspiring charlatans that his words were lost forever amidst the unctuous din of their platitudes, and the self-important claptrap they preached from their pompous pulpits was much like sludge—deep, dark, and hazardous to the health.

He slammed a fist on the desk top. "Let's see how they like that, eh, Dr. Mallory?"

"Rough stuff," I agreed.

"One more," he said, leafing through his notes. "Yeah, yeah, here it is. I wrote this for all those folks I saw come into my church and leave halfway through the service. My heart went with them, Donald, because I had nothing to hold them. And nothing for a preacher on Sunday means the end of the line. Ready?"

"Fire away."

"You got it. I call it simply, Verses. This is one through five . . ."

> I heard a song of Jesus
> A whisper from afar.
> But misty time so clouds his fate
> That I am left to speculate
> And wish upon a star

He closed his pad and looked me directly in the eye. "Well?"

"I like that. And the rest certainly buries the needle on the zingometer, all right."

"And?"

"And that's about it," I said. "It's all well and good, but I'm not sure that's what it's going to take."

He banged the desk angrily. "What are you trying to tell me, Mr. Mallory?" He held up his notes. "This stuff is terrific. This will knock their eyes right out of their sockets."

"So will the cancan," I said. "So what?"

He was miserable. "What is it you want from me?"

"Hey," I objected, "I don't want anything. This was all your idea, remember? I just happen to think people want meaning, not a mallet in the face."

"Meaning, huh?"

"Yeah," I said. "Got any?"

He shrugged. "In my heart, yes. In my head, well . . . I'm not so sure."

"Well, maybe that's what you need to try," I said. "Let your heart do the writing."

He shook his head violently. "No, no," he said, "that's going backwards, right back to the mysticism and vast unknown from whence religion sprung in the first place. It goes directly against what I am trying to accomplish. No, if religion is going to survive, it must adapt. It must be willing to deal with reality and answer hard questions. To step right up to old Mr. Science and go toe to toe. Trouble is, I don't know how to do that."

"What's this hang-up you have with science?" I asked.

"I told you before—science has all the big answers these days. If you want to know the origin of life or the destiny of mankind, you call a physicist. You wanna know what kind of flowers to send to Aunt Lucy's anniversary gala, you call me."

"Bull," I said. "Listen, how imposing can science be when it can't even answer a child's simplest question."

"Yeah, what's that?"

"Why? Look, science can tell us that the universe started with a big bang, but it can't tell us why. Sure," I continued, "it can tell us that the initial phase of the whole thing was a point of infinite density, a singularity—but it can't tell us why, or what happened before that. And it doesn't even try. Know why?"

"Why?"

"'Cause physics is trapped inside itself. It can't even begin to address certain questions because it doesn't have the means. So they just pretend the questions aren't there."

He folded his hands and gave me a long solemn look. "Are you religious, son?"

"No," I answered.

"And yet you have within you a sense of awe, a notion of God's majesty. The church has lost you to science."

"No, the church has lost me to truth."

He smiled. "Yet God is truth."

I folded my arms across my chest. "Tell that to Galileo," I said.

He nodded. "I understand what you say, but the church has come a long way since the Inquisition. You're not being fair."

I shrugged. "Only in terms of method," I said. "The mind-set, even the message is still the same. Religion is simply opposed to thought in any matter that conflicts with established dogma. Always has been. And if it's opposed to thought then it's opposed to truth. Why is the truth so scary?"

"The truth doesn't scare me," he replied.

"Then preach it," I said. "I dare you."

He looked at me for a long while with his chin in the palm of his hand. Finally he said, "The truth from the heart, huh?"

I was just about to answer him when the phone buzzed. It was the intercom. "Yeah?" I said. It was

Henri and he wanted me to join him for a meeting posthaste. "Excuse me, Pastor, I'll be back in a moment."

I excused myself and walked down the hall to Henri's office. He was behind his desk. Kiddo Kenny London was laying on the sofa with his feet dangling over the end, and another gentleman I didn't recognize was sitting in an armchair. "Donny," said Henri, "this is Mr. R. C. Smythe, local account executive for A.A.A. And, of course, you know Kiddo Kenny, my financial genius."

"Kenny," I said.

"Donny baby."

I shook hands. "Nice to meet you, Mr. Smythe. Great organization you got there. Just last year one of your boys towed me out of a snow bank."

"Ah, no," said R. C. Smythe with a humorless grin, "not that triple A." He pulled out a business card and handed it to me. "I'm with Americans for an American America, the Christian political syndicate. Heard of us?"

"'Fraid not."

R. C. Smythe crossed his legs. "We don't seek publicity, Mr. Mallory. We try to influence various situations within this great republic from behind the scenes. Thus I'm not surprised."

"So what's it all about?" I asked.

"It's about Americans for an American America!" Henri shouted. "Didn't you hear?"

"What the hell is that supposed to mean?"

Kiddo Kenny London sat up. "Geez, Donny baby, get with the program already. It's about being for America. It's about being for Americans who are also for America. See?"

"Oh, thank you very much, Mr. London," I said. "Now it's all very clear."

Henri poured everyone a glass of wine. "Mr. Smythe is here for our money, Donny, and I wanted to know what you thought."

"Here for our money?" I said.

R. C. Smythe smiled that humorless smile again. "Offering, actually. We much prefer to call it an offering." He turned to me. "As I was explaining to Dr. Lafayette, we of the Christian syndicate are presently implementing certain, shall we say, arrangements with other like-minded Americans across this great land of ours in order—as Thomas Jefferson so aptly put it—to form a more perfect union. But, of course, that takes money. Lots of it."

"What kind of arrangements?" I asked.

"Well, our syndicate has been deeply and religiously involved in certain key local political contests. And Mr. Mallory, through the power of prayer and the strength of the Great Jehovah, our syndicate has prevailed and the American we backed was elected."

"That's clout, Donny," Henri offered, nodding his head.

I turned to R. C. Smythe. "You buy elections?"

He screwed up his face. "Influence, Mr. Mallory. We influence. Buy is a very ugly word."

"Very actionable," Henri added.

"Exactly," continued R. C. "And we have discovered over the years that our influence tends to be much more influential at the local level than at the national. So that's where we are concentrating our prayers and offerings this go round."

"But you didn't tell him the great part, R. C.," bubbled Henri, barely able to control himself. "Tell him the best part."

"Well," R. C. went on, "we of the Christian syndicate feel it our charitable and Christian duty to reciprocate earthly tidings wherever and whenever possible or, in the words of our trusted corporate council, 'legally exculpable.'"

Henri jumped to his feet. "Get it? It means they know where their bread is buttered, Donny. We take care of them, they take care of us. Right R. C.?"

"More or less."

Henri grew very still. He closed his eyes and put one hand above us all to lead in prayer. "The first dynamic principle of economic righteousness flows strongly here among us," he said. "Oh, I can feel it in the room. God is happy with this deal." Then his eyes popped open and seemed to expand twofold. "In the great and immortal words of Jesus H. Christ himself, 'One hand washes the other.' Right R. C.? That's what makes America great!"

"Well, I'm not sure I recall tha . . ." said R. C. Smythe, but he stopped in mid-sentence as Kiddo Kenny London rose from the sofa, clearly galvanized by Henri's recitation, a look of wonder in his eyes.

"I'm moved," he said, holding his heart. "Get this, fellas," he continued, struggling for words, "I, I'm not a religious man . . ."

"No," said Henri.

". . . but listening to what Henri just said made me damn proud of him, and damn proud to be an American, too. And, Mr. Smythe, I'd love to be a member of a fine and patriotic organization like Americans for an American America, but I have to know just one thing."

"Wonderful," said R. C. Smythe, "and what is that?"

"What's my percentage?"

R. C. Smythe was confused. "Excuse me?"

"My cut, my percentage, my take?"

"Well, I'm really at a loss for words." said R. C.

Kiddo Kenny stepped to the center of the room, his hand still over his heart. "'Cause it's like Henri was saying, R. C., America is strong and revered worldwide because it is the great land of percentages. Everybody gets a cut. You get yours, I get mine. See? Democracy. That's why I love being a broker, because it's just as American as apple pie. Any action goes down, I get a cut. Even your interest groups are jumping on the bandwagon now because they understand the great principle of percentages. America, we are a nation of ten percenters."

"That's beautiful, Kenny," Henri said sarcastically, "and it shows you to be just the freaking leech you are. America is more than just a nation of ten percenters like you. By God, it's a nation of doers, of visionaries, of men like me who roll the dice every day and create wealth and health out of the sheer force of our iron wills."

Henri's words made my stomach heave. "Listen to this crap," I said. "How about both of you giving us a break?"

"It's true," argued Henri, leaping up behind his desk. "America is a country of rugged individualists like myself. Men who play hard and fast with the rules in order to build on a Herculean scale. Look out there!" he demanded. "Everything you see around here has been built by men like me, and I'm no ten percenter." He turned to Kiddo Kenny. "Excuse me, Kenny, but guys like you are nothing but parasites, living off the creative genius of minds like my own. You're nothing but in the right place at the right time. You do nothing but be in the right place at the right time."

Kiddo Kenny's face turned crimson. "I happen to be a financial genius," he protested. "I work my balls off day and night trading everything from apples to zebra pelts in order to make investors like you fatter than you already are—which, in your case, may be a physical impossibility." He turned quickly my way. "By the way, Don, babe, I have access to a few hundred crates of smashing new Uzis that are going for a remarkable discount if you're interested."

"Machine guns?" I said.

"Yeah."

"No thanks, Ken."

"Well, then, back to you, fat man. Just exactly where do you get off parading around as someone who builds anything or helps anyone? You're nothing but a thief. Only person you ever help is yourself—and that's to your clients' wallets. You got some nerve calling me a blood sucker."

"That's a lie and a slander!" wailed Henri, tramping purposefully around the corner of his desk to confront Kenny.

"Oh yeah," Kiddo Kenny yelled.

"Yeah!"

"Oh yeah."

"Yeah!"

"Gentlemen, gentlemen," protested R. C. Smythe, boldly holding up both hands as if to stop a runaway train. "Let us not be at one another's throats about this. It pains me to see two devout Americans quarreling when they both have semi-valid visions of what America is."

Henri pulled the fat cigar from his lips and looked into R. C.'s eyes. "Semi?" he said.

"Yes. America is certainly a place where ten per-centers and bold men of vision may flourish, but more importantly, it is a land of cultural and religious purity. It is the prize of Abraham, the gift of the Father, my friends, and we must always strive as a first priority to keep her unaltered and undiluted by heathen customs and ways. We must, above all else, preserve."

Just then the door flew open and Pastor Frickenfrayor burst into the room, face aglow, eyes flashing. He pointed at R. C. Smythe. "Fraud!" he screamed. "Impostor, charlatan! You, sir, are a disgrace." He leaped over a chair into the middle of the fray. "Be off with thine false preaching, infidel. Thou make'st me want to puke. America is not a place for religious intolerance and exclusion as you so cleverly portray it. It is the Lord's intention that America be a shining example of religious tolerance and inclusion. You blaspheme with your tarnished and bitter message."

R. C. blew up his chest like a strutting fowl. "Who is this maniac?" he demanded. "How dare he defame me!"

Henri stepped in between the two. "Look, R. C., he's just one of my nuts. Must have broken out of his cell, is all."

"A NUT! Why, sir, I am the very mouthpiece of the Lord here on earth," howled the pastor. "I am his virtual right hand."

R. C. put his hands on his hips. "I happen to represent Americans for an American America," he said, "so who are you to question my statements?"

"Pastor Daniel Frickenfrayor," responded the pastor, "instrument of our Lord. And I'm not questioning your statements, Mr. Smythe, I'm calling them cow dung."

R. C. Smythe was furious. His cheeks rippled like stormy seas. "Dr. Lafayette," he yelled, "I want you to sue this buffoon for slander on my behalf." He turned to Kiddo Kenny. "Mr. London, I would appreciate your appearing as a witness to this unprecedented slander at the trial in order to attest to the outrageous villifications cast upon me by this imbecile."

"Sure," said Kiddo Kenny, "for ten percent of gross."

"Stop right there," I yelled. "Just hold it, all of you." They all stopped where they stood and looked at me.

"You're all wrong," I continued, "and you're not even close. Try and understand this. America is not money changing hands or the domination of one particular point of view—religious or whatever—over all others. America is not easy wealth, Kiddo, nor is it just a stage for tycoons, Henri. America is not even a place. It's an idea, an idea that remains unfulfilled." My heart started to pound, my palms sweat.

"America is the simple idea that all people can live together in freedom, achieving individually to their greatest limits, while respecting the limits, thoughts, rights and achievements of others. If America has failed, it is not because the idea is imperfect, but because we, collectively, have failed her. It is not enough that we have respect for our own ideas—that, indeed, seems to be in ample supply—but that we have equal and unqualified respect for the ideas of others. That, gentlemen, is America."

I was done. I had never spoken so clearly or forcefully about anything in my life. I took a long, slow breath.

All four men stood with their mouths open before me. Then R. C. Smythe said, "Well, that was about the stupidest thing I've ever heard. America, not a place? America, not the land of Christian virtue?"

Henri laughed openly. "An idea, huh?" he scoffed, wagging his tongue about like an idiot.

They all laughed. "So what's my cut of this idea?" asked Kiddo Kenny London.

They howled some more. "Gentlemen," said Henri, "please forgive my youthful assistant. He is easily carried away. You see," he continued, wrinkling up his face uncomfortably, "he used to be a teacher."

"Oooooh." said R. C. Smythe.

"Oooooh," said Kiddo Kenny.

"Poor lad," said Pastor Frickenfrayor.

"Why don't we continue this intriguing discussion at the cocktail bar?" offered Henri. "Gentlemen . . ."

They left the room and I slumped against the wall. I felt empty. I had spoken from the heart, offered the clearest and most dramatic explanation I could muster and they thought me nothing but a fool for it. What serious hope did I have of accomplishing anything? Why stay?

Then something moved in the shadows. It was Marcy Trimble standing back by the bookcase in the dark. I hadn't noticed her before. She moved forward just slightly into the light and I could see a soft glow in her blue eyes. She gazed at me gently for a few moments and I was transfixed as never before. Then, as if some unseen hand had reached into the room and tapped her on the shoulder, she was roused and turned to go. She walked quickly to the door. But before leaving, turned again to face me. She appeared confused. She smiled quickly, almost lovingly, I thought, and then was gone.

8

"These Christian scam dogs are real honest-to-goodness artists," reflected Henri at breakfast the following morning, between enormous mouthfuls of jelly roll. "They're good. Very good. Christ, kid, they got it down to some kinda' science or something."

I sipped my coffee thoughtfully. "You're obviously impressed."

"No, not impressed. Inspired."

I sniffed the air. "Is that money I smell?"

His eyes lit up. "Big money," he corrected. "I believe I may be close to fulfilling the first dynamic principle of economic righteousness."

"That big?" I said. "How?"

"It's just a feeling right now. But that Smythe character got me to thinking. He knows what he's talking about, Donny. You know, the behind the scenes, the buying influence at the local level and all. He understands clout. Of course, he doesn't understand the first dynamic principle of economic righteousness, but what's his loss is our gain. I'm still not sure exactly how I'm going to make the big splash, buckwise, but I understand now how to grease the skids, as they say: Influence!"

"Seems kind of risky to me, investment wise," I observed.

"Strawberries?"

"I'm stuffed."

"True. But all investments involve an element of risk. The question is really one of potential return. Until last night, I never understood that the most potentially lucrative investments were the ones outside the normal financial loop."

"Like buying people off."

"Exactly. Look, you fix a traffic ticket or buy a broad for some young city councilman. What's it cost, maybe a couple hundred beans, tops. Five years later he's the mayor. Ten years down the line maybe he's gotten to Congress. Who knows?"

"Yeah, go on."

"One thing's for sure, ten years down the line he won't want jackshit to find out about what you got on him. And, of course, if you're smart you've been pumping bucks into his campaigns—legally and illegally—so you really got him by the short hairs. See? If you take a fall, so does he. All the way to the bottom. 'Course, he's got a lot more to lose than you. You're rich, he ain't."

"So you put the screws to him."

"Of course. You get whatever you want. You need a government contract for ball point pens. Bingo. You want a special, untested drug released early for investment purposes. Bang, it's done. Get the picture?"

"That's nothing but blackmail."

He flipped a napkin into the air. "Sometimes you really disappoint me, Donald. Of course it's blackmail. Blackmail is what America is all about. It's the oil in the engine, the gas in the tank. And, my God, just think of the return on your investment. You put out a couple hundred smackers, and a few years down the line you're raking in millions." He looked toward heaven. "Now *that's* righteous."

I shook my head in dismay. "So you're throwing in with R. C. Smythe and his Christian syndicate?"

"Yes and no. Yes, I'll give them some money, but no, not all. Let's face it, not every solid target for graft is up to their, let's say, cultural standards. I want to be free, free to build, to create, to bribe anyone I feel like. I will not discriminate."

I rolled my eyes. "That's very democratic of you."

"It's only right."

"So, when do you get started?"

"I already have," he replied. "Ms. Townsend is presently cataloguing a list of all state and local officials which she will then cross-index with my local connection in the police for any tendencies of a sordid or embarrassing nature. You know, booze, women, drugs, payola. Whatever. Then I will begin to zero in. Shouldn't take long."

"Well, good luck," I said.

"Thanks. What's your day look like?"

"Two sessions of your famed polka catharsis, then I'm off for the afternoon. I like Saturdays," I said. "How about you?"

"Well, after an hour or so of dial-a-dollar with my new list, I'm heading over to the university library, aisle D, table 6, chair #3 for a few moments of sublime reflection. Then this evening I have purchased the rather considerable favors of Ms. Kitty Fouchet for my continuing carnal delight. A wonderful day, all in all."

"You're perverted, Max," I laughed.

"The whole bleeping world is perverted, and you're no exception. I've seen the way you look at that tail, Marcy."

AMERICAN RAIN

"Men look at girls. So what? It's natural. A trapeze and leg irons in your bedroom, now that's something else."

"Ahh, the leg irons were just a gimmick." He patted his stomach. "The trapeze, unfortunately, has become but a fond remembrance." He chuckled. "If I tried it again we might all be in big trouble."

"Yeah," I agreed, "you'd probably bring the house down around us."

He smiled, then looked at me seriously for a moment or two. "Speaking of bringing down the house," he said, "how are we looking in the books?"

I put down my coffee cup. "Incredible," I said. "If I hadn't seen it with my own eyes I would never have believed it. You're making a freaking fortune."

"We," he corrected. "I've been paying you fair and square. You've seen the checks."

"Yeah."

He pulled up closer on his chair. "So tell me," he asked, "how do you feel about the business?"

"It's an abomination."

"Well, it happens to be an abomination that's putting *beaucoup* bucks in your back pocket," he pointed out. "I suppose it's sheer folly on my part to think you'll ever be anything other than morally superior."

I started to raise a hand in protest but he waved it aside. "Never mind," he said. "Listen, here's a tip. That chick Marcy you're so enthralled with likes to paint. She spends a lot of her Saturdays down at the old Guilford Reservoir just down the road."

My heart bounced. "Is that so," I said. "Appreciate it."

"The least I can do. One other thing. I got a call this morning from some local group of concerned citizens. Sounded like a bunch of beggars to me. Anyway, I told them to talk to you. Said you were in control of the purse strings. They'll be by sometime later this afternoon. Just get the hell rid of them. Charity, can you imagine?"

That morning the clock would not move. I stared at it, glared at it, threatened to choke it's cord, but nothing could make it move. The two sessions of polka catharsis took forever. The wine cooler wind downs that followed seemed actually to go backwards in time. Dr. Myron Wilmer had a difficult go of it at both, severely gouging several clients with his ski tips during a particularly raucous spin during the catharsis, and later losing complete control of his emotions after Mrs. Pizianni adroitly stole them right off the bottoms of his feet. Fortunately, I caught her in the driveway trying to lash them to the roof of her Volvo, and was able to return them unscathed to the petrified physicist. But he sobbed uncontrollably for at least an hour anyway.

Regardless, I herded them all out by noon and grabbed a light salad for lunch. Then I jumped into a ratty old pair of gym shorts and dashed out the front door. It seemed like a good day for a run. Maybe to the old reservoir.

I trotted down to the street. The day was hot and humid. Animals lazed. Birds had all but deserted the tree tops for cooler climes. I started to run, slowly at first then with more conviction as my muscles unlimbered. I cruised down green, summer streets where occasionally the sound of children splashing in unseen sprinklers arose from behind tree-lined backyards. I puffed my way down Charles Street. The pavement radiated a steady, withering heat. Sweat dripped down my legs, then filled my eyes. Baltimore in July.

Somehow I spotted her long before I should have been able to. How does that work? I saw her as I jogged up Millbrook almost a quarter of a mile away through two gardens, a stand of elms and at least one game of softball. She was down by the water, wedged against a sea of lush, green vegetation. She was working intently on her easel.

My spirits soared. I ran slowly around the far edge of the reservoir hoping she would look up and spot me. But no such luck. So I looped the park and tried it once again, this time loping with great conviction along that stretch of the road best exposed to her potential gaze, but again it was to no avail. When a third circuit produced the same result, I was forced to collapse in a small grove near a water fountain, sucking huge mouthfuls of air, and staring into the merciless blue sky. My shirt was soaked completely through, my hair matted, my body temperature probably soaring right off the chart. For a minute or two I considered myself a serious candidate for cardiac arrest. Vaguely I heard the sound of the fountain being pumped a few feet distant.

"Hello."

I sat up. It was her. Quickly, I brushed the hair back from my forehead. "Oh," I stammered.

She handed me a cup of water. "Are you OK?"

"Oh, ah, sure," I said. "Just taking a blow."

"You look very hot. Go ahead, drink it all."

I downed the water. "Thanks."

"I thought I recognized you," she said. "Isn't it awfully hot out here to be running?"

I shrugged. "I enjoy the heat," I lied.

"Your face is very red. I have a towel, shall I soak it full of water for you?"

"Oh, no." I pointed to the trees. "It's just the shade here. The contrast, you know? I'm really all right."

"Would you like a little more?"

"That'd be great."

She filled the cup again as I wiped the sweat from my arms and tried to make myself more presentable. "Thanks," I said when she returned. The water was wonderfully cold.

She knelt in the grass nearby. "Do you run often?"

I finished the water and sat up Indian style. Her hair was long and silky, skin smooth and rich. It was difficult to concentrate. "I'm getting back into it," I said, lying again.

She smiled. "You picked one heck of a day."

"Yeah, guess you're right." I laughed "So what brings you down here?" I asked.

"Nothing."

"Nothing? Is that your work over there? I saw someone working at an easel."

She shifted uncomfortably. "Well . . . yeah. That was me. . . . I was painting."

"Really? That's great."

"Oh, I just mess around with it."

"I'll bet you're good," I winked. "Can I see?"

"Would you like to?"

"Yeah."

"Well . . . OK."

We walked down toward the water. Her hair bounced. She smelled fresh and wonderful. I smelled foul. "Sorry I'm such a mess," I said, wiping more sweat from my face and arms.

She chuckled. "Exercise in ninety-seven degree weather does that."

We stopped at her easel. She appeared to be about half finished with a landscape, a painting of the water and the trees that meshed the two in a brilliant display of color. The glint of the sun on the water was dazzling. I thought it was very good. "Wow," I said.

"Wow?" she repeated. She smiled warmly. "I haven't heard anyone say wow in a long time."

"Well, I guess I'm not much of an art critic," I said. "But I think that's sensational. You're very talented."

She blushed. "Thank you."

"Do you paint a lot?"

"Enough."

"Can I see some more?"

"Well, I don't have any more of them here right now. One at a time, you know."

"Maybe some other time?" I said.

". . . Sure."

I glanced back at the canvas. "When do you expect to be finished?"

"Oh . . . tomorrow. Or maybe the next day."

I folded my arms. "With talent like that you should be doing this full time, if you ask me. You're wasting your time at the Center."

Her face clouded. "Well, I have precious little choice," she snapped.

I drew back. "How do you mean?"

She turned on me sharply. "You mean you don't know?"

"Know what?"

"I can't leave. I'm part of a deal."

"A deal?"

"Yes, a little arrangement Dr. Lafayette worked out with my family. My father, really."

"Oh, come on."

"It's true," she protested. "My father is the dean of a local law school," she said. "I won't say which one."

"Oh boy," I said. "Don't bother, I think I know."

"And Dr. Lafayette caught him in an embarrassing situation. Please understand, I love my father but he is weak. He has problems, and Dr. Lafayette would have ruined him. That animal wanted my mother too, but I wouldn't let her come. I can fend him off better than she could have. So I must work as his secretary for one year. That's the agreement. And that's all it is."

I was deeply embarrassed. "That's absolutely incredible," I said, "but I've seen how he operates, and he told me the story about your dad. He just didn't tell me about you."

"Oh, I'm just a minor detail to him."

"Look," I said, "you're free to leave. He can't possibly hold you to an arrangement like that. Just walk."

"But he would destroy my family. Believe me, it would literally kill my father if word of this ever got out. He's not strong." She clenched her teeth. "It's just rotten blackmail."

"Yeah, blackmail. That's what America is all about," I said.

"What?"

"Nothing," I said. "Just a little joke."

"I'm not amused." She stared at me for a few seconds, eyes narrowing. "Just what are you doing here?"

"What do you mean by here? The park, the Center, the State of Maryland?"

"Take your pick."

"I'm here because he more or less roped me into it. Not as bad as you, but strapped in nevertheless. Oh, I could probably walk right out the door but he'd make things tough on me. And besides, I like you. Hey," I added quickly, "there's the ice cream man." I pulled a soggy five dollar bill out of my sock. "Can I interest you?"

She thought about it for a long while. "You're not like him, are you?" she asked finally.

"Not entirely."

She fought back a smile. "Well . . . I suppose so then."

I bought two ice cream cones and we sat on a bench in the shade for over an hour. We watched the people come and go. Across the way some kids had a game of softball going. The heat finally drove them into the shade.

I told her about the years I had spent in teaching. Then I told her about leaving in order to fulfill my destiny and why I hadn't even made it past the first day on the road or farther than Charles Street. She understood. She warmed up. I kicked at the dusty sidewalk. "I could leave," I said, "it just seems convenient not to."

She laughed. "Tell me about it. Sometimes I think freedom is nothing more than a word, just a term people use to describe something that doesn't exist and never will." She sighed. "No one ever explained to me that life came with all of these strings attached."

"Yup," I agreed. "Some good ones, some bad. I meant what I said about liking you. Hope you didn't mind that?"

". . . No."

I looked up and down the street nervously. My heart raced. "I hear there's some sort of festival or other down at the harbor tonight," I said. "Could I interest you in an educational look see, and maybe a not so educational glass of beer or two?"

She smiled warmly. "Why not." She looked up into the clear, shimmering sky. "It will be a nice night for the harbor. "But," she added quickly, "will I have to call you Doctor all night?"

"Only if you want to get me arrested."

She giggled. "Do you know my address?"

"I got it out of the files," I said. "How about eight?"

109

"That would be fine," she said. "And now I'd better pack up my things before the paint melts."

I helped her pick up her materials and then ran home at a near sprint. I ran like a machine, my feet hardly touching the ground. I ran two miles in ninety-seven degree heat, smiling all the way, never even breaking a sweat. I laughed out loud. I was either in love—or in a dehydrated state of shock. I hit the front stoop of The Center for Psychiatric Retribution on the fly and flung open the door with a bang. Three people were seated in the lobby, waiting. I stopped short and remembered the citizens group Henri had referred to. "Yes?" I said.

There were two men and a woman. The man in the middle stood up. "Dr. Lafayette?"

"No, I'm sorry," I answered. "I'm Don Mallory, Dr. Lafayette's assistant. How can I help you?"

The other man stood. I recognized him. It was David Winthrop of Winthrop's Hardware down on the Block; the man with the sandwiches. "We represent a group of concerned and active citizens who are trying to help out downtown with some of our city's more uncomfortable problems," he explained. Specifically, we are dealing with the shortage of housing and food for some of the less fortunate and we have found that it's very expensive."

"I'm sure it is," I said, "but what brings you here?"

The woman stood and joined the men. "A friend of mine works for Mr. Kenneth London, a broker. I was led to believe you knew him."

"I do."

"Well," she continued, "Mr. London suggested to my friend that Dr. Lafayette was a philanthropist and might be interested in backing our efforts."

I almost swallowed my tongue.

"I can assure you, sir," added David Winthrop, "all donations go directly to the needy. We are not professional fund raisers. We get nothing from this. In fact, we give daily ourselves."

"What is the name of your group?"

David Winthrop shrugged his shoulders. "We have no name."

"How many people do you represent."

The woman smiled. "Well, actually, we're it."

I had seen David Winthrop in action, so I knew they were telling the truth. I wanted to help but I remembered what Henri had said. Since these people were of no immediate use to him, he would never consider sending even a dime their way. "Listen, the government, . . ." I started to say, but David Winthrop was way ahead of me.

"To begin with, sir," he said, "the government does not care. And even if the government did care, most of these folks are well beyond it's reach. Some of them are quite beyond anyone's grasp. Believe me, Mr. Mallory, I live amongst them. They are on the street near my store late at night, and they are there in the morning when I open up. They eat garbage when they can find it. They live in filth. It is not pleasant."

"I gather," I said.

The woman spoke up again. "We're not pretending to offer any sort of solution to all of this," she said. "I'm not sure there is one. We're just trying to help out as best we can. To feed the ones we see and to develop some shelter areas in our neighborhood. Not much. But even that is expensive."

"And Mr. London is helping you?" I asked, half amazed.

"Well, no," said David Winthrop. "We apparently caught Mr. London at an inappropriate moment. He merely suggested we try Dr. Lafayette."

"Believe me," Mr. Mallory," added the first man, "we don't enjoy asking for your money. We are not professionals at this. We do spend a lot of our own money. If we had more, we wouldn't be here."

"I appreciate that," I said. "Listen, I'll have to speak to Dr. Lafayette about releasing any vast sums to your organization. He's pretty tight, you know."

"We were not aware of that."

"But in the meantime, I'm certain the good doctor wouldn't mind if I disbursed a token on his behalf. Could you wait a minute or two?"

They could.

I went back to my office and pulled out the corporation check book. Henri had entrusted me with the everyday bills and disbursements as well as the general bookkeeping for The Center. He trusted me with all the accounting because, he said, I was one of the few people he knew who was still stupid enough to be honest. Next to the checkbook were the paychecks Henri had given to me. They were all neatly folded and clipped together. I had been paid handsomely for my efforts, not to mention my share of the House of Cards scheme, but I hadn't done anything with any of it. I pulled the checks out and looked at them. It was more money than I had made in my entire teaching career. How crazy. But I hadn't cashed any of the checks because I had been ambivalent about the entire operation. I didn't mind helping in all of this craziness, but an accomplice was something else.

But as I held the paper that represented so much money, my sense of ambivalence lifted. I had an idea. I would funnel what funds I could to people and groups that needed it. Simple as that. I would negotiate a better deal for myself with Max, a better percentage of the take and more authority as well. Then I would steer my share of the money to wherever I thought it would help most. I suddenly felt good about myself. I grabbed the checkbook and went downstairs.

"Here you are," I said, approaching them.

All three looked at the check and their eyes lit up. "This is very generous," she said. "Please do thank Dr. Lafayette for us."

"I will," I said. "I would suggest that you check back with me in a few weeks. Perhaps by then Dr. Lafayette will be in a position to help your cause further. The doctor is a very decent man. Tight, but decent."

"We certainly will," said David Winthrop. "I would like to personally thank the doctor for his generosity. Not many people have given us even the time of day."

"No!" I said. "That would be a bad idea. The doctor is extremely tight-lipped when it comes to his philanthropy. Believe me, he considers it to be in very poor taste to even discuss it. Your thanking him would be an enormous embarrassment. He simply considers decency a duty."

"That is remarkable," said the woman. "You don't find gentlemen like Dr. Lafayette around anymore."

"No," I agreed. "In fact that may be an understatement." I showed them to the door.

As we stepped outside, David Winthrop turned to me. "Mr. Mallory, I can't but help feeling I know you from somewhere."

"Beats me," I said.

He smiled as all three turned and walked down the steps to their car. I waved goodbye. As the car rumbled to life at the curb, I rubbed my hands together anxiously. Now I had a few games of my own to play. Step, by meager step, I thought, as they drove away. The best things are built brick by brick. They would be back. Others would follow. Everything takes time. Perhaps destiny had not forgotten me after all.

9

"Get ready, kid," Henri said as I came down the stairs first thing Monday morning. "The Rollins settlement is this morning and I don't expect it's going to be easy."

"What's the big deal?"

"For some reason the insurance adjustors who represent the board of education are less then impressed with our case and consider my financial demands to be exorbitant as well."

"Oh, come on. Don't tell me you filed a suit on that garbage?"

"Well, sure."

"For how much?" I asked.

"Twenty million."

"Imagine. And they didn't just write you a check, huh?"

"No," he replied. In fact they're coming over to meet Wilbur, his family, and to discuss the case eyeball to eyeball. Could be tough sledding. Wha-da-ya think?"

I poured myself a cup of coffee and sat at the table. "You're talking major league fiasco here," I said. "Nobody could take that pack of morons seriously."

"I hear you," he said, fidgeting in his chair. "But still they're apparently worried enough about the case to come over. That's something."

I shook my head. "Nope. This is going to make World War II look like kid stuff. Better reload your pistola there, partner."

The entire Rollins mob arrived around nine and Henri took them into the library to try and coach them, as best he could, on the civilities of public meetings, but it was like trying to teach lobsters to sing a sonata. From my office I heard him repeatedly pleading for them to stay in their chairs, put down the scissors, stop slapping one another, and to keep their private parts to themselves.

Within half an hour, the gentlemen from the insurance company arrived. They appeared tight-lipped and apprehensive. They sat in the lobby without speaking. Ten minutes later I went out, introduced myself, and brought them back to the library. One was Jason Will, Vice President of Claims. The other was a Mr. Keith Vincent, Vice President of Accounting. I introduced them around the room, and Henri showed them to two chairs set up directly in front of his desk. The Rollins family was arrayed behind them on different chairs. Wilbur sat by himself in one corner, a sock stuffed into his mouth. Carl sat in the other corner, hands tied behind his back. The insurance executives looked around the room, glanced uneasily at one another, and sat.

Henri stood up. He began grandly, strolling slowly around the room. "Gentlemen," he said, "you have before you here—er, rather, behind you—a family destroyed—yes, I say destroyed—by the gross, reckless, and altogether sinister negligence of your insured." He pointed to Wilbur. "The child who cowers now in the corner like wounded prey was once the pride of his class, a virtual specimen of manliness and academic excellence. A renaissance child, if you will. Why, his mother had high hopes of his gaining early admissions to Harvard University, and the phenom, Wilbur, routinely spoke in those days of personally finding a cure for cancer while also running for high elective office. Now look what you've done."

Mr. Will spoke up. "I will not argue, Dr. Lafayette, that the child appears at this time to display no recognizable manifestations of human intelligence. However, his genetic and social limitations are not the result of any action or lack thereof on the part of our client. In short, sir, you have no case."

"As well you know, Mr. Will," countered Henri, "I serve the child's family not only as competent council, but as their trusted psychiatrist as well. I am perfectly prepared to testify on the child's behalf that he has been hideously traumatized at the hands of your client. I believe you have my detailed diagnosis as far as that is concerned."

Mr. Will held up a thin medical report. "You mean this rag, 'Stunted Lifetime Expectations vis-a-vis School Board Inadequacy'?" he asked. "Why, I don't believe I've ever read more rubbish, hocus pocus, and outright lies in one document before in my life. Do you actually intend to introduce this trash in court?"

Henri stepped back as if struck. He waited a moment and then spoke very quietly. "I did not agree to this meeting to have my reputation impugned, Mr. Will," he almost whispered. He looked at Vincent. "Sir," he said, "your compatriot seems to be laboring under the impression that I do not know SLANDER!! when I hear it."

"Now, now, now," said Vincent. "Dr. Lafayette, I'm sure Mr. Will meant nothing derogatory by his statement. Did you Jason? . . . Jason?"

"Like hell I didn't!" Will yelled. "I meant every goddamn word of it."

Henri looked at me. "Make a note for me if you would, Donald, to sue these gentlemen for slander," he asked. "It should be an open and shut case, I think, what with all these witnesses."

Will stood up and pointed at Henri angrily. "File your damn slander suit, asshole. Go ahead, I dare you. I know what you're running here. You come after me and I'll go straight to the papers. I'll ruin you tomorrow. You know you don't have a prayer so why don't you just cram it."

Vincent leaped to his feet and grabbed Will by the lapels. "Jason!" he wailed, "have you lost your mind? Have you gone completely loco?" He shook Will for a moment or two, then turned to Henri. "I assure you, Dr. Lafayette, we did not come here with any intentions of impugning your integrity, and Mr. Will is certainly not speaking for Intergalactic Underwriters when he addresses you so scurrilously."

"Get your hands off me, you twerp," said Will, yanking himself free from the terrified accountant. "I'm tired of pandering to crooks like these. Both of you make me sick."

Vincent stepped back. "You know what was agreed to at the home office, Jason. The chairman wants this case settled, and you agreed. What's gotten into you?"

"That was then, this is now. I just can't go through with this kind of crap anymore. Understand?"

The accountant drew himself up. "I warn you, Jason," he threatened, "if you continue on in this suicidal manner, I will have no choice but to relieve you of your position." He looked at Henri. "There's legal precedent for such drastic action, isn't there?"

"Removing a commander in the field when deemed unfit for duty," affirmed Henri. "It's in *The Bill of Rights*."

"*The Bill of Rights*, Jason!" Vincent repeated ominously. "You see? Step out of line one more time and I'll be forced to invoke it."

"*The Bill of Rights* my ass," said Will, glaring at the trembling Vincent. "You want my job, Keith? Take it. Go ahead, it's yours."

". . . What?" asked Vincent, swallowing hard.

"TAKE IT!" howled Will. "Go ahead, Keith. See how long you last dealing with this lunacy every day of your life. For Christ's sake, Keith, just look around you here." He pointed to the Rollins family. "He's got one nut tied up in the corner over there, and his jewel of a plaintiff here has a sock stuffed down his throat so he won't say anything stupid. I swear, Keith, you couldn't smell manure if you were standing three feet deep in it."

"Hey, did he call me manure?" yelled Carl, bouncing up and down on his chair.

"Shut up, Carl!" snapped Henri, inching closer to the desk drawer with the revolver in it.

Will began shaking his head mournfully. "Keith, think about this for a second. Here we are, all ready to pay a case where a stooge doesn't show up for school for almost two years simply because this two bit swindler, Lafayette here, comes up with some absolutely cockamamie legal mumbo jumbo. What are we, nuts? Keith, if we pay on this, we'll pay on anything. Do you hear me? Let's make him try the bastard in court."

Vincent put his hands on his hips. "You know what the chairman said," he snapped back. "He said the case is iffy. The chairman said he doesn't know for sure just what a jury would do with it. He's afraid a jury would try to find a way to pay the kid and then we would have established bad precedent for a profitable line of insurance." Vincent tapped his foot on the floor impatiently.

Will put his hands to his head. "God, if a jury would pay even a dime on this case then we're all finished."

Vincent smiled smugly. "Jason," he said, "Intergalactic Underwriters can survive one bad judgement."

"I don't mean the company, you idiot," snapped Will. "I'm talking about the nation here. I mean the whole blessed world, Keith. How the hell can we go on like this? How can people *think* like this?"

Henri stepped forward. "So you gentlemen admit you have a loser on your hands," he said. "Do you have an offer for me, Mr. Vincent? Perhaps you could get your checkbook out and we could put the entire matter to rest with no further unpleasantness."

Will's mouth dropped open. "Listen to this guy, Keith." he said. "He has no shame. He's beyond belief." He walked up to Henri. "Tell me, Lafayette," he asked, "if this kid here with the sock in his mouth is not responsible for what happened to him, then is anyone anymore? Huh? Tell me, Lafayette, is there anyone in the whole wide world who, in that fat brain of yours, is considered accountable for his own actions?"

Henri said nothing.

Will spun suddenly and ran to the window. He threw it open and cupped his hands over his mouth. "Is there anyone OUT THERE who is not a victim?" he screamed, then collapsed against the wall. "Oh God," he moaned, "look at me. I'm losing it."

"Jason, calm down." counseled Vincent. "You're overreacting. It's just business."

"That's right," agreed Henri, taking Will by the elbow and leading him back to his chair. "This is all just business. Don't go taking it so personally."

Will collapsed onto his seat. "I can't help it," he said. "Look, I know it's business, but we're all paying the price, aren't we? I mean, nothing works right anymore and no one cares because it's all just business now. Used to be someone cared. Keith, tell me, where did it all go wrong?"

"It didn't," the accountant replied emphatically. "The chairman simply wants the numbers on the quarterly profit report to look nice. That's all."

Will threw his hands up. "But it's a sham!" he insisted. "We do things that will eventually kill us just to look good for one lousy quarter. It's crazy. These damn reports are supposed to show us how well we're producing, not be the product themselves. Christ, the tail is wagging the dog all over this country, Keith. From education to oil drilling, soon we're going to pay for it."

"Now stop overreacting, Jason," said Vincent. "Business is business. You must understand. Numbers are simply the professional way of doing everything these days."

"Professional, ha," laughed Will. "Look at this place. Why it's nothing but a den of thieves and lunatics."

"I resent that insinuation," said Henri, nose in the air. "I happen to run a highly professional organization and represent some of the finest and most respected clients in the entire state."

"Yeah, name one?" taunted Will.

Just then the door flew open and Marcy ran into the room. She pointed to the phone. "I'm sorry to interrupt," she said, looking at me anxiously, "but we have an emergency phone call from Dr. Myron Wilmer. He insists on speaking to you and Dr. Lafayette."

I jumped to my feet. "What's happened?"

"He's at a convenience store somewhere down town from what I can tell," she continued, "and he says he's

121

lost his focus. He's scared to death that he will disappear within the next few seconds."

Henri looked at Will sheepishly. "Hold that thought concerning my clients, will you."

I grabbed the phone. "Yes, Dr. Wilmer," I said. "What seems to be the problem?" Every set of eyes in the room were on me.

"Dr. Mallory?" Wilmer asked.

"Yes, I'm here."

"Is Dr. Lafayette there as well?"

"Yes," I affirmed.

"I can't hear him."

"Hold on," I said. Reluctantly, I routed the call through the voice box on Henri's desk. "You will be able to hear everyone now," I said.

"Great. Dr. Lafayette," Wilmer said, "my focus has dimmed."

"I'll strangle that fucking mutant with my bare hands," said Henri.

"What? What was that?" asked Wilmer.

"Sit down, Dr. Lafayette," I demanded. "Nothing, nothing. Go on."

"Oh, well, I came into this convenience store for a quick hot dog with chili and when I reached the canned goods aisle, I suddenly found myself staring into the endless void I am so fearful of. What a shock! I realized at once that I was having serious doubts as to the elementary structure of my skis. You see, I saw them suddenly not as a bulwark against oblivion, but merely a ragtag collection of nothingness. It is a problem I had not previously considered. You know that if I seriously doubt my capacity to sustain myself as a physical entity, I will not. In short, if the skis go, I go. Goddamn you, Heisenberg!"

Henri began rubbing his temples furiously with his finger tips. "Just hang up on that bastard, will you please. I'm starting to sense serious vexations in my cash flow."

"No," I said. "Doctor, you merely need your focus retuned. Get it? Away from the abstract world of particle motion and onto something more, well, . . . earthly."

"Will a chili dog do?" he asked.

"No," I said. "Something with more umph."

"Well, hurry, Doctor, things are starting to blink out all around me."

I thought quickly. "Is the clerk there?"

"Yes, she is."

"Put her on."

I asked the clerk if they had girly magazines behind the counter. They did. Then I explained to her that she had become a vital cog in a medical emergency and that she had to proceed with all dispatch to the counter, snatch up a copy of *Nymph Magazine*, open it to the centerfold, and hold it up for Dr. Wilmer's review."

She said, "Are you a sicko, er somethin'?"

"No!" I said. "I beg you, please hurry. This is an emergency!"

". . . June or July?" she asked finally.

"July."

"Oh hey, hon, I seen that one." she commented. "You ask me, dem boobs ain't real. That's a silicone job, Mister."

"They'll do."

She handed the phone back to Wilmer.

"What's going on?" he cried. "I haven't got long."

"You'll see," I said. "Just watch her."

There was a short period of silence, then: ". . . Oh, my gosh," he said. "That's incredible."

"How's your focus doing?" I asked.

". . . Returning. Why . . . those are enormous. I had no idea."

"Beats quarks, doesn't it?"

"Well, it certainly beats staring into the endless void," he agreed. "By a long shot."

"Are things still blinking?" I asked.

"No. I think it's over. Yeah, I'm OK. My goodness, Doctor, you've done it again. And with another novel, innovative approach. Thank you again, Herr Doctor. Just one more thing?"

"What's that?"

"Where do I get a subscription?"

"Check it out," I said, and hung up.

Will rubbed his face mournfully and motioned to Vincent. "Do you believe this? Are you proud of yourself now, Keith? Why, this is nothing but an insane asylum and we're part of it. In fact, we're funding the damn thing." He looked at me. "Just what the hell was that all about?"

"Dr. Wilmer is increasingly frightened that he does not actually exist. That nothing does."

Will rubbed his face again and snickered. "And here I'm just the opposite," he said, "increasingly frightened to death that I do, that all of this," he went on, motioning to the world around him, "is so very real, unalterable and out of control. I should meet this guy, Wilmer, maybe we could average each other out." He smiled weakly. "Go ahead, Keith, it's all yours. I'm done."

Vincent edged up on his chair and looked at Henri. He made an offer. Henri countered. Vincent made a final offer. Henri countered. Vincent made another final offer. Henri accepted. Will went limp. The case settled for $500,000. The case was worthless and everyone knew it. Henri popped the cork on a bottle of champagne to celebrate. He winked and offered the first toast to Intergalactic Underwriters.

Everyone shook hands and said goodbye. Henri and Vincent each took an arm and helped Will down the steps and into the car. He was numb. Adding insult to injury, Henri slipped his doctor's business card into Will's breast pocket. "You may need a consultation," he said with a sneer. Will wept openly as the car sped away.

That night after dinner I wandered out onto the back porch and flopped down on a chaise lounge. I was tired. The Rollins settlement had both amused and appalled me. The older you get the more you come to see how utterly irrational the world really is. Logic and precision in human affairs seems mere fiction. I felt sorry for Will.

I watched the sun set amid a gathering of turbid clouds to the west. The air outside was very still, the leaves limp. Thunder rattled in the distance. Rain was near. Perhaps it would break the heat.

Henri followed me out with a cup of espresso in his hand. Slowly he eased himself down on the chaise next to me, carefully positioning his enormous bulk on it as the deflated chair sagged and squeaked under the burden. He sighed. "Another day, another dollar, hey kid?"

I smiled. "I still can't believe you got five HUNDRED thousand dollars out of Intergalactic Underwriters for that garbage case."

"Like candy from a baby, Donald," he said. "Although Will had me going there for awhile. Guys like that worry me."

"Why?"

"'Cause he knew what he was doing. Couldn't you tell. He had my number. Competence, Donny, it's the death knell of my business, the dreaded *X* factor. Fortunately, the numbers guy, Vincent, took over and with him it was a cakewalk."

"So you're a richer man today than yesterday. The beat goes on."

"Yes, but somehow it seems less satisfying this time around. Both Carl and Wilbur were furious with my percentage of the haul—er, rather, my contingency on the settlement—and threatened to go to my arch rival, Ian Stanforth, and sue me for malpractice. The ingrates. I countered by threatening to cut their balls off, but straightforward threats don't work with trash like that."

"And after all you've done for them," I said.

"Indeed."

I laughed to myself and stared out over the street lights. "Rain's coming."

He looked around. ". . . Yeah, I used to come out here with my dad when I was a kid. After he got home from work, you know, he'd come out on the porch here and read the paper at night." He grew silent and distant. He seemed lost in the thought, in the past. It was a side of him I'd never seen before. "Dad was a good man," he added finally. "He did very well for himself."

"Yeah," I agreed.

He looked at me and his eyes sparkled. "But I'm doing better." He reached over and slapped me on the knee. "And speaking of doing well, I heard you got little miss tight twat out Saturday night. How'd it go?"

"Just fine."

He rolled his eyes suggestively. "What's she, some kinda red hot sleezeball or something? D'ja bang it in the back seat?"

"'Course not," I said. "We just went to the festival downtown. Walked around and had a few drinks. Talked."

"... And?"

"And that's it. She's nice."

"Come on." He looked at me sideways. "You mean she's got a nice ass."

"Listen, dirt ball, I like her. We had lunch together today and we're going to the theater on Saturday. End of conversation."

"The theater? Aghhh!" he gagged. "Make me sick already."

"Just don't heave it this way."

He laughed, then grew silent again. The rain came, but it was just the edge of the storm, a soft constant drumming on the roof. We sat and listened for a long while. "You seem awfully quiet," I observed. "There a problem?"

"Just thinking," he replied. "And depressed just a little."

"About what?"

"About the business. How I have not, despite numerous hours of brain storming, been able to hatch my Grand Scheme. It's out there, I know, at my very finger tips it seems sometimes, but still I have nothing."

"Your Grand Scheme?"

"Yes, I have the means all worked out and ready to implement—the influence buying and trading, the blackmail, etc.—but still they are like horses waiting idly in the stable with no wagon to pull. I need to complete the first dynamic principle of economic righteousness, by God, Donny. It is my imperative in life."

"You mean to tell me," I said, "that all of this is no good."

"No, it's fine. But it's still subject to the evil influence of competence, and the hours are long. The Grand

Scheme will be a mechanism of beauty, impervious to 'the slings and arrows of outrageous fortune.'"

"Shakespeare aside," I said, "you want the impossible."

"No!" he countered. "It is possible, I just have to think."

I looked back outside. "Max, it's like you want to be paid a fortune for doing nothing. Like sitting here on the porch and being paid just because it rains. Every time it rains and for every drop."

He opened his mouth to respond but stopped in mid-thought. He stared at me. His eyes got big. Then bigger. His face turned red. Sweat beaded on his forehead. His nostrils flared and his ears got hot. "My God!" he yelled, leaping from the chaise, "That's it! How simple. How perfect. The rain. Who would have ever thought. . . . Donny, you're a genius." He paced swiftly across the porch. "Paid every time it rains. Imagine! Just sit on your can and watch the cash register spin as drops hit the roof. It's doable, by God."

He turned and ran toward his office. For the rest of the night the phone lines were on fire. American Rain had been born.

10

"GOLLLFFF!! . . . anyone?"

I flew from beneath the covers, heart pounding wildly. "What?"

Henri stood at the foot of my bed, attired in knickers, with what appeared to be a three-iron in his hand. "Golf anyone?"

"Are you out of your everlovin' mind?" I asked, still breathing hard. "You 'bout scared me to death."

"A lad like yourself ought not be concerned with his ticker. But seeing as how you are, I think a little exercise is just what you need, especially since your girly friend isn't giving you any these days."

I rubbed my face and moaned. "My God, it's 6:30 A.M. What the hell is going on?"

"I have scheduled a golf outing for this morning with my good friend R. C. Smythe and the honored Senator from West Virginia, Clayton Crowntooth."

I sat up straight. "*The* Clayton Crowntooth, the Minority Leader in the Senate and longtime heavyweight on the Hill?"

"The very same. And I want you to come along as my business associate and partner."

I sat on the edge of the bed. "I take it this has to do with that rain thing we were discussing last night?"

"Indeed it does. I didn't sleep all night. I was on the phone, calling in every chip I have out there and getting ready to purchase some others. I am laying the groundwork for the greatest capitalistic venture in the history of mankind. I'm going to create a virtual money machine, a cash cow of such colossal magnitude that Adam Smith himself will get a virtual hard-on in his grave at the mere mention of my name."

"You are one sick cowboy," I said. "Do you honestly think you're going to collect on the rain? How?"

"The Scheme Magnifico was hatched last night in one moment of blazing insight. My accomplishment will go down in time, I'm sure, alongside the brilliant insights provided to mankind by such genius as Newton and Einstein." He pointed to his temple. "I have it all up here," he said. "Don't worry. In due course, I'll explain it in detail. But for now, let us busy ourselves with the graft at hand."

"You intend to buy Clayton Crowntooth?"

"Lock, stock, and barrel."

"And how many more?" I asked.

"As many as it takes," he answered.

The country club was outside of town in the Green Spring Valley. Jules drove. The morning air was dry and clear—rare for August—and we arrived a half-hour before our tee time. I got out of the car and stretched. The sky was blue. Birds chirped above. As soon as we pulled up outside the clubhouse, uniformed attendants grabbed our golf clubs and whisked us away to the first tee. Complimentary coffee and Danish sat by the putting green. I grabbed a cheese Danish and watched as the attendants brought our clubs around. I turned to Henri. "Impressive place," I said. "Who's the member?"

"Smythe," he answered. "He wines and dines all the hotdogs out here."

"Speak of the devil," I said.

R. C. Smythe and Senator Crowntooth were at the far end of the practice green working on their four-footers. Smythe spotted us first. "Henri, Donald," he called, waving for us to join them. "Grab a putter and let's whack them a bit before heading off. What do you say?"

"Right-O," Henri yelled. "Tallyho, gentlemen."

"Tallyho, tallyho," they both called back.

Henri and I grabbed our putters and started their way. "What's this tallyho shit?" I asked under my breath.

"Country club talk," said Henri, smiling as we walked—as if his face were made of plaster of Paris.

Henri, gloriously attired in black and red knickers, green socks, and an avocado shirt, marched purposefully across the green looking very much like a tie-dyed tank in low gear. Then he stopped suddenly and saluted Clayton Crowntooth with a flick of the fingers. "Senator," he exclaimed, "I happen to be one of your greatest admirers. You are a man of astute and uncommon political genius. I am honored."

"Why, the honor is all mine," replied the senator, sporting that gawking sort of grin he was famous for. He put out his hand. "Put'er there, Doctor. Just call me Buck."

"My," said R. C. Smythe. "Only the senator's closest friends get to call him Buck."

Henri bowed at the waist. "I'm deeply moved."

The senator was short and intense. His eyes were calm, but busy, darting from face to face, image to image. He seemed to miss very little. He was famous for his backwoods, almost bumpkinish methods and dress, which he played to the hilt. But under all that syrup and molasses, I'd heard there was a mind as sharp as a broken bottle. More than one political opponent had gone down to defeat, I guessed, by underestimating him.

"Buck," said Henri, pumping the senator's hand, "I'm just glad as hell to meet you. I'm also glad you could make it this morning on such short notice."

"Why, Dr. Lafayette, I wouldn't have missed it for all the anthracite in Kanawha County," the senator replied. "No siree bobcat," he continued. "When R. C. called me and explained the dimensions of your financial interest in my campaign, well sir, I just had to meet you eyeball to eyeball. 'Sides, golf is an earthy enterprise, a humble test of man against Mother Nature. Positively uplifting, you ask me."

"You know I have oft times felt the exact same way, but until this very moment lacked the precise words to adequately describe it, Buck." said R. C. Smythe. "My, but you have a way, don't you. And by golly, you're right. Why, I tell you I have never felt as close to my Lord as I do when I have a driver in my hands. It's true."

"Here, here," applauded Crowntooth.

Henri smacked his hands together excitedly. "Well, let's get going here gentlemen," he said. "But I hope you don't expect Don and I to play up to your, no doubt, professional standards. It has been quite a while, after all, since either of us has played."

"Amateurism," said Buck Crowntooth, smiling broadly, "how clean and wonderful. I admire true amateurs, Dr. Lafayette. Why, there's no need to apologize at all. As far as I'm concerned, it's all very refreshing. By golly, I'm an amateur, too. So's R. C."

"Salt of the earth," said R. C.

"'Course, I admire professionals as well," continued the senator. "Their drive for perfection and so on."

"They are to be commended, indeed," agreed R. C.

We all walked over to the first tee, congratulating everyone, praising everything. We yanked out our drivers and went to work. R. C. knocked one more or less down the middle, The senator went off to the right, and I wound up in the left rough.

Henri took a few wild practice strokes, looking very much like a dangerous man. Then he knocked the caddy master flat onto his back with a shot that soared from the tee at a right angle to the course, bounced off a fence, then ricocheted back onto the fairway about twenty-five yards from where we stood. Henri marched to the edge of the tee and waved his driver menacingly at the caddy master. "Move, damn it!" he screamed. "If you weren't such an old bag of bones, I'd of had another twenty yards on that shot."

I quickly helped the caddy master to his feet, jumped into the golf cart, and wheeled up to Henri. "Get in," I hissed.

It had obviously been a long while since any of us—other than R. C.—had played golf, and the rust on our swings showed. We were all over the place, across this fairway, down the next, crashing into trees, fences, nearby houses.

Henri, in particular, had a difficult time hitting the ball as it had a tendency to disappear from view beneath his enormous stomach whenever he approached it. I laughed. It was like a golfing version of Heisenberg's Uncertainty Principle. I wondered what Dr. Myron Wilmer would have made of it.

"I can see the damn thing from over there," Henri said, pointing to a spot a few feet distant, "and I can hit the damn thing from right here, but I can't see it and hit it from here. Best I can manage is to get a piece of it every other shot or so. I need a scientist or something to figure this out for me."

"Well," I offered, "Dr. Wilmer would probably tell you that the reason you can only hit it fifty percent of the time is because it is only there fifty percent of the time. Or better, that it is only fifty percent there."

Henri glared at me. "You wanna get lost?"

"Forget it," I said. "Go ahead, take a swing. Kill someone. See if I care."

He reared back and took an enormous swing, sending the ball slicing with a tremendous whack off to our immediate right where it almost decapitated a young man at a water fountain. "Moron!" Henri screamed at him when the fellow leaped to his feet with a look of disgust on his face. "You'd think you'd get a little more courtesy at a joint like this, eh, Donny?"

Fortunately, no one was seriously injured. We got by the front nine and made the turn toward the back. As for the golf, well, no one really seemed to care how poorly they were playing. We were not there for golf. We were there for business and the distinct aroma of greenbacks hovered just above us as we played. At the fourteenth, we ducked into a small shack for a glass of ice tea.

R. C. smiled and crossed his legs. "Buck, Henri here is a real American."

"That's what I understand. It's real nice to have real Americans behind you in a tight campaign. For sure."

Henri inched forward. "Like the one you're in now, Senator?"

Buck grimaced. "'Fraid you're right there, Henri. My opponent has drug up some horse manure about my taking bribes and kickbacks. 'Course, it's all a bunch of foolishness. . . ."

"Foolishness!" agreed R. C.

"... but it does seem to be having an effect with the electorate," Clayton Crowntooth went on. "The polls—damn'em!—have got me in a bit of a tail spin, don't ya know, and I just can't seem to work the old magic this time 'round. I know a good TV blitz would put me over the top, but the money's drying up, son. When you're down in the polls, seems like no one's got nothing for you."

"How does two million dollars sound to you, Senator?" asked Henri.

I almost swallowed my glass. Clayton Crowntooth's eyes snapped open wide. "Two million dollars, Dr. Lafayette?" he asked slowly.

"Sure. Right now. I'll write you a check."

Buck regained his composure. "Now, Doctor," he said, "you wouldn't be considering this here two million dollars to be some sort of bribe or other would you now, 'cause I can't go taking no bribes. I ain't a bribe-taking man, right R. C.?"

"Right on, Buck."

"No," said Henri.

The senator smiled at R. C. "Two million dollars is very generous, R. C. It would have quite an impact on my campaign."

"Not only that," added Henri, "but you know that one particular journalist who's been hounding you day in and day out about this bribe business?"

Buck's face darkened. "Yeah."

"Well," Henri said, "my sources tell me he's got a few skeletons in his own closet. Women principally. It seems the campaign trail gets pretty lonely for journalists, too. I'm sure, however, that something can be worked out so his family need not be dragged into such sordid business. He seems like such a reasonable man in print, you know. Something like a big change in his tune towards you might do. What do you say?"

Buck fought back tears. "Henri, I promise you, if you can make that low down son of a bitch eat his words, I'll owe you forever. God, I'd give anything to see that."

R. C. slapped the table and let out a whoop. "By golly, Senator, did I tell you Dr. Lafayette was a damn fine American or what?"

"Damn fine," Buck agreed.

R. C. leaped to his feet and grabbed Henri's hand. "Damn fine real American, by golly."

"You're up," someone yelled.

We all grabbed our clubs and headed for the next tee. We hit away and started back up the fairway. Buck put his arm around Henri's shoulders. "Because you are such a damn fine real American, Henri, I'm going to tell you a little something that I generally keep to myself," he said. "Politics is simply the art of compromise. That's the long and short of it. You've always got to be willing to compromise on everything," he confided, "if you ever want to make it on the Hill. Of course," he went on carefully, "there are certain things—principles and such—that must never be compromised, no matter what. However, times will occasionally arise when even these things we hold so sacred must be, well, *negotiated* in order to better serve our country. And no one has ever accused me, Doctor, of being unwilling to serve my country, if you get my drift?"

"I do indeed," Henri replied. "Occasions arise when out of love of country and patriotic fervor you find it necessary to accept money, momentarily setting aside your cherished principles, in order to serve a higher good."

"My God, son, but you are clearheaded," said Buck, slapping Henri on the back. "You done hit the nail on the head."

"I certainly admire your dedication and self-sacrifice," said Henri. "Not many men would be willing to lay their lives open to such criticism simply to better serve their nation. My gosh, Senator, you are truly a patriot."

"You and me gonna get along real good, Henri. Yesssahh. Now, if there is anything whatsoever I can ever help you out with, please don't hesitate to let me know. We gonna do business."

"Well . . .", said Henri.

"What's that?"

"Oh . . . nothing."

"Look here R. C.," said Senator Crowntooth, "I can't hardly impose the influence of my office on this good gentlemen. You are simply too altruistic for your own good, Henri. Now please, how may I help you?"

"Well, there is this small environmental issue that I am interested in," said Henri. "It has to do with rainfall."

"Say no more," said Clayton Crowntooth. "My record on the environment is a sterling example of leadership and compromise. I believe in the environment, Henri. What was it I said about the environment in that speech in Wheeling last year, R. C.?"

"Said the environment was nice to have around, Buck."

"That's right. Nice to have around. Tough, hardhitting stance from a no nonsense senator, Henri. 'Course I'll back you on this rain thing. Can we talk percentage?"

"No," said Henri. "Cash, up front. I'll make you a rich man, but the take is mine."

"American as all get out!" Clayton exclaimed. "When does it go down?"

"This fall, right after the elections," Henri said. "The president wants that new missile appropriation to pass you guys have been fighting. On the other hand, you want the tax on gasoline increased. Word is, the two may be packaged in some sort of compromise bill that might sail through untouched."

The senator shook his head in agreement. "Good chance of that," he agreed.

"Well, all we have to do is attach my little environmental bill to the tail of that big boy and let it go through untouched as well. I'm banking on everyone being so happy with the overall compromise they won't look too closely at an ambiguous, petty environmental issue that's of no real consequence to either party."

"You got what'cha call a plan there, Henri. Might just could work, too. 'Course, I can round up the troops on my side, but I can't speak for the fellas on the other side of the aisle."

"I'll take care of that," said Henri. "There's more than enough grease to go around."

"Ha!" laughed Clayton Crowntooth. "Grease to go around," he repeated, laughing again. "Got to remember that. And here I am lecturing the good doctor on politics. Seems like the wrong jaws have been flapping around here."

We finished the back nine, had lunch, then packed up our clubs to go. "Senator," Henri said, "the first thing we have to do is get you re-elected. That check I gave you is solid as a rock—and there's more where that came from if you need it. Once you're back at the helm, we'll talk about you becoming a rich man." We all shook hands goodbye. "I'll be in touch," said Henri.

"That's absolutely incredible," Marcy said, finishing the last bite of her chocolate mousse. "You mean he actually intends to cash in on the rain? It will never happen. How the heck could he ever make that work?"

"He's got some sort of governmental contract or other in mind. Beyond that, I don't know right now. But I'll tell you this," I went on, "he's spending money on it like he's got his own mint. He's dead serious about the whole thing."

"Well, if you ask me, he's criminally insane"

"Couple of weeks ago, I would have agreed with you. Now, well, I'm not so sure. He appears to have some heavyweight backing. I never understood how much money talks."

She laughed. "If I didn't hate him so much, I would probably find him amusing. Maybe even interesting. But now . . ."

"Yeah, I know how you feel.

We finished our dinner and I called for the check. The Mechanic Theater was only a few blocks away so we decided to walk.

Outside the air was warm and calm. The western sky was streaked in red above the city and night was just starting to fall. The air was balmy. She walked close by my side, her hip brushing against mine as we strolled slowly down the sidewalk.

"It's not only him. I fault my father as much as I do Henri. And I know that I'm not blameless in the entire affair—I suppose I could just walk away—and I don't."

"Yeah."

"It just seems like such a shame. We could both accomplish so much if it weren't for all this stupid crap we've gotten ourselves stuck in."

I stopped. "Look, I agree with you, but it isn't getting us anywhere. Let's just forget it for tonight. What do you say? For one lousy night, let's forget about Henri Goldleaf Lafayette III, about the absurd curve life has thrown you, and just live. Sometimes I think I've been thinking too much, you know? Like right now, for instance. I want to suspend everything, if even for only a few hours. I just want to be out with you. That's all. Because I like you a lot, because the night is young and warm, and because you look great in that tight dress.

She took my arm and smiled. "Well, if that's the way you feel," she said, "I suppose I can manage for an hour or two. Which way is it to the theater?"

"Screw the theater," I said.

"But you already bought the tickets."

"So what? Let's toss'em in the can and head out."

"Where?"

"Dancing," I said. "Feel like it? Let's go on one of those late cruises out to the bay and dance on the top deck. What do you say? I'll buy some champagne and it will be great. We can watch the lights, feel the breeze, and dance until we're plain old tired of it."

"Sure," she said.

So that's what we did. We boarded the Chesapeake Princess and headed for the top deck. It was very crowded but I fenagled a table by the rail and ordered a bottle of champagne. We toasted. She laughed. The band played rock tunes, I think. I don't really remember. It didn't matter. We danced and drank. We walked together to the stern of the ship and watched the lights slowly drift past. I held her close. The warm bay breeze blew through her hair. Then suddenly we were back at the dock. Three hours gone in a flash.

So we decided on a nightcap and walked down to The Brig. She sat very close to me. I felt the warmth of her legs. We finished the drink slowly, then headed back to the car.

Late at night in the parking garage, we were like the last two people on earth. I pulled her close and kissed her. I felt the full tautness of her breasts through the sheer fabric of her summer dress, and held her tight. "Your place or mine?" I asked with a wink.

She smiled. "Surely not yours."

"Yours then," I said, and started the engine.

She lived in a small apartment in a converted old Victorian on Roland Avenue. We were quiet so as not to wake the landlady. "It's not much," she whispered, "but it's home."

Inside, the apartment was full of her paintings. They were stacked in the hallway, hung on every conceivable space of wall. They were bright and beautiful. But I wasn't interested in them. When she brought me a can of beer, I held her arm. She stepped back.

"What's the matter?" I asked, surprised.

She tried to smile. "Oh . . . nothing."

"Nothing bullshit." I touched her elbow. "I thought we had something going here."

She went stiff. "Sure. Yes, I like you a lot."

"You got a funny way of showing it."

"I'm sorry," she said. She stepped closer, struggling for the right words. "I do like you, Donny. I do." She swung her hair to the side. "It's just that, well, sometimes I need time to adjust. You know?"

"To adjust to what?

"To . . . to all these strings," she blurted, "these damned commitments."

"I'm not asking for any damned commitments," I said stepping close. "I don't care about tomorrow or next week. I just want you now, right here."

I pulled her against me tightly. She didn't resist. I kissed her hard on the lips and her thighs arched forward. Her body relaxed. I reached down and squeezed her rear as slowly her hips rotated toward me. Her breath came out in a gush. The heat was overwhelming. I reached for the clasp on the back of her dress, gave it a tug, and the dress slipped slowly to the floor. I kissed her breast.

"You were saying?" I murmured, breathing heavily.

"Nothing," she whispered. "Nothing at all."

She took my hand and led me slowly to the bedroom.

The next morning I awoke very early. The air conditioning unit in the bedroom window was blowing loudly but ineffectively, making a hollow kind of rumble. But it wasn't that. It was the sun, I think. The sun on the headboard of the bed demanding that I face a new day, a few untidy pieces of my life that had to be looked after.

She slept very quietly next to my arm. She was curled. I could feel the firm curve of her rear against my leg. It made me hard and I wanted to take her then, to hear the bedsprings groan rhythmically as she wrapped her legs around my back. But she slept so soundly that it seemed a sin to wake her. Her hair smelled like flowers.

Along the roof line of the house, birds twittered in the early morning sun. I stretched carefully under the blankets and put my arm around her shoulder. She snuggled close in her sleep. I think I could have stayed like that forever, precisely in that position, covered and warm, awash in her love. But I knew it would have to change. And uncertainty is scary.

I could not love her and be a party to her misery. That had to end. The means of gaining her release from the arrangement Henri had struck with her father were easily within my command. She was right. He did not consider her an item of importance and would, no doubt, be willing to listen to a better offer. I had one in mind.

But her freedom scared me. She was too talented and beautiful to hang around unnoticed. She would soar, I knew. Success would take her far away, and I would be left with only fleeting recollections. And so I lay on the bed and listened intensely to her breathing, and the gentle patter of birds on the shingles above, trying to memorize every detail. I knew this might be the first and last of such occasions. Why, I wondered, did love have to be such a pain in the ass.

11

It was two weeks later. The phone rang in the middle of the night. I fumbled my way across the sheets and found the receiver by the eighth ring. "Yes?" I answered, groggy and confused. I glanced at the clock. It was 2:30 A.M.

"Dr. Mallory?"

"Yes."

"So sorry to bother you at such an hour, but I haven't been able to get through to Henri. R. C. Smythe here. How are you?"

"Asleep," I said.

"Sorry about that, but I've been with the senator since yesterday morning and something important has come up."

I rubbed my face. "What's that?"

"Our position. Have you seen the latest polls?"

"No."

"Well, the senator is right back in the thick of things. He's making this a real horse race. Looks like it'll go right down to the wire."

The clicheometer in the back of my head rang furiously. "Enough, R. C., I get the point. So?"

"So, we're so close we can almost taste it. The opposition is hanging on by their fin . . ."

"Can it, R. C., and get to the point."

"Well, did you know that Outspoken Females for Freedom is scheduled to have a major fund-raiser in Baltimore on Tuesday?"

Instinctively, I reached to protect my crotch. "OFF?" I asked.

"Yes."

"Yeah, come to think of it, I did hear something about that," I said.

"I've just learned that some sort of row has developed between the organization and their original sponsor. Seems they're in a difficult position because their membership, such that it is, is already on the way. They would do almost anything not to have to back out at this late date. Plus, their membership is way down. They need this fund-raiser desperately."

"So what's any of this got to do with the price of beans, R. C.?"

"Isn't it obvious, Donny? The senator and I would like Henri to intercede on behalf of the woman's group and sponsor the fund-raiser, with the condition that the senator be allowed to speak. It's probably just the juice we need to put us completely over the top. Press coverage would be at a maximum and we could dilute the woman's vote our opponent seems to have."

"Let me get this straight," I said. "You want Henri Goldleaf Lafayette III, the man who at this very moment is probably sailing across his room on a trapeze with Ms. Kitty Fouchet, to become a sponsor for OFF, a group of man-hating lesbians? That's absolutely incredible."

"Politics makes strange bedfellows, Mr. Mallory," twittered R. C. "I admit it may seem a bit of a gamble, but we're banking on the fact they're desperate and trying to move to the political center. Beggars can't be choosers."

Again the sharp ping in the back of my head. "There is in all of this the ring of desperation," I said. "You must realize Henri has never seen a woman he didn't like. A lot."

"It will be seen as desperate only if we lose and then it won't matter a hoot. If we win, on the other hand, it will be viewed as a bold step by a confident legislator. What's to lose?"

"All right! All right! All right! I said. "I'll talk to him first thing in the morning."

"Great," said R. C. "But I can't emphasize enough how important it is that we move quickly on this, Don. By noon, the opportunity may have been lost."

"I understand, R. C. You have my word. First thing."

Henri held up an entire slab of French toast, surveyed it happily, then devoured it in a single gargantuan chomp. For thirty seconds he munched it to death, then washed it down with a few mouthfuls of burgundy. "Why not?" he said. "You know I like dames. Could always stand to import a little new talent."

"Yeah, but this is OFF," I said, again reaching intuitively to protect my crotch.

"What's that? What-er-you doing there?"

"It's just a reaction. Haven't you ever seen the news when a few hundred of those lesbians get together and start screaming OFF! OFF! OFFFFF! Scares the bejesus out of me."

"Lighten up, Donny. It's just some chicks in town for a convention. Good pickings, you ask me," he insisted.

"Get them wasted and we'll all be bouncing from bed to bed. Remember that square dancing group from Kansas?"

"Don't ever confuse this with that!" I objected. "Ain't close to being the same."

"Oh, sure it is," he argued. "Chicks at a convention act the same as men: they want a good stiff drink and some guys running around in jockstraps so they can pinch an ass or two. A little clean fun is all. Don't worry, we'll give them plenty of that. I might strap on the old jock myself, come to think of it."

"Max," I objected, "these witches are likely to tie you to a bus by your balls and drag you clear to Philadelphia if you do just half the stuff you have in mind. You are everything they revile in the male species and then some. You ask me, this whole situation is like you charging a keg of dynamite with your dick on fire."

"Ha," he laughed. "That good, huh? I like a wench with some umph in her ass."

"You're completely missing my point here. I'm not talking about sexual appetites. I'm talking about intellectual storm troopers."

"Strawberries?"

"No," I answered, waving the lush fruit aside.

"They're fresh."

"No, I said."

"OK, OK," he said, putting down the bowl. "Look, you're overreacting. What's gotten into you?"

"I'm not overreacting," I insisted. "It's just I think you're making a huge mistake with this OFF thing. These women have fangs."

"Look," he said, "I ain't never heard of OFF and I don't care. A bitch is a bitch. I'm gonna troop them on in here and prove you wrong."

I tossed up my hands then sat back and smiled. "OK, you fat fuck, have it your way. But when you and your balls aren't playing on the same team anymore, don't say I didn't warn you."

"Fine, you warned me. Now, what's next."

"Well, I talked to R. C. again this morning, and he says you are supposed to contact the local chapter president, Molly Brickowski, to set it up. He says just call her 'Brick,' 'cause everyone else does."

Henri's eyes bulged. "I'm horny already. Just give me the damn phone number so I can hone in on this Brick filly and I'll be taking it all the way from here. I smell a home run, kid." He glanced my way. "Don't you have anything constructive you can be doing while your old uncle is taking care of business?"

I was miffed. "Depends on what you mean by constructive," I replied. "Some folks would say that nothing constructive ever gets done around here. As for me, I'm seeing Frickenfrayor later on."

"Frickenfrayor, that nut! Listen, you tell that silly beanbag to get going with that Bible of his. The meter's running. It's put up or shut up time in the Bible biz. Why, at the rate I'm bribing people these days, I'm gonna need a nice slice of Bible royalties pretty soon."

"Cool it," I said. "Frickenfrayor is one of the few sane people you have around here. I happen to like him."

"Yeah, well, don't be taking any of his lame excuses and whining about this lack of production. Lean on the bastard."

"Cram it," I said.

"What did you say to me?"

"I said cram it!"

"Oh . . . OK. Check back with me."

"Yeah," I said.

Pastor Frickenfrayor came in later that morning and sat quietly in front of me. He seemed subdued but cheerful. "I've received a special invitation," he confided.

"What sort of invitation?"

"To deliver a guest sermon for a local congregation. It came from a close friend of mine." He wrinkled his face. "It's been a long time, Donald."

"Oh?"

"You see, I haven't actually preached to a congregation in years. I was too controversial, they said. Or too volatile. Or too argumentative. Too everything. And they were right, of course. I was." He shifted uneasily. "The invitation took me by surprise."

"I can tell it means a lot to you," I said.

"Yes. . . . Yes, it does. You know, at first it didn't. Didn't mean much of anything. It's just a small congregation and I thought, well, what's the big deal? But then it started to grow on me enormously." He leaned forward and looked at me intensely. "Donald, I'm a preacher. Understand me, son, it's not just what I do, it's what I am. Yet I haven't preached in front of a congregation in years. Perhaps it has been for the best but now, well, now I want it to work. I want to leave them with something special. No more bombast, no more self-serving gospel, no more hyperbole. Just the pure and simple truth."

"Can't beat that," I said.

He arched an eyebrow. "I hope," he said. "Fact is," he went on, "I can't be sure. I've written this special little sermon and I wanted to run it by you before I deliver it. It's still rough, mind you. I call it, 'Sermon on Light.' It's going in the new Bible. See what you think."

He pulled the sermon out of his briefcase and read it over once carefully before starting. "Ready?" he asked finally.

"Shoot."

Before heat, before substance, before life itself, there was light. Light floods down upon us each morning from the heavens bringing warmth to our bodies, life to the meadows and illuminating vividly the world in which we live. But what we see or, for that matter, whether we see at all, is not so much dependent upon light as it is ourselves. That is, you and I. Some of us see the world with wondrous clarity, while others see but dimly. Some use the sun's light to pursue truth, while others seek to obscure it. I have been both blessed and cursed with a wandering soul and an anxious mind, and at one time or another, I must confess, have been guilty of them all.

Sifting down through the substance of my life, a simple fact has become self-evident to me: Above all else, we should pursue the truth. For proof of this you need look no further than the abundant sunshine and warmth of a May afternoon. The message is as timeless as is dawn itself. It is a mystery that I did not see it before. But for years I did not.

Because knowledge was imperfect, I foolishly turned my back on the pursuit of truth. I worshiped instead a mere sliver of time—an imperfect, hand hewn reconstruction of events that was originally intended to explain and inform —but over the weeks, years, and centuries came to limit and close our understanding. The hand of man closed what the mind of the Creator had opened. Truth became exclusive and exclusionary, something held and dispensed by a powerful few. That the sun-light that illuminated our footsteps mocked these confining efforts, went by, as far as I can tell, completely unnoticed.

As a result of this, our culture developed two mutually exclusive paths to the truth. One was the domain of the chosen, the other open to all through thought and trial. Religion and Science. One was obsessed with the holy while fearful of knowledge, the other obsessed with knowledge while fearful of anything that even so much as smacked of the divine.

Why? Why should the pursuit of knowledge be a soulless, antiseptic trek, reviled by the faithful as we cower before the latest glimpse of reality like small children before an angry storm? And why should a simple belief in faith and the majesty of creation have no place in the pursuit of truth? It should not.

My message to you today is a simple one: Do not fear the truth. Open your eyes and see what is to be seen. The light that floods our lives is there for a purpose. Use it and grow. And with a growing appreciation of the world around you, the perverse notion that truth can be the hallowed property of the few, to be dispensed or not dispensed at their whim, will melt away forever. Good riddance, I say.

But just as blind and foolish as is the notion that religion is somehow unassailable by fact and logic is the current belief that given enough time and resources, every question will have an answer. Every doubt, every mystery, will be ultimately erased from the universe by the pained but systematic pursuit of knowledge through science. For knowledge is imperfect and will always be so. Every discovery creates more questions then it answers, every fact spurs new inquiry.

Ultimately, science will not—can not—answer our questions about the world just as the gospels cannot quench our craving for the truth. One day we will ask ourselves why. Why is there one more question? Why must I ask? Why? And on that day we will no longer be divided by discipline and approach, but be united as one before the majesty of truth. For at the heart of religion, there must be truth, and at the heart of truth, we will be united in religion. Then we will truly walk with God. Thank You.

Just then we both heard a tremendous ruckus out in the hall. We turned as Dr. Myron Wilmer burst through the door and stumbled into the office atop his trusty skis. I stood up. "Dr. Wilmer," I said, taken back, "what in the world are you doing here? I wasn't expecting you. Is there a problem?"

He blinked and blinked and blinked. "I'll say there is."

"You've lost your focus again," I surmised.

"Yes. Completely. And I'm due at the Physicists Association Dinner in less than one hour." He threw his hands up in the air. "Here I'm supposed to deliver a speech on time flux potentialities and I can hardly put one foot in front of the other for fear of disappearing into oblivion".

"Ah, this is Pastor Frickenfrayor, Doctor," I said.

"How do you do," said Myron.

"Just fine," responded the pastor.
"Doctor," said Dr. Wilmer, "I need a real pick-me-up. Something with a kick to it."
"Well, I don't know," I said, scratching my chin. "This is all so sudden."
"Yeah," the doctor said apologetically, "I'm sorry to barge in on you like this. I'm kind of desperate."
"No problem at all," said the pastor.
The doctor started banging his way across the floor toward my desk in search of a seat, but caught his right ski between the leg of Pastor Frickenfrayor's chair and a coffee table. It wedged tight. "Ouch," he wailed, as his leg twisted.
"Hold it!" I yelled, leaping from my seat.
I ran to his side. "Let me help," I insisted, holding him up. I tried to wrench the ski free but only managed to send the doctor reeling off balance. He waved his arms wildly, knocking the pastor's sermon from his lap and onto the floor. "Whoa!" he shrieked, pumping his elbows about violently as he lurched back and forth like some odd form of enraged fowl. Suddenly his briefcase flew into the air as he vainly tried to recover his balance. Just as he managed to catch himself on the front edge of my desk, the briefcase descended with a startling THONK! on his forehead. The wallop opened the briefcase, sending the doctor's notes flying all over the carpet, and sending him reeling back and forth across the floor, half-stunned. He came to rest against the far wall, eyes crossed, breathing heavily.
"Are you all right?" I asked, going to his side.
His eyes gradually unglued and focused properly. He smiled. "Why, I'm back again!" he said. "I'm fixed. My focus is A-OK." He stomped boldly back and forth across the carpet to test his theory. "Yes," he announced, "I'm well again." He turned to me. "How do

you do it, Herr Doctor? You are truly unbelievable. Another dazzling and unique medical strategy employed in just the nick of time. You have saved me again." He pumped my hand in thanks. "Let me just gather up my notes and I'll be on my way now."

He grabbed the papers from the floor and stuffed them hurriedly into his briefcase. "Adios, Herr Doctor," he called, angling for the door. "A pleasure, Herr Pastor."

"Likewise, . . ." answered Pastor Frickenfrayor, but the doctor had thumped and bumped his way out of sight.

I shook my head. "So much for your high-powered science," I said. "What a piece of work."

The pastor turned to me. "Why on earth does he wear those skis?"

"It's a long story," I replied. "Suffice it to say, he's scared to death that reality does not exist."

Frickenfrayor's mouth fell open. "Well, . . ." he said.

"Anyway," I continued, "I do like your sermon. Far as I'm concerned, it hit the mark. Can I get a copy?"

"Sure," he said, fumbling through his notes. "Well, I could have sworn I had an extra copy here, he said, looking through everything to no avail. "I'll be. 'Fraid I can't find it, Donald."

It was not until several weeks later that I found out Dr. Wilmer had accidentally scooped up the pastor's sermon and stuffed it into his briefcase, along with the rest of his speech for the dinner that night.

"Forget it," I said to the pastor. "Send me a copy when you get a chance."

"I'll do that, son. Wish me good luck."

"You got it," I replied warmly.

I showed the pastor to the door and ran into Henri on the way back. "Everything is set for tomorrow morning," he said. "No problem. The babes will all be checking into their rooms in the A.M., and the senator is scheduled to address them early. After that, I have scheduled a wonderful dinner followed by a little entertainment. I've ordered enough caviar to feed the Russian infantry, sixteen ice sculptures of Venus with gazongas out to here, and fifty-seven cases of Jack Daniels. Vaa-vaa-voom!"

My position, I decided, was much like witnessing a train wreck from afar. I could kick. I could scream. But it was apparent there was little I could do to head the destruction off. "Fifty-seven cases of Jack Daniels?" I asked.

"Just to wet their dainty whistles. I'm also spiking the punch with tequila."

"And exactly what sort of entertainment do you have in mind?"

"I've hired the Banana Boys," he said.

"Have you lost your mind entirely?" I yelled. "Do you mean those guys who dance and cavort around in nothing but sequined jock straps sporting bulges the size of Uncle Frank's Kielbasa?"

"Exactly," he replied.

I shuddered to think what the women from OFF would do when the Banana Boys started doing their thing. Riot came to mind. "It's your funeral," I said. I decided I had to make a move before the opportunity went up in smoke. "But should this thing prove successful . . ."

"Wha-da-ya mean, should? This thing will knock'em dead. I'm going to be the talk of the town."

"Be that as it may," I went on quickly, "when this rain thing gets set up, how am I going to fit in?"

"I'll need you, kid. More than ever. You and me, we're gonna run it. You on the numbers, me on the style end."

155

"Yeah, well, I have a few conditions," I said.

"Conditions?"

"Yeah. Like a bigger cut and more control. That's what I want."

He rubbed his chin, then smiled. "You been hanging around the old master too long. You're stiffing me, aren't you?"

". . . No . . . I'm . . ."

"Stop it," he insisted. "You're stiffing me. I can't believe it." He stepped forward and for the briefest moment gave me a hug. "I never thought I'd see the day. I knew you had it in you, but I never thought I'd see the day. 'Course, the answer is no."

I laughed. "Then you can run the fucker yourself. You're talking big bucks here, Max. Monster bucks. You'll never keep track of it. It'll run you right into the ground."

"All right! All right! Five percent of net and that's it."

"No way," I countered. "Twenty percent of gross and I control all investment capitol. Take it or leave it."

"Christ, you've become a maniac, a butcher. . . . OK, I'll take it."

"And one more thing," I said. "The girl goes free. No more deal on her."

He smiled again. "Sure. The girl walks, but you stay. One year. You take her place, at considerably better wages, of course. But you stay."

I swallowed hard. "Deal," I said.

12

"The Patuxent Room, Sir," the doorman said, bowing just slightly.

"That's for the senator's speech, right?" I asked.

"Yes, sir," he affirmed. "The dinner will be held later in the Wye Room, and after that, it's back to the Patuxent Room for the evening festivities."

I was impressed. Somehow Henri had wangled us into the Carroll Downtown Hotel, one of the oldest, most sumptuous, and exclusive hotels in town. Everything was polished wood and shiny brass. My feet sank into the carpet as I walked. "Marcy," I said, "can you believe this?" Just then, I spotted a huge sign in the middle of the lobby. It said OFF in enormous red letters. Reflexively, I reached to protect my crotch.

Marcy snickered. "What in the world are you doing?" she asked.

"I don't know," I admitted. "It's just some kind of unconscious reaction I seem to have."

"To what?" she wondered.

"To OFF."

She rolled her eyes. "That's not what it means," she said.

"Oh yeah. Well, it may not mean that to you."

"It has to do with freedom and equality," she insisted stiffly.

"Sure," I said.

She stopped in her tracks. "Did you know I happen to be a member of OFF?"

"You are?" I asked, dumbfounded.

She didn't get an opportunity to reply because Henri came whizzing across the lobby toward us and grabbed my arm. "You're looking lovely, Marcy," he said. "Nice ass."

She turned and gave me one of those *this is hopeless* looks. "What's up?" I asked.

"Money! Money, money. Let's talk."

"Excuse me for just a second," I said, as Henri dragged me to a corner. "What the hell's this all about?" I shook loose my arm.

He put his face very close to mine. "I think I just may have dropped the ball," he said. "Big time."

"What are you talking about?"

"There are so many congressmen and big shots here today to hear the senator's speech that I went overboard. I bought them all. I just couldn't help myself. I went nuts!"

"How nuts?"

"Five million dollars worth."

"F-f-five million dollars! You don't have five fucking million dollars."

He gritted his teeth. "I know, I know," he replied, starting to perspire. "And now the gents from the hotel are leaning on me for cash up front. For lunch alone I've ordered Maine lobster and New York strips." He started to shake. "Christ, Donny, do you have any idea how much *twelve hundred* Maine lobsters cost?"

"Get a hold of yourself," I said, rubbing my chin furiously. "We'll think of something."

"Of what? WHAT?"
"Have you talked to Kiddo Kenny London yet?"
"No."
"Well, we need to. We can liquidate some bonds this morning for cash, and maybe he'll have some hot tips. Go ahead and pay the hotel. My guess is, most of the bribe checks you wrote this morning won't be cashed until this afternoon—or maybe even tomorrow. That gives us some working time."

"You're right, you're right. I'll insist that the bribees stick around for the whole affair. After all, I just bought them, didn't I?"

"Yeah. Now you have to make it stick. You call London; I'm going to talk to Marcy. I'll be right back."

I walked back down the hall. "Problems," I said.

"What's up?" she asked.

"Henri's in way over his head. He's gone ahead and paid off half the stinking planet and now can't make ends meet."

"What will you do? Does this mean the fund raiser is finished?"

"No. Not, at least, as of right now," I said. "But check back in half an hour and if the doormen are tossing me onto the sidewalk, you'll have your answer."

She looked glum.

"Look, believe it or not," I said, "I've been through this before. Maybe we can pull it off again. Go ahead to the meeting. I've got some phone calls to make. I'll catch up with you later."

I went looking for Henri and found him on the far side of the lobby hanging onto a phone. "How fast, Kiddo?" he was saying. "Yeah, yeah, all that's great, but how fast can you move them?"

"Move what?" I asked. "What's he got, Max? Just what the hell is he moving?"

Henri put his hand over the receiver and leaned my way. "Tanks."

"Tanks?" I repeated. "You're buying tanks?"

He leaned my way again. "We're buying new Soviet armor, moving it via Pakistan to Chad. Fifty nifty tanks."

"You want to wind up in jail for the rest of your life?" I screamed. "Give me that phone," I ordered, yanking the receiver from his hand.

"What the hell is this all about, Kenny?"

"Donny baby, don't get all ruffled," said Kiddo. "Just a little international arms trade is all. If we pull it off, we're looking at three to four million apiece."

"And if we don't, we'll all wind up in the slammer for the rest of our natural lives," I said. "The whole thing stinks. Cancel."

"If you say so, baby, but . . ."

"No buts, Kiddo," I said. "Cancel it now, then liquidate all the bonds we're holding post haste. Check the big board for anything that looks good. We're gonna trade on volume. We should be good for at least two mil until tomorrow when these checks start to clear. I'll get back to you. Got it?"

"Got it."

I hung up. Henri gulped hard. He was sweating profusely. I put my arm around his shoulder. "We'll make it," I said. "I'll handle everything. Now you go back in there and act the perfect host. We'll pull it off."

I ran back and found Marcy waiting at the doors to the Patuxent Room. Hundreds of women had gathered already. I touched her elbow. "London's working on it," I said.

"And?"

"And it's going to be a long day. Go ahead and enjoy the speeches, but before you go in I want to tell you something."
She tilted her head. "What?"
"I love you," I said, "but that's not all."
She blinked.
"You're free of that stupid deal. No more Center. I convinced Henri it was immoral."
She looked at me for a long time. "Are you serious?" she asked finally. "How?"
"I told you. I just convinced him it was wrong."
"And he won't go after my father?"
"I promise. Ask him if you don't believe me."
She wrapped her arms around my neck and gave me a huge kiss. "I love you, too." "OK," I said. "Now hurry off to your leftist lesbian manifesto therapy and I'll get back to business."
She laughed. "Will I see you?"
"Yeah, I'll try and get back." I held up my ticket. "Here, I've got the seat right next to yours. Don't let anybody take it."
It was done. I had no time to fret or worry about the consequences. I loved her and that would have to do.
I ran back to the lobby and grabbed the horn. "Kiddo," I said, "what's it look like?"
"Nothing real hot on the big board," he answered. "Sorry. Now, I do have some activity heating up in the previously owned gems and paintings mart."
"You mean stolen goods?" I asked
"No. Previously owned, Donald."
"Look," I said, "this is going to be legit. I may be out in left field and we may have to reach mighty high to catch the ball, but it's going to be legit. Understand, Kiddo?"

"Comprendo, baby," he acknowledged. "By the way," he went on, "how's the senator doing?"

"He's not on till later," I said.

"Get it straight, baby," said Kiddo Kenny. "Henri told me he was moving up the main event to keep the bribees in their seats until you could come up with the big fix."

"That's news to me, Kenny," I said. "I'll have to check it out."

I ran back to the Patuxent Room and opened the door. I had never heard a place so large and so packed with people be this deathly silent. It was like stepping into a mausoleum. At the front of the room, Senator Crowntooth was speaking, waving his arms in animation, but the reaction of the assembled members of OFF was chilling. When I stepped into the room, the sound of my shoe scraping the carpet caused a few hundred heads to turn. I slipped down the aisle and found Marcy.

"What gives?" I whispered.

She rolled her eyes. "Just listen."

". . . and my Mammy, a fine woman, a big woman, by golly, smacked some horse sense into this knuckle head of mine from time to time. So I understand in my heart what it is women of today want from their government. They want understanding, and a position—other than on their backs, ha ha—they can be proud of. And Clayton Crowntooth—please ladies, call me Buck—is just the man to deliver. Yessirree bobcat . . ."

I put my head down. "At least no one has thrown anything," I said.

"Not yet."

"He's just warming up," I said. "He'll get better."

". . . America has always been a land where a broad with a nice set of gams and a size 36 *"D"* bra could get by nicely. But I want it to be a place where gals like yourselves—you know, maybe a little on the pudgy side and kind a square lookin' in the butt area—can get by almost as well. Now don't that remind me of a story . . ."

"Oh God," I moaned as a ripple of angry electricity went through the crowd. "I'm getting out of here before all hell breaks loose. Catch you later."

I slipped down the aisle again and quickly beat a retreat to the exit. I ran for the phones, but Henri grabbed me halfway through the lobby. "What's going on?" he demanded.

"I was just headed back to call Kenny," I said.

"Well, what did you decide on? The hot Rembrandt or the diamonds?"

"Neither," I said. "I'm going to trade on high volume and make it legit."

His face got red. "But he had some . . ."

"Never mind what he had," I interrupted. "I'm going to do it, and I'm going to do it right. Don't worry."

"Don't worry!" he cried. "The bill from lunch alone is two hundred and twenty thousand dollars. They just handed it to me."

"Does that include the tip?"

He looked straight up. "The kid's making jokes," he said. "I'm going down the tube and the kid's making jokes."

"Look," I said, "you'd better get back in there and smooth things over. The senator is about to be tarred and feathered."

"Crowntooth?"

"Yeah."

"I thought he was doing real good. They do look a little square in the . . ."

"Stay out then," I said, "but don't stray too far because you and R. C. are probably the only ones who like what he's saying in there. He may need you to run interference."

I sprinted back to the phones, but they were all tied up. When I was finally able to reach London's number, it was busy. Finally, I got through. He was out to lunch. I looked at my watch and started to sweat. It was getting close to one o'clock. "Shit," I said. I ran into the dining room but was too tense to eat. I gulped a cup of coffee and called London again.

"Heyyy, Donny," he said. "How goes it?"

"That's what you're supposed to be telling me, Kiddo. Hope you have something prime."

"I got a couple sweet deals, Donny, but nothing that will raise the kind a coin you need by closing. Can't be done."

I slammed my hand into my mouth and bit my knuckles. "What then?"

"Tanks," he said.

"No," I insisted, "I'm not buying any Soviet armor. There's just got to be something else."

"OK, OK," he said, "how 'bout after-market auto parts moved in bulk?"

"Do you mean stolen parts?"

"What, do they brand these babies? How the hell do I know where they came from? I'm just a lousy broker here, Donny."

"Forget it," I said. I racked my brain. "How about a horse?" I asked finally.

"A horse, huh?" I heard him rustling through the sheet. "Nah," he said, "nothing looking too hot here today. Sorry."

"How about that horse we won on before. What was his name?"

"House of Cards," he said. "I think he's running up in New York somewhere. Maybe Belmont."

"Check it."

"Here it is," he said. "Yeah, House of Cards is going off in the sixth race this afternoon at Belmont. Hold on and I'll check the computer for the latest odds. . . . Ah, here it is: six to one. Not bad, kid, but the horse ain't scheduled to win, you know."

"Bet him," I said. "I have a feeling. Lay down a big boy."

". . . A million, kid?"

"Yeah, do it."

He whistled. "If you say so, baby. It's done."

I hung up the phone and started to perspire. I undid my tie and steam rose from my shirt like a fog. What was I doing? Had I lost my mind? Then I thought, the bet's down. It doesn't matter. We would either have it made in the shade or be out on the street—nothing in between. I glanced quickly at the clock. It was just slightly passed two. The race would start in a little over an hour. I took a deep breath, headed back to The Patuxent Room, eased my way down the aisle, and sat next to Marcy. She put her hand on mine and I gave her a wink. Crowntooth was winding down.

". . . and so you see, gals, the path through the forest of inequality leads through the wild and wonderful State of West Virginie and directly to the open door of Clayton 'Buck' Crowntooth. By golly, I care about'cha. That's right, little ladies, 'tain't no other candidate out there with my sort of heartfelt concern for the needs and wants of the women folk such as ya'll. By golly, come on, back me now. Whatcha say, clap for me now. Back me now! Stand up and let'er rip!"

Not a soul moved. Silence. Absolute, endless, palpable silence.

Buck Crowntooth stood in a sea of dead air before a thousand females who more or less hated his guts. He was smiling and blinking, winking and grinning as though he were the most welcomed, admired and adored leader of our times. I had to hand it to him—he was a pro. When after thirty seconds not a single person had clapped or stood, Buck waved to the assembly as though they were family, said goodbye—"Love ya'll. Thankee. Thankee."—and walked off the stage.

A short, box-shaped woman with violent red hair assumed Buck's place at the podium. "LADIES," she boomed, "our next scheduled event is the televised address from California of our past president, Linda Glicken. The speech will air in exactly forty-five minutes. Please be back and seated. DISMISSED!"

"Who's that?" I asked Marcy.

"Molly Brickowski."

"Oh. So that's the Brick, huh?"

"That's her."

I smiled. "Good luck, Henri," I said.

"What?"

"Nothing. Just mumbling."

"Well, I'm famished," Marcy said. "That was the longest, stupidest, most irritating speech I've ever heard."

"That good, huh? Come on, let's get out of here."

The room emptied quickly. We walked into the lobby and made our way toward the dining room. Henri emerged from the crowd and grabbed me by the arm again. His face was wet with perspiration. "I've been looking for you," he said. "What's up?"

"Marcy," I said, "go ahead and grab something. I'm not hungry anyway. I'll be out here." I watched as she walked away. "We're all set," I finally assured him.

He wiped the sweat from his brow with the back of his hand. "Whew," he said. "So you came to your senses and bought the tanks?"

"No."

"What then? Drugs? Machine guns? Or did you decide to put some money behind that generalissimo down their in banana land?"

"No."

He frowned. ". . . Well, what then?"

"House of Cards," I said.

He grabbed me by the lapels. "That stinking horse?"

I pushed him away and straightened my jacket. "Keep your freaking hands off of me and, yes, I bet that stinking horse. I had a feeling."

"A *feeling*!" He put a fist in front of my face. "Well, it may be your *last*."

I slapped his hand away. "Stick it in your ear," I said. "It worked before, it will work again."

"Are you absolutely nuts? That other deal was a set up, a scam."

"No," I insisted, "you heard it yourself. They just took the lead off of him, is all. The horse can run. He's a winner. And besides, it's done."

"Excuse me . . ."

We both turned. It was Molly Brickowski. "Dr. Lafayette," she said, "please pardon my intrusion, but I couldn't help overhearing. Am I to understand that the financial underpinnings of the entire OFF meeting and fund-raiser are riding on a horse race?"

"Well . . . I . . . ah . . ." stumbled Henri.

"Tell her," I said. "What difference does it make? She knows anyway."

"Yes," said Henri, "I'm afraid it's true. It appears my young assistant here in a wild and reckless fit bet all of my resources on a horse by the name of House of Cards. If the horse fails, I'm afraid we'll all be out on the street, my dear. But please, don't judge him too harshly. He has made extraordinary progress under my tutelage and I don't want to harm what good I have done him, even if he has placed my entire financial empire at peril."

Molly Brickowski put her hands on her hips. "You are an extraordinary man, Dr. Lafayette," she said. "Even though this foolish twit has endangered your very financial survival, your concern is for him. Very admirable, I must say."

Neither Molly Brickowski's square suit nor her square blouse could hide the considerable bust which she now thrust unintentionally at Henri. He stared at her knockers. "And I am equally as impressed," he replied, eyes bulging.

She stepped back quickly, pulling her suit together. "Excuse me?"

Henri bowed, then stepped close. "I know, Madame President, that you are a woman of considerable stature . . . and learning. I understand fully your position in the community and yet somehow, suddenly, I don't care." He stepped even closer, touching her thigh gently with his fingers. "I must be out of my mind to say such a thing, but the heat I feel in your presence is so intense I can't think straight. I am willing, nay compelled, to toss my education and career to the wind. You are, Madame President, an extraordinary creature."

Then he quickly stepped away. "I'm sorry, so sorry," he gasped. "Please, forgive me." Max turned to me. "Donald, let's go find the communications room in this hotel. The race will be starting soon. I'm sure we can pick it up on cable TV if we tinker a bit. . . . Adieu, Madame."

Molly Brickowski wobbled in place, eyes aflutter, as we made our way to the communications room. We found it in the basement.

"Do you know what you're doing?" I asked, as he picked the lock.

"What's the big deal? A widget here, a wadget there. Crank a few knobs and we'll be cooking."

"Is this really necessary?" I asked, looking around nervously.

He grabbed me by the lapels. "My whole rain deal is hinging on this race, you nitwit," he screamed. "Yes, it's necessary. I can't just sit around, waiting to see how it goes. I have to see it."

I pulled away. "Well, I don't. I can't stand to watch. I'll go crazy."

"To each his own." he responded, wiggling knobs, twisting dials. "Go on then; get out of here. Go see if that redheaded wench is in heat yet."

I left. Hurrying to the bar, I ordered a shot of whiskey. I tossed it down, closed my eyes, and felt its liquid fire burn through my body. Then I found the elevator and made my way to The Wye Room where the televised address by Linda Glicken was scheduled. I looked at my watch. The race would be starting in seconds. My heart pounded. I blinked several times, opened the door, and stepped into the dark room. Down front, the pudgy face of Linda Glicken talked from a large screen.

". . . so our efforts must continue, must be redoubled, if our cause is to bear fruit. We are the champions of womankind, we are the vanguard of liberty and justice here on earth. We ARE . . ."

Suddenly Linda Glicken's face froze then disassembled in a trillion fuzzy directions as the screen unfocused, streaked, then focused again. But where Linda's jaws had just been flapping, eleven straining thoroughbreds now flew around a white fence, mud filling the air behind them. The jockeys were struggling, the horses packed tightly against each other. The race was close.

And then a voice, high-pitched and nasal: "... on the near turn it's Shoemettle by a nose, followed by Fandango, Conga Line, Ernie's Business, House of Cards, Lover's Leap..."

I jumped to my feet. "Yes!" I yelled, "Go baby. Go!"

The room was buzzing. "What's happening? What's going on? Where's Linda?"

"Order, order," Molly Brickowski demanded, running to the podium. "We must have order."

"... as they close, it's Shoemettle, followed by Fandango, Conga Line, House of Cards coming hard on the outside, Ernie's Business, Lover's Leap..."

I went wild. "Yeah! Go House of Cards! Come on baby." I jumped up on my chair.

Molly Brickowski stared at me, then turned and looked at the screen closely. Suddenly, it struck her. "Yaaa!" she exploded, throwing both arms in the air. "Go House of Cards!"

"... as they near the club house, it's still Shoemettle by a nose, followed by Fandango, House of Cards closing like a wild machine on the outside, Conga Line now fading, Lover's Leap..."

"Gooooo!" I yelled, "Go! Go! Go!"

Following Molly's lead, the other women began slowly chanting and cheering. Others clapped.

"... as they near the finish line, it's Shoemettle and Fandango neck and neck with House of Cards closing furiously."

"Ahhhhhhhh!" cried Molly.

The clapping became thunderous.

"... Shoemettle, Fandango and House of Cards, all neck and neck..."

"Do it! Do it!" I implored.

"... Shoemettle and House of Cards as Fandango fades ... Shoemettle and House of Cards ... Shoemettle and House of Cards."

I made two fists and closed my eyes. I held my breath.

"... at the wire, it's ... House of Cards."

I opened my eyes. "Yahh-hoooo," I screamed.

The place went crazy. Women who had no reason to cry began crying. Others jumped up and down on their chairs. Molly leaped in the air like a school girl, red hair bouncing wildly across the stage. Marcy came running up to me. "Is this it?" she asked, laughing uncontrollably. She hugged me. "Was that your investment?"

"Yes!" I yelled. "We did it!"

Amid the raucous jubilation, I spotted Henri plunging down the aisle to my left, virtually flying onto the stage. He pointed at Molly. Then he approached her slowly, grabbed her by the neck, and firmly kissed her mouth for a full thirty seconds. As he did so, he carefully slipped one hand under her coat and fondled her breast. Quickly jumping back, he held both hands over his head in a victory salute. The cheers were deafening. There he stood, in the center of this crazy moment, claiming a prize no one understood, awash in applause meant for no one in particular, yet utterly victorious. That's when I knew there would be no stopping him.

13

"Stunned," said R. C. Smythe to an assembly of reporters, "absolutely stunned. Have you ever seen a crowd so entirely enthralled, so involved in a speech before? Today we witnessed political history in the making, my friends. The senator connected with these women in a way no other politician past or present has ever been able to do."

"But, Mr. Smythe," protested one reporter. "are you sure the women weren't just a bit put out by the senator's words?"

"Rubbish. Absolute left-wing, dirty-tricks garbage," snorted R. C. "I challenge you, sir, to report the truth of what occurred here today. Why, the senator's performance was spellbinding. A simply breathtaking exhibition by a politico at the very apex of his powers and acumen."

"And how about this Dr. . . . ah?"

"Lafayette," said R. C. "That's Dr. Lafayette. He is an extraordinary human being, a philanthropist whose concern for women is so honestly heartfelt it brings a tear to my eye. He is a unique man who seems to possess an almost electric presence, an ability to galvanize a crowd and whip them into near hysteria. Did you see him on that stage? Did you see the way those women reacted? Why it was mayhem—total, spontaneous mayhem. The man has power, I tell you, a sense of self and charisma not unlike that wielded by Roosevelt, Kennedy, and Elvis—just to name a few. He's a great American. Don't forget his name, friends. He's going to go far."

I chuckled and walked on. I had to admit the fundraiser was going well. The dinner went off without a hitch. Everyone was still mildly euphoric over the horse race and the influx of cash it added to their coffers. During the banquet, Henri made an official donation of two hundred thousand dollars to OFF and gave another one hundred thousand to Senator Crowntooth's campaign as well. Everyone clapped politely.

Of course, some of the women didn't care for the goings on. But their numbers were limited and their voices were soon drowned out by the more prudent members of the organization—the ones who understood the one unavoidable truth of American politics: money talks. So flash bulbs flashed, reporters reported, and money multiplied.

After dinner, The Patuxent Room was rearranged for the evening's entertainment. Henri had imported a rock band, and three or four open bars were set up around the perimeter of the dance floor. It was certainly a departure for OFF—and there was some grumbling—but most of the participants didn't seem to mind. Around nine o'clock, the festivities started to warm up. By eleven, the party was cooking. Jack Daniels was going by the case, and even Henri's special punch of vodka, gin, bourbon, tequila, and lemonade had found plenty of takers.

Still, it was an odd affair: a strange marriage of hard driving, primal rock occasionally interrupted by a speech or slogan session of sorts. Although the two would not, under normal circumstances, cohabit— because of the abundant drink and the general sense of euphoria that carried on into the night—they seemed perfectly wed. The thumping, carnal rock and roll— now just a pulsing rhythm in the background—kept perfect beat to the rhythmic rounds of sloganeering. The women never dreamed politics could be so fun. Even those who took everything seriously were starting to joke and giggle. Others swayed gently to the music as they talked.

I was feeling good. Marcy and I laughed and danced our way around the floor. We sipped wine. I began to relax. I began to think the impossible: Henri might just pull it all off. He might even have OFF in his back pocket before the night was over.

By midnight, the press had put down their pencils and joined in the revelry. Led by Henri, the men started dancing with the women. Henri immediately pounced on Molly. They slid smoothly back and forth across the floor. People clapped and cheered. They were an item. Everything was wonderful. Everyone was happy. Then it happened.

Around 1 A.M., Molly went to the podium to wish everyone well and close down for the night. She turned on the microphone and tapped it a few times. Biiiiinnngggg Biiiiinnngggg. For no reason in particular, and from far in back of the room, the chant began: "OFF, OFF, OFF." It was the booze and good times talking and it spread almost immediately. "OFF, OFF, OFF." Molly held up her hands to stop the chant, but that only served to encourage the chanters. "OFF! OFF! OFF!" Soon all the women were clapping and stomping their feet in unison. "OFF! OFF! OFF!" It became deafening. "OFF! OFF! OFF!" Everyone was clapping, stomping, shouting, and laughing at once. Molly tried to stop it, but her efforts were useless. So she joined in. "OFF! OFF! OFF!"

I was standing on the side of the room with my arm around Marcy's waist. I was drinking a bottle of beer and laughing. The whole thing seemed so impossible to me, so wild and joyous, that I was almost swept away in the pounding emotion. But suddenly I had a horrible thought. I looked for Henri. I couldn't see him anywhere. "Oh my God," I said to Marcy. "Oh no!"

"What's wrong?" she said, grabbing my arm as I turned this way and that. "What is it?"

"I just realized what's going to happen next," I shouted at her, barely audible above the pounding din. "God Almighty, I know exactly what he's going to do."

"What?" she screamed, cupping her hand around her ear.

"OFF! OFF! OFF!"

"I know what that maniac is up to!" I yelled. "Oh God." I pulled her close to my ear and shouted for all I was worth: "Banana Boys! You stay here. I gotta find him. Maybe I can get to him before he gets to the stage. maybe it's not too late. Wait here!"

"OFF! OFF! OFF!"

I ran through the assembly as fast as I could. But the crowd was so large and tightly packed I didn't get very far before I spotted him. Instantly, I knew it was all over. He was on the other side of the room, just stepping onto the stage. He motioned to the band. They joined in the chant with a slow base beat. Boom, boom, boom."

"OFF! OFF! OFF!"

Boom, boom, boom.

Behind him were the Banana Boys dressed in nothing but their clingy, yellow skivvies. They danced on stage, gyrating lewdly to the thundering beat, thrusting their pelvises at the audience. Naturally, Henri thought the chant he was hearing was an animal demand for his clothes.

"OFF! OFF! OFF!"

Boom, boom, boom.

At first no one saw them, but then Henri led the procession to the center of the stage. There he stopped, pointing provocatively at Molly, whose mouth had dropped open almost to her knees. She froze, obviously shocked. He turned and started removing his shirt. Then his shoes.

"OFF! OFF!"

The band slowed down.

The Banana Boys danced to the front of the stage and began making obscene motions as Henri removed his socks and whipped off his belt.

"Off!"

The band stopped.

When Henri ripped off his pants, pure pandemonium hit the hall like a missile striking an ammo dump. Women started running everywhere, some charged the stage, others dashed for the exits. Many were screaming. A few cried. Some grabbed chairs and began flinging them at the Banana Boys. One group started grabbing the Banana Boys, ripping their G-strings off, having a good look for themselves. Bottles were broken, people run over, tables overturned, pictures fell from the walls, lights smashed, food flung—it all happened in seconds. Five women carried off one of the Banana Boys while the others fought their way backstage through a bombardment of bottles, food, chairs, and female undergarments. The last time I saw Henri, he was standing at center stage, an enormous bra hanging from one ear, furiously kissing Molly Brickowski.

AMERICAN RAIN

I ran back through the stampeding crowd and found Marcy under a chair. Behind me, cops flooded the room, whistles screeched, and sirens blared outside. I grabbed Marcy's hand and yanked her up, pointing towards the window. "Let's get the hell out of here!" We made a break for it.

Marcy laughed so hard she had to bite the pillow. She wiped the tears from her eyes with a corner of the sheet, then caught her breath. "I'll never forget the sight of that fat monstrosity dancing and stripping as long as I live." Another wave of laughter took her. "Ohhhhhhhh," she moaned.

I chuckled myself. Weeks later, it was still funny. It had taken the police over two hours to restore order—pulling naked Banana Boys out of closets; tripping over broken glass; fighting off hordes of drunken, hysterical women. Marcy and I watched carefully from the shadows across the street as countless bodies were piled into paddy wagons for their trip downtown.

The next morning, the press went wild. Every major newspaper in the country carried the story on page one. Pictures of Henri and petrified Banana Boys surrounded by screeching females were everywhere you looked. Editorials, jokes, and television interviews multiplied like rabbits. The following evening, a camera crew from Detroit showed up just to film the clean up—such was the interest across the country. From California to Maine, Americans were howling over the incident.

The national leadership of OFF was so mortified it went into public mourning. And at first I thought it was over for us, too—Henri, me, Crowntooth, R. C., the "Brick," right on down the line—but then a strange thing happened. The following Monday, the phone lines began to go crazy at OFF. Switch boards were swamped from Portland to Miami with pledge money and new enlistees. In one forty-eight hour period alone, the Outspoken Females for Freedom took in more cash and new members than it had in eight years. Chagrin promptly turned to euphoria at the national office. And the event suddenly changed from the apocalyptic into a cause celebre. All sorts of politicians and rock stars claimed to have been there. A T-shirt came out. By the next Friday, the people at OFF were smiling. For what had originally seemed a complete debacle became one of the greatest publicity coups of the century. And there was Henri, center stage.

"Now dear, repulsive Henri," Marcy marvelled, shaking her head in amazement, "is the very toast of OFF. And why? Because he danced around practically naked with a bunch of guys hung like gas pumps—all in an attempt to humiliate us. Can you believe it?"

"Speaking of guys hung like gas pumps . . ." I said, reaching for her under the sheet.

"Stop it!" she laughed, slapping me away.

I rolled over on my side. "You're right," I agreed. "The guy's like a cat or something, you know? He always lands on his feet. It's a talent."

"Well, I'm just sick of the two of them together," she went on. "Yuukk!" Marcy grimaced in distaste. "The pinching and cavorting, the humping they do in public, it's simply disgusting. To think Molly Brickowski, a stalwart of the feminist cause, could sink so low so fast is more than incredible. It's frightening. Who'd have guessed it?"

I reached for her again and found her hip. "And who are you to talk?" I teased.

I pulled her to me. She gave me a long slow kiss. "Fill'er up," purred Marcy.

Later, while she was showering, I went to the window. Marcy lived in one of those old houses innocent of screens. When the window glass was raised, it was just you and the air outside. I liked that. So I sat by the window and felt the new coolness in the morning breeze. September. Fall was closing in. Where had the time gone?

Marcy's apartment was now sparse and tidy. No paintings. She was all packed. She was moving up the road to her grandmother's old place in Frederick. It would be perfect, she said. Upstairs there were several rooms where she could live and work. Downstairs was a small shop opening onto Church Street where she could sell her paintings. In the backyard, she even had a garden to grow. Freedom. It was exactly what she wanted. She came out of the shower and spotted me. "Stop brooding and come with me," she said, drying her hair.

"And do what?"

"Anything. Does it matter? We'll be free, and we'll be together. What were you going to do when you left New Jersey last spring? You can do it now. You can do it with me."

"I can't," I whispered. I rubbed my hand along the window ledge. "The elections are coming up real soon. He needs me. Maybe after that."

She shook out her hair. Rainbow droplets of light fell everywhere. "He's just using you, you know. All you have to do is walk out that door, get in my car, and come along." Her eyes suddenly sparkled. "Frederick is beautiful in the fall," she enticed. "The Catoctin Mountains, the Blue Ridge. You'd love it. I remember when I was a little girl," she breathed dreamily. "Going to the farm, I thought there was nowhere else in the world where the sun could shine so bright or the grass could grow so green. That was before Grandmother sold the farm and moved to town, but it's still just as bright and green there. Please come."

I looked out the window. "It's not that far, Marcy. You said so yourself. I'll be able to come up on the weekends. At night sometimes, too. We'll be OK."

She lowered her glossy, black lashes. Shadows fell across her cheeks. "Well, I don't understand," she said, "but it's up to you. It's just I think it's important to be free. Absolutely free." She beamed. "I can't wait."

I shrugged. "I'm not sure there's any such animal."

She stuck her tongue out at me and marched off to get dressed. I turned back to the window. Soon the leaves would turn. Then winter. What else would change? Would I be able to balance my one year commitment to Henri and a long distance love affair at the same time? The uncertainty made me fret. I would give anything not to lose her. In a way, it was funny. I had left New Jersey to find my destiny, romance the farthest thing from my mind. Now here I was. My priorities had totally reversed themselves.

Marcy came back from the bathroom. Smiling, kissing me, she tried to reassure me, "We'll be fine. I love you. Don't worry so much."

I kissed her back. "Yeah."

She finished with her lipstick. "Well, today's my last day and I hope it will be a good one. For instance," she continued, "I hope I don't have to listen to Molly's outrageous moaning all day long. It's embarrassing."

"Give her a break," I said. "She likes getting laid."

"But it never ends, Donny!"

"She's making up for lost time."

She folded her arms, exasperated. "But how can they screw so much? It's positively inhuman."

"Yeah? Well, tell me what Max does that is human?"

"You have a point there," she admitted. "But poor Molly. I just can't believe she's fallen for him like this."

"Truth is, I think he likes her," I said. "Don't ask me why, but he does. It's amazing to see, but she's actually taken his mind off money for a few hours a day. And that's saying something. Who knows where it will lead?"

She laughed and cocked her head. "The world is a funny place, isn't it?"

"Hilarious. I'm only now starting to understand how funny."

She wrinkled her nose at me and took my arm. "I'm tired of that blue mood," she said. "Let's go to work."

So we went to The Center and the day went much too quickly for me. I wanted it to slow down, to linger. I wanted to savor having her near this one last time. But the hours marched by as relentlessly and hectically as ever. To this I, of course, overreacted. I grew sad and melancholy. I couldn't concentrate on anything except her leaving.

After work, we took a short walk down Charles Street and had dinner. Then we watched television for awhile before going to bed. She fell asleep almost immediately while I couldn't sleep at all. I tried every position I knew, but nothing worked. Finally, I got quietly out of bed and went to the window. I gave it a gentle tug and it slid open. The night air was cool and moist.

I guess I'd been sitting there for nearly an hour before the phone rang. Startled, I jumped across the room and grabbed it from the table before the ringing woke Marcy. "What?" I demanded, angry at the intrusion.

"Dr. Mallory?"

"Yes, who's calling?"

"Dr. Myron Wilmer here."

I saw red. "How in the blue blazes . . ."

"I'm sorry to bother you, Doctor, but your answering service said you could be reached at this number."

I felt like screaming *idiot!* at him, but instead I snidely inquired, "Oh, lose your focus again?"

"No," he replied, rather matter-of-factly. "Quite the opposite. I think I have actually located it."

"So, what's the problem?"

"No problem, just news."

"What news?"

"Bad news."

"Spit it out then," I hissed, afraid to yell and wake Marcy.

"I am standing here now without my skis."

"But that's great," I said.

"No, it's horrible."

"But that's what you wanted."

"True. But it's great and it's horrible."

"How?"

"Great I don't have to wear skis, horrible because I understand why."

"Why," I asked, simmering.

"I can't tell you that."

"Oh," I said, slapping my forehead. "What is it then?"

"Do you remember the physicists' dinner I told you about?"

"Yeah."

"Something very strange occurred that night."

"Go on."

"Well, you may recall I was scheduled to provide a talk on time flux potentialities?"

"Sure," I said.

AMERICAN RAIN

"You see, I was very nervous—I'm not used to speaking before large gatherings, especially with skis on my feet—and my notes were jumbled due to that little episode we had back in your office. So I just started reading, not really knowing where I was headed, just finessing it, as they say. But before long, I realized something very odd."

"Yes, yes. Get to the point."

"Well, you see, the notes I was reading from were not mine at all," he said. "In fact, I was reading something I had never even seen before. I noticed much later it was entitled 'Sermon on Light.' However, at the time, I was utterly dumbfounded. And do you know what else?"

"What?"

"So were my colleagues. That's right. My brethren were absolutely speechless. I had never seen such a thing transpire in twenty-two years of attendance. So I read on."

"And?"

"And my speech turned out to be profoundly moving. Why, even the old Prussian, Ziegfield Von Pippin, had tears in his eyes by the time I finished. And the reaction! Why, they didn't clap. By gosh, they pounded the table tops, they stood on their chairs! It was unbelievable. To this day, I still have to remind myself it was a group of physicists I was addressing and not a convention of creationists. I was advised later, almost to a man, that they had all at one time or another felt the very same thing. I was astonished!"

"But why?" I asked.

"Because physicists don't *feel*. We *think*. We deal in quanta, quarks, electrons and such. In finite realities. We can dissect the universe into it's constituent properties and rearrange it again, if we must. But we don't feel

183

anything about it. Feelings are for Cub Scouts and social workers. Or so I thought."

"What do you think now?"

"... The majesty of creation. That was the term that did it, that changed everything, I think. The notion that creation is not just dips and dabs of matter and energy but, whether taken as a whole or broken down into its tiniest parts, all creation has majesty. Let me tell you something. . . ."

"Please do."

"There are times when I'm here at the lab late at night, working on problems or maybe setting up experiments for the next day, when I feel a sense of something profound. Are you listening?"

"Yes, go on."

"It's almost as if I sense or feel something of the Creator in my work. I have never said this to anyone. Please keep it in your strictest confidence."

"I will," I promised.

"Thank you. But as I was saying, I sit in my chair, maybe working out the math for a particle collision, and the sensation has come to me more than once that what I am really working on—the vectors, the intricate arrangements that just seem to go on and on—are for me a rare and intended look at . . ."

"At?" I demanded.

"... At the Creator's thoughts . . . and of late I am more convinced than ever that it's true. Which brings me to the skis. It also brings me to my present state, and what I have come to learn, and explains my need for an appointment post haste."

"But I want to hear more," I almost shouted. "Why have you taken them off? What have you learned?"

"In due course, good Doctor," he said. "At our next appointment, I shall tell all. I have learned a great deal. You will see. Can you keep a big secret, Herr Doctor?"

"Why?" I asked suspiciously.

"Because it's the biggest secret you'll ever hear."

14

"Heyyy," said Henri, ogling Molly as she entered his office in the new pair of skintight blue jeans and high heels he had just purchased for her. "I dig the glide in the stride, you struttin' with de pride now, woman." He stood and did a rhumba sort of number as she sashayed around him in a circle. "You get my mojo working, momma. That's right!"

"Well, I'm not so terribly sure of these, Boopy dear," she said, frowning at her reflection in the window. "I look awfully . . . cheap, don't you think?"

"Not on your life," protested Henri. "Sequins happen to be the latest look this fall, my little sparrow."

"But Boopy dearest," she continued, "my boobs just seem so stuck out and, well, obvious in this tiny, sheer, sequiny whatever-you-call-it you bought for me."

Henri's eyes grew wild. He began to pant. "Yes," he said. "Exactly, my comely little kumquat. Why, the carnal emanations emitted by your sensual curvaceousness have positively short-circuited my medulla oblongata. As I speak, steam is parboiling my internodal connections, destroying my senses. But still I cannot look away."

AMERICAN RAIN

She gave him a hug. "You're such a charmer, Boopy Doopy," she cooed. "How in the world could any woman ever resist you when you always know exactly what to say? You're such a *catch!*"

Henri beamed.

"Still," Molly demurred, looking down at her new jeans, "this bull's-eye on the crotch does seem just the tiniest bit uncomplimentary."

"Oh, no!" argued Henri. "Not a chance, my tempestuous tomato. They *are* you, your very essence."

"Do you really think so, my rampaging stallion?" queried Molly. "You don't think it smacks of just the itsiest bit of sexism? I'm fearful the other sisters in the movement will consider me a scandal."

Henri grabbed her by the rump and yanked her close. "You are a scandal, my provocative pinto bean!" he bellowed. He threw one arm in the air. "You are a wild and lusty nymph, an unbridled love machine in overdrive. You are everything. To hell with them if they don't like it!"

Molly started shaking her bottom. "Oh Boopy, you do get me going, now don't you."

I looked out the door and saw Marcy standing in the hallway with a look of absolute revulsion on her face. She put a finger in her mouth and pretended to gag. Then she stalked off.

Henri kissed Molly hard on the mouth and commenced rubbing her rear end. "Oh, but you are a hot and earthy hombre, Henri" growled Molly, pulling at his shirt. "Such *fire*, such *machismo*."

Henri took a deep breath. "Only because you inspire me so, my dimpled dew drop," he replied, grabbing Molly's hand and shoving it into his pants."

Molly's eyes bugged. "Oh!" she cried, "my inspiration is apparently enormous."

"Yes!" Henri fired back hotly, "as you see, my enraged pleasure pole is now fully extended and prepared to thrust again and again into your wanton core of desire, my passionate pony."

Molly closed her eyes. "Ride me then, you sex-crazed cowboy. Take me, Henri. Saddle up!"

Henri pulled away. "Go now to our palace of pleasure, my pretty provocateur, and disrobe. I shall follow at once, but first I require a word or two with my trusted associate, Donald."

Molly ran to the door then turned. "Leg irons as usual, Boopy Dearest?"

"But of course, Cherry Pit."

Molly closed the door behind her and Henri returned to his desk.

"You are a very sick man," I said. *"Very."*

He shook his head. "Guess again, linguine brain. She's the most exciting thing around, untouched and unplowed. Forbidden fruit!"

I made an ugly face. "Yeah, well I don't know how much more of this gooey shit I can stomach. The two of you are nauseating."

"Get used to it, small time, 'cause it's going to be hot and heavy around here for the foreseeable future."

"Not for me," I replied. "I'm leaving for Frederick in an hour or so with Marcy. I can use the fresh air."

"I heard. That's why I called you."

"So speak to me," I said.

"Boinking your little filly out there in the sticks is your business. Just be sure to have your sorry behind back here by Monday morning."

"For what?" I asked.

"I'm going to start plucking the strings on the banjo of big bucks."

". . . Which means?"

"Which means that Crowntooth is a shoo-in for reelection in just a few weeks. So now's the time to write our little rider on rainfall and get it into committee. I've already called for a meeting. Everybody who owes me and can help will be there. Republicans, Democrats, liberals, conservatives, atheists, the religious right, gays; you name'em, they'll be there. Monday at 9:00 A.M., we're going to give them their marching orders. It will be great!" He rubbed his hands together hungrily. "It's all coming together, Donny," he crowed.

"This I've got to see," I admitted. "I'll be there."

He looked at me seriously. "You'd better be," he warned. He put his arm around my shoulder. "I'm counting on you, Donny. This is where we jump off into the economic stratosphere." Just then a soft rain started to fall gently on the roof. He closed his eyes. "Ah," he said. "That, my boy, is the sound of pay dirt."

"Look at that view!" Marcy called from upstairs. "Can you believe it?"

I dragged her bags up the stairs and wiped my forehead. "Do you really need all this lead?" I asked, pointing to the suitcases. "I thought you were going to paint, not conduct radioactive experiments."

"It isn't lead," she replied. "That's just my clothes. Wait till you get to my art gear if you think that's heavy."

I went to the window to scope out the view. The mountains rolled away to the west in unbroken waves of blue. I had to admit, it was beautiful. Already the leaves were beginning to turn in the higher elevations, aspens dotting the hillsides like flakes of gold. "Very nice," I said. "Fall's coming."

She moved to my side for a look. She smiled and breathed deeply, as if she could taste the coming season. "Soon those hills will be wild with color. It's like New England," she insisted. "People come from all over to see it." She leaned against me. "I remember quite clearly that from a certain ridge on Grandmother's farm, you could see from Thurmont clear to South Mountain—an unending sea of color. Gosh."

"Gosh?" I repeated.

"Yeah, gosh," she said, sticking her nose in the air. "Or maybe I should say inspirational, because that's how I see it."

"Well, then you should be cranking out paintings like an assembly line."

"I will," she promised.

I laughed.

"Why are you so skeptical of everything?" she asked, stepping back. "Don't you see? Can't you just feel how clear and free the air is up here?"

I took a sniff. "Frankly, no," I said. "And I'm not skeptical of everything."

"Well, you certainly are of me."

"I'm not skeptical of you," I insisted. "I'm skeptical of our relationship, with you up here and me down there. That's all. And, well, maybe of this whole freedom thing of yours too."

"What freedom thing?"

"This insistence you've developed that the whole freaking world will be milk and honey if you can just be in Frederick," I surveyed the street below us. "Look, it's a nice town, but it isn't necessarily the promised land to me. After all, you painted tons of canvases in Baltimore under the most adverse circumstances."

"And now I'll double that!"

"Maybe. Maybe not. That remains to be seen."

"See, you are skeptical."

"Yes, of that," I said. "But not of everything. Marcy, it just seems to me that if you're meant to paint, you paint—be it in a closet or a cell. All the pretty trees in the world don't make an artist. I've seen you when you get going. Why, it's like nothing could stop you."

She squared her shoulders. "I know what I'm talking about," she said. "You'll just have to wait and see."

I sighed. "OK."

We unpacked most of her things and had both floors swept out by nightfall. I opened the upstairs windows and a westerly breeze filled the rooms with fresh mountain air. She went out for a six-pack of beer and we both opened one before dinner. I leaned against the wall and watched her. She was radiant. Dusty, dirty, sweat soaked, but radiant. I smiled. No matter what, I promised myself, no matter how far off the mark I thought she was, I vowed not to take that away from her.

The rest of the trip went well. That night we strolled down Market Street and found a small bistro for dinner. A band played jazz in the back as the Orioles struggled soundlessly on the television above the bar. She dazzled me with her spirit. Her eyes blazed. She seemed so sure of herself, so energetic and free, that she had me doubting myself.

The next day we unpacked all of her equipment and by three, it was time for me to head out. It was hard leaving. The town was beautiful. She was beautiful. I kissed her long and intimately. "Call me tonight," she said.

The ride home was only an hour, but it seemed like four. I missed her terribly already. When I got back, I drug into the house and dropped my bags in the foyer.

Something moved to my right. A man stood up. "Dr. Mallory?"

"Yes," I replied, slightly startled. When he stepped into the light, I recognized him. It was David Winthrop. "Mr. Winthrop. What can I do for you?"

He shook my hand then hesitated. ". . . Well, to begin with I have come to thank both you and Dr. Lafayette for the generous donations you have been forwarding to us. I assure you, they are well utilized and very much appreciated."

"And second?" I asked.

He smiled sheepishly. "And second, I'm afraid I have come to ask for more." He looked away.

"I'm sorry," I said. "I didn't mean to put you on the spot like that."

He seemed very tense. "I put myself on the spot, Doctor. I am not well constructed for this sort of begging."

I smiled. "You're not begging, Mr. Winthrop," I said. I looked around. "Look," I went on, "I've had a sort of long afternoon here myself and could use a cold drink. Would you care to join me?"

He held up both hands. "Why not?"

I showed him the way to my office and pulled out a bottle of sour mash whiskey, grabbed some ice from the kitchen, and poured the whiskey over it generously. "Cheers," I said.

He nodded.

We both sat. "Mr. Winthrop," I said, "you need not apologize here. Ever. Frankly, I admire what you do. It takes guts and immense fortitude. I couldn't do it. Not for a minute."

For a moment he looked at me as if slightly shocked, then he bowed his head slightly. "Thank you," he said. "But fortitude, I'm afraid, plays no major roll in my actions." He held out his hands to me. "It's just something that's there and has to be done. That's all."

"So what's up?" I asked.

He sighed. "Just more of the same, Dr. Mallory," he said. "We had hoped that additional funding would come through, but I'm afraid it hasn't. Just a lot of empty promises as usual." He laughed humorlessly. "So here I am. We are only halfway done with the shelter and entirely out of funds."

I leaned forward. "We can help," I said. "Put your mind to ease. Tomorrow I will consult with Dr. Lafayette, but I'm sure he will authorize the funds you require. He is very much impressed with your work."

David Winthrop smiled. "You are both so kind. I appreciate your candor. As you can see, I am not good at this at all."

I held up the bottle. "Another?" I asked.

He hesitated. ". . . Why not?" he said.

I poured us another drink each. "Can I ask you something?" I said.

"Be my guest," he answered.

"Why do you do it?"

"Do what?"

"This work. This community group."

He grimaced. "It's something I strongly believe in."

"I'm sorry. I don't mean to pry," I said. "But why?"

He stood up and walked to the fireplace. He leaned against the bricks. "I owe most of what I am to my father, Dr. Mallory. He was an uneducated man, in the traditional sense. But a man who revered education nevertheless. He drilled us on the classics and insisted we complete our school assignments daily. He built Winthrop's Hardware up from nothing with little more than the sweat of his brow and dogged persistence against a world that hated him simply because of his color. Yet he never turned bitter—or let the unfairness of his life inhibit his instinct for love, learning and giving. He put me and all of my brothers and sister through college on an income that was scarcely capable of feeding us from one day to the next."

"Impressive," I said.

He smiled. "My father was a simple man," he continued, "with simple beliefs. In fact, there was a time, Doctor, when I thought he was nothing but an old fool. I'd studied history and math, psychology and social theory. I knew Plato, Shakespeare, and Moore as well as the modern philosophers. As a result, I considered his rather basic understandings of the world to be just so much simple-mindedness."

"What exactly was so simple?" I asked.

"My father believed in a rather ancient idea, Dr. Mallory. He believed the world was a struggle between good and evil, and that in the end, one would come to dominate the other."

I raised an eyebrow. "By what means would one dominate the other?"

He held up his hands. "By these means," he replied. "By the everyday acts of men and women through time eternal, Dr. Mallory."

"You mean, for every evil act, a good one must be recorded somewhere to even the ledger, so to speak?"

He smiled. "Exactly. . . . Simple, isn't it?"

"Yes."

"Well, I thought so, too, Doctor. After all, the world hardly accepts the idea of good and evil anymore. There are only circumstances—some pleasurable, some less so. And thus I was schooled and so I believed, until . . ."

"Go on."

"Well, until my father passed away and I was summoned home to bury him. I took over the store then—it had to be run—and I began to walk in his shoes, as they say. Now, years later, I have come to see the world quite differently than I had viewed it before. If I'm not a full-blown adherent of my father's simple-minded notions, I am certainly less critical of them. Do you believe in destiny, Doctor?"

"No," I answered.

He shook his head. "Neither do I," he said. "Do you believe in free will?"

"Yes."

He smiled. "Then we are brothers, you and I. But of a dying brotherhood, I'm afraid."

Standing and pouring myself another drink filling his glass as well, I said, "I believe that we are free to choose. Yes. I also believe there is a lot of good and bad luck running loose, much that cannot be anticipated by anyone, no matter how cunning or well-informed."

"I agree," he said. "The unfortunate family destroyed by a drunken driver, for instance, has no way of anticipating his presence before the fateful swerve. But the action, I believe, cannot be interpreted—as is so often the case—as a willful act of God or part of some divine plan. It is quite simply the wretched, mindless act of a fool."

". . . And as such could have been avoided?" I asked.

He looked at me for a few seconds.

"Exactly," he said finally. "And that is the tough part, isn't it? To bury your children and know it did not have to be. Most people would go insane, having to face that fact. But I believe it to be true, nevertheless."

"And so?"

"And so I act," he said. He drew himself up and there was fire in his eyes. "I do what I can because it's all I can do. In the face of bestiality, we offer comfort. Where there is hunger, food. Ignorance, learning. But mind you, Doctor, I am no saint, and I am no pacifist. I will fight if need be, and I will protect myself and my family from the evil I see everyday. On every corner. Do you understand what it's like?"

"Somewhat," I said.

"I saw a man murdered for no reason the other day." he said, sadly. "Why? Simply because he was there and vulnerable. Life means nothing, Dr. Mallory. I see people robbed of all dignity, of all humanity, not only by squalor, drugs, and ignorance, but by each other as well. And I see it daily. And just when I want to scream out, when I want to grab my children and leave for anywhere else, I notice some small act of decency performed by someone I would never have guessed capable of it. Then I realize all over again that the struggle is real; that good and evil are truly out there competing for the world, for our lives; and the outcome still waits to be decided. So I do what I have to do. Just like all the rest."

"I don't know if I believe that," I said.

He smiled. "That's fine. I'm not sure I believe it entirely myself." He squinted as if to focus on something minute. "But, strange as it may sound, I can tell you with great certainty that there are times when I can almost feel evil in my presence. On the street at night. I can see it in the lifeless, murderous eyes of the junkies in the shadows. I can sense it lurking in the darkness, something remorseless, vicious. It's awful."

Suddenly, unexplainably, his face exploded in a smile. "And yet amidst all this human carnage there is constant kindness and achievement. I see mothers who will simply not give in to the conditions surrounding them, who love and nurture their children despite tremendous odds. I see people who care, men who love and protect." He laughed out loud and held up his glass. "Let me tell you. . . ." he said, draining the last of his drink.

"Yes, yes, go on," I said, refilling his glass.

He walked back and forth across the carpet, eyes ablaze. "Let me tell you about this woman. Lord, she must be close to ninety years old now. Wilma Loraine Monroe." He laughed again and drained his glass. "She resides in one of the most horrid sections of our town. The area has been entirely consumed by gangs of drug dealers. Their henchmen patrol the sidewalks with automatic weapons and a thirst for blood. They have no pity, mind you. They would spare no one."

"Yet every day this elegant elderly woman shoos them from in front of her apartment with a broom and sweeps the area clean. They threaten her, they stick weapons in her face, but still she sweeps. Ha! I tell you, the first time I saw her I was transfixed, Doctor. Because it was the first time I saw the world for exactly what it was. Oh, some dismiss her actions as foolishness, as mere stubbornness, but I saw it that day for exactly what it was. Just, my friend, as my father had seen it before me."

"An act of faith?" I asked, starting to understand.

"Precisely!" he replied. "A little old woman who refuses to give in to the chaos swirling around her. Who, broom in hand, fights back the enveloping evil by a daily act of faith. She believes in the sanctity of life and the promise of civilization. That's when I understood."

"What?"

"That the war would not be won by grand schemes or slogans. That it would be won by people like Wilma Loraine Monroe. Small people. Everyday folk. But people who could stare right into Hell's own eye and not blink, Dr. Mallory. They are out there, battling as we speak, and I believe in them. They are my religion. They are why I do it."

We stared at one another for a long moment. He put down his glass. "I tend to carry on at times," he apologized. "Forgive me."

"Not at all," I replied. "I admire you. You are a man of great character. I pale before you."

He held up his hand. "No, no. Not at all, Dr. Mallory," he said. "You are a good man. A helper, a listener . . . a thinker, I suspect. The truth is, I wish I could be more like you and not so enraged by the things I see. You and Dr. Lafayette are decent people."

"Who?"

"Why, Dr. Lafayette," he replied. "He has helped us enormously."

"Oh, yeah, yeah," I said. "That's right."

He shook my hand. "Please let me know about the funds at your earliest convenience."

"Of course," I said, and showed him to the door.

That night I was filled with a strange awareness. I could not sleep. So I went to the window to watch the stars. The moon was full, shadows sharp on the lawn below. The entire universe seemed crystal clear, yet I sensed something I had never before encountered. Evil? Was that what everything was about? And if so, on which side of the ledger would my life eventually fall? I felt sad. I missed Marcy. I looked out into the darkness but it offered no answers.

15

"Please! Please!" cried Henri, waving his hands overhead as he entered the library, "may I have your attention, ladies and gentlemen." The room immediately grew silent. "If you could all just try and locate a seat, we can get cracking with the business at hand."

Everyone shifted around, but it was useless. The library was packed to bursting. People were pressed against walls and crammed into doorways. "OK, OK," Henri called, waving a mallet, "let's gather on in here now, folks, so's we can all hear. That's right. That's it folks. Just remember, we're all here for self-aggrandizement, so let's not be shy."

People dragged their chairs to the center of the room, scooting forward with their knees. "Wonderful, wonderful," coached Henri. "Senator, slide over there a little, would you? Great. Yeah, good to see you, Mayor. Hello, Reverend. Hi there, General. Now that's better. Look, you twinkies from the gay alliance can shove in with the geeks from the minister's conference over there along the wall. That's it. OK."

Henri walked to the front of the room and whacked the mallet on the desk. "This meeting has officially been called to order. I'm going to turn it over now to the famous Senator Buck Crowntooth of West Virginia, who will explain just what the hell you're all doing here."

Buck stood up and walked to the desk. He gave his suspenders a snap and chuckled. "Looks like we're all stuffed in here thicker than ticks on a 'coon hound," he said with a smile. "But that's OK, huh folks, 'cause we got's this here bill," he went on, holding up a piece of paper for everyone to see, "to ram through Congress seein' as how it's about as American as tenny shoes and environmental as all get out to boot."

Drew from the gay alliance raised his hand with a question.

Senator Crowntooth snapped his suspenders and pointed to Drew. "Shoot."

Drew crossed his legs. "Well, what precisely does 'environmental as all get out' mean?"

Buck scratched his chin thoughtfully. "Well, hell," he said, "it means . . . Well, you know . . . Help me, R. C."

R. C. Smythe stood up in the back of the room. "It means American as all get out. When the senator says environmental, he means American. And when he utilizes the term American, he also means environmental. Same thing. The senator is one hell of an American, environmentally speaking. You know, like George Washington and the apple tree."

"That's right, R. C.," agreed Buck Crowntooth, "Ol' Georgie did cut himself an apple tree, now didn't he. Environmental as all get out."

"Speaking of cut," said Kiddo Kenny London, "I love the bleeping shit out of this chit-chat, but let's get on with the money mambo we all came to dance to."

"*Cherry* tree," I said.

Drew pursed his lips. "Just where in the world did George Washington come from?"

"Virginia," said Henri.

"Virginia," sneered Linda Glicken, sitting next to Molly behind me. "Another disgusting, demeaning, sexist example of the usage of the female gender throughout history. Just one more thing to tromp on."

"Cherry!" I said loudly.

"I beg your pardon!" cried Linda Glicken. She stood up and whacked me with a newspaper.

Drew shifted petulantly. "I don't give a fig about your fat twat or your nonexistent sex life," he hissed at Linda. "I want someone to talk to me about George Washington."

Buck Crowntooth rolled up his sleeves as if to box. "Watch yourself there, twinkie boy. You're talking about the father of my country now, not just another sicko perversion you're used to consummating with your limp-wristed friends. Don't no one talk to him about George Washington, lest he whip it out and do some awful kind of indecency right here in front of us all."

"Oh, you're all so ill," Drew huffed. "I just wanted to know how George Washington got into this is all."

"I don't know how George Washington came into this conversation, but I do know he died almost penniless," snapped Kiddo Kenny. "We keep farting around here, so will we all. Let's do some dealing."

"Cherry tree!" I insisted again. "I wanna get it straight."

"Oh, I can help with that," said Drew.

"Such offensive language," objected one of the ministers along the wall. "I'm afraid we of the ministerial conference will have to excuse ourselves from this meeting. It is simply below our dignity." They all stood up.

Molly Brickowski jumped to her feet, wobbling noticeably in her high-heeled leather boots and crotch-hugging hot pants. "Take one step out of this meeting my Boopy called," she threatened, "and I'll give you a religious right to the kisser, Bible breath."

"How dare you," cried the minister. "I'll do just as I please."

Drew covered his mouth. "Oh, oh, a fight."

Just then Henri marched to the center of the room with his huge revolver held overhead. He fired one time—Ka Boooooooom—then lowered the gun to eye level. Plaster dust drifted slowly down on all of us from an enormous hole in the ceiling. Silence returned. Henri smiled at the minister. "You were saying?" he asked.

"Nothing, Dr. Lafayette. Nothing at all."

"Good," said Henri. "Now all of you can just sit back down, but first, I want you all to repeat after me—Money!"

"MONEY!" everyone yelled.

"Excellent," Henri declared. "Now that we're all on track, it's back to you, Buck."

"Right, Henri," said the senator. He held up the paper again. "I have here in my possession the bill we've all been working on," he said. "Now, I intend to personally introduce this little environmental measure as a rider to the gasoline/missile compromise that's been all but agreed upon already. With the help of my adversaries on the other side of the aisle—seven senators stood in the back of the room and waved—it should sail through virtually unopposed. No use me goin' into the details of the bill with ya'll. Let's just remember it's environmental as all get out, and important to our mutual benefactor, Dr. Lafayette here."

Everyone in the room clapped dutifully. Henri smiled and holstered his pistol.

"Now," Buck continued, "we should have no problems 'cause at least half the Senate and most of the House is in cahoots on this, but politics bein' politics, well, we can never know nothing for sure. That's where ya'll come in. The minute the main compromise is reached, I will immediately introduce our happy little rider as an attachment. My staff has been advised to contact each and every one of you at once. Get on the horn, folks. Scream at your representatives, wail at the press." Senator Crowntooth turned to Henri. "We got some media types here today don't we, Doc?"

Henri pointed. An entire row stood up.

"You folks need to get out the word," urged Clayton. "Write it up. Talk it up. This is the greatest bill since the beginning of time, and it needs to be passed without a change, and so forth. That's the line. Got it?"

"Got it!" they all yelled.

"But here's the thing, folks," Crowntooth went on. "We don't mention our little addition, OK? The less publicity the better. Just beat the drum for the missile/gasoline package as a whole, and forget that little ambiguous rider that's been attached.

"But what about the president?" asked Kiddo Kenny. "How do we know he won't scuttle the whole deal?"

Buck smiled coyly and looked over at Henri.

"Let's just say that eventuality has been taken care of," said Henri, stepping to the center of the room again. He smirked. "I would have had him here today, in fact. But hell, who needs him?"

Buck Crowntooth laughed out loud. "And shoot, folks," he declared, "Henri here was decent enough to make sure the ol' boy will retire in dignity, if you get my drift. No, Kiddo, won't no objections be coming out of the White House."

Then Buck passed out a list of instructions to every bribee in attendance. "This here gives you a list of addresses and phone numbers for all the influential folks on the Hill and across the country," he said. "Come D-Day, I want to see Ma Bell light up like a sparkler on the Fourth of July. God bless ye all. And let's do right by the good Doc here."

Buck then dismissed everyone but a few key people, and we all huddled in Henri's office. Buck lit a cigar and leaned back on one of the enormous leather chairs. He was content. "Henri," he said, "this here environmental measure of yours is what I call a piece of work."

"Thank you," said Henri.

"Yup," Crowntooth continued, "the construction of this thing is nothing short of beautiful. Ain't no appropriations bill, so it don't have to go through the House, which means the money hounds won't be looking at it too close. It just requires a minimal 'redistribution of allocations,' as I believe the wording goes, from every federal agency, or state and local government receiving federal funds for anything. We identified the redistributions clear down to entities like county park commissions and sheriffs' departments. And since the actual cost of this thing to any one department is nothing more than nickels and dimes, I doubt anyone will ever catch on to it—let alone object. Assuming they knew what in the world it even is, which they won't, 'Cause it's worded so damned ambiguously. Get this: '. . . cause to be established an environmental entity for the accurate recording and verification of national precipitation units on a daily basis, for which a debit will be recorded and duly collected by a consultant of the government's choosing in accordance with table x, graph 14 as herein attached . . .' Ha!" Buck crowed, slapping his knee. "Art is what it is. Pure art."

Henri smiled. "As Buck pointed out, the whole angle of the scam is that it dongs everyone just a little. And we've arranged to take the funds directly out of budgets before allocations to the various federal, state and local whatever are deducted, so they won't even miss them."

"How are you getting a hold of it?" asked Kiddo Kenny, smacking his lips.

"Computer," said Henri. "It cost me a bundle, but I've purchased software that will enable me to calculate each department's debit by formula per hundredths of a centimeter of precipitation, and instantly reduce their approved appropriation per budget accordingly for the next month, week, or whatever. Not only that," he went on excitedly, "but the green guys will be flicked electronically my way to a special account daily. No waiting, no hassle, no delay. A river of money every time it rains, snows, or even so much as fogs. That's where you come in, London."

"How so?"

"You'll have instant access to all funds via my computer hookups," explained Henri. "I expect every dime to be wisely invested and utilized to the utmost percentage point available. Do a good job and you'll be wealthier than even your wildest dreams. Screw it up, and I'll shove that ugly face of yours against the red-hot engine block of my Rolls, and saw your head off with the fan belt."

Senator Crowntooth shook his head. "Understand what we're talking about here, boys?"

We all sat quietly.

"Well, I went ahead and put a pencil to it," Buck continued, "and I come up with a little over two billion or so per year. Give or take a few hundred million here and there."

"A few billion?" I said, astonished.

"Yup," affirmed Buck, "and all legit . . . kinda. Well, more or less."

"When it rains, it pours," Henri said, smiling ear to ear. "My life's work will soon be complete."

All went as planned. Crowntooth was elected by a safe margin, and, at once, the maneuvering and infighting went into high gear. The gasoline/missile compromise took some doing, but in a few days was worked out. Henri was on the phone the whole time, begging and cajoling, demanding and bargaining, never for a minute allowing the prize to get too far out of sight.

The rider was introduced immediately as promised by Crowntooth and went virtually unnoticed. A few junior senators raised some initial doubts, but they were quickly assured by senior legislators from both parties that the rider was an innocuous nothing, a meager "toss-in" drafted and attached only to appease certain environmental activists who might otherwise have attempted to torpedo the gasoline/missile deal. "Compromise at its finest hour," were Clayton Crowntooth's exact words.

Overnight, we were in business. Things went so fast it was hard to keep up. Henri, absolutely confident of his new scheme, sold his entire practice to his enemy and arch rival, the noted trial attorney, Ian Stanforth—but not before gutting the records and grossly misrepresenting the entire scope and profitability of the business. Henri laughed all the way to the bank, figuring it would take years for Stanforth to figure out the rouse. And by then, Henri would be virtually untouchable behind his billions.

He sold the practice, but not the house where we continued to reside. And he moved all his old employees into new quarters in the International Building, the tallest, most influential tower in town. We leased the two top floors, although our need for space was even less then in the house. But Henri wanted flair; cost mattered little.

I'll never forget going down to the office with him that first day in the Rolls. At the door of the International Building, two uniformed guards hired by Henri for no purpose other than to assist us from the car, did just that, tipping their caps and saluting as we headed for the elevator. We zipped to the twenty-seventh floor and got out at the main entrance. There Ms. Townsend sat at an enormous marble receptionist's desk. Above her, the name of our new firm covered half of the wall in huge golden letters: AMERICAN RAIN.

Henri looked at the sign and sighed. "Something, huh kid?"

"American Rain?" I said.

"Remember this day, Don," he replied. "Twenty years from now, we'll own half of the world. We'll be bigger than Ford, US Steel, or any of those rag-tag Fortune Five Hundred outfits. We'll be bigger than most of the countries in Europe and all those countries south of the border. We'll redefine bigness, Donny. Do you have any idea what two billion dollars a year, properly invested over a twenty year period, could do?"

"Just vaguely," I said.

"Well, specifically, we could buy the Netherlands, for example. Or New York City, or all the hot dogs in North America." He giggled. "Get it? We will be able to buy anything we want." He grabbed me by the arm. "Come on," he said, let me show you our new offices."

We rode the elevator up to the next floor. It had been completely redesigned by Henri for our specific use, and now the entire twenty-eighth floor—some forty thousand square feet of office space—consisted of just two offices: Henri's and mine. I had never seen or imagined anything quite like it before.

First mine. There was a running track around the outside, should I feel the need for a jog. An exercise room (complete with sauna, steam room, and full time masseur) overlooked the city, while a private dining room gazed out over the harbor. The work area was the size of a small warehouse, all marble and mahogany. Batteries of electronic monitors and television screens surrounded my desk, which was the size of a small aircraft carrier. Henri walked to the enormous leather chair that was to be mine and gave it a twirl.

"From here," he explained, pointing to the lights and monitors, "you can follow the rainfall activity anywhere in the country, as well as the computer-generated, up-to-the-second estimates of the dollar output for each storm, shower, and cloud." He beamed at me.

"Impressive," I acknowledged.

He twirled the chair again. "And over here," he went on, pointing to a raft of screens and televisions on the other side of the room, "you can monitor the markets worldwide. Look," he explained, pushing a button, "here's Tokyo, and London, and Munich, and so on. Information from every capital in the entire world will be fed here instantly so you always have a clear idea where to move the money, from one second to the next, for maximum profitization. Finally, over here," he said, pointing to a final bank of blank screens, "will be an up-to-the-minute rundown of every dollar we've invest-

AMERICAN RAIN

ed. The computer will provide you with profit projections on a daily, weekly and yearly basis, and will also red star any investment, no matter how small, that is not performing up to expectations."

"That's incredible," I exclaimed.

"Not only that," he continued, "but if you just push this button, the computer will give you a full breakdown of solid performers to choose from, should you decide to move any currency from this to that and so on. And it's all updated every fifth second, recalculated, and totally refined electronically."

I whistled in appreciation.

"All of this will enable you to work closely with Kiddo Kenny and monitor the leech's every move—should he decide to get cute with us."

"I had no idea," I said, "anything like this existed. Wall Street doesn't even have some of the information you have. And it's displayed here every ten seconds!"

"Tell me about it," he replied. "Cost me a bundle, not to mention all the foreign goons I had to bribe. But it's worth it, every dime. Now, we just have to make it work." He slammed his fist on the desk top. "Talk about your profit centers," he said. "American Rain is going to be the biggest, fastest grower in the history of capitalism. Donny? . . ."

"Yeah."

"You're an important man now," he said, placing his hand on my shoulder in a fatherly gesture. "Everything rides on you. Understand?"

"Sure," I said.

"I took the liberty of taking out an insurance policy on your behind just in case. Two million big boys. That's how much I think of you."

"I'm not sure if that should make me feel easy or uneasy," I said.

Then we went down to Henri's office. There was a living room and a lounge. These led to a game room and a bar, which, in turn, were followed by another lounge and a spa. Through French doors, we entered a wine cellar, then out again to a bedroom. At the far end was an enormous gourmet kitchen, fully staffed, and a dining room with a harbor view which could easily seat fifty people.

"But there's no desk," I observed. "No place to work."

He arched an eyebrow. "You don't seem to understand," he said. "My roll from here on out is one of grand, perhaps even grotesque, consumption. My part of the work has been done. From now on, I intend only to reap the rewards which, by all reasonable estimations, should be nothing short of mind-boggling."

"Ah," I said, suddenly understanding. "The dynamic principle of economic righteousness. Fulfilled."

"Fulfilled entirely," he whispered. "Soon I will be as one with my Lord. From this window, I will sip expensive cognac and watch the rain fall on the harbor. I will smile knowingly as each and every drop cascades into my wallet. Mine is the ultimate success, Donny. Nirvana."

"OK," I said, and he left. I went to the window and stared down at the city below me. From that height, I imagined, it would be easy to think you could own the world. That your particular shuffling of cash was somehow important and central to the game as a whole. You could believe you, as the shuffler, were better than the rest because of the mere size of your desk and your great distance from the street.

I had to laugh. It was ironic. For the money meant nothing to me. Not that I was pure or above it in some virginal sense—I appreciated good things and what it took to get them as much as the next man—but I had come to understand so clearly that what I truly wanted in life was fifty miles away in Frederick. That single fact made what I had become—the money, the office, the power which would eventually be mine—utterly beside the point.

And what made it ironic was I could easily imagine a thousand men and women giving away a lifetime of effort, dying to achieve even one-tenth of what I had been virtually handed, while turning their backs on love, forgetting their families, and racing away as fast as their feet could carry them from the very things I had come somehow, and suddenly, to cherish.

The older you get, the more you see. I wondered if this fact wasn't one of life's little tricks, a hopeless inversion. Or was it merely a variation on the same old truth: people always wanted much more intensely the very things they could not have?

I could walk out the door and go to her, but I would not. I had promised to stay, and my word meant something important to me. Perhaps I was being stupid or naive. But it was something I clung to in the hurricane of life like I would a raft in a storm at sea. I knew keeping promises seemed dated and old fashioned in the circles I now moved, but I also knew it was the one reason Henri had brought me into the business and trusted me to begin with. Honor among thieves? Perhaps. But in his own way—at least as far as his relationship with me was concerned—he had always been straightforward and honest, scrupulously adhering to the letter of every promise or agreement made.

So I wouldn't let him down. For the remainder of my sentence, I elected to follow this simple rule: to make each day better than the last by improving myself and the world as best I could. For the next year, that would have to do.

I turned back from the window and instantly noticed the office had come alive. Screens ran red with numbers, monitors flashed, computers projected at dizzying rates all around me. American Rain was in business. There would be much to do.

I went to my desk and put my finger on the intercom. "Ms. Townsend," I called.

"Yes, Dr. Mallory."

"Please get me David Winthrop."

16

"Flight 401 for Dallas is now boarding at gate 4B," came the announcement over the loudspeaker. "All passengers . . ."

I grabbed my briefcase and scurried quickly up the escalator. I checked my watch. With a little luck, I would make it. If only my bags would do the same.

For three weeks, it had been like this. Run, run, run. New York for a meeting with our law firm; Los Angeles for a meeting with the accountants; and now to Dallas to "interface" with the computer people. In two days, I was due back in New York. I was starting to feel a little ragged.

I found my seat on the plane and tossed my briefcase in the compartment above me. First class. I ordered a drink but passed on the magazines; I'd seen them all before. Around me, well-dressed men and women began working, sifting through position papers, editing monthly reports, analyzing mountains of statistics. One by one, they glanced my way. I had seen the looks before and knew what they were thinking. The slicker with the thousand dollar suit, the Rolex, the solid gold cuff links, was from another league. He was not going to sweat his way across country, fighting exhaustion and Draconian deadlines. No. He was having a touch of scotch and listening to Beethoven. Who was he?

I had learned to feign complete indifference. It was the key. In my three weeks of travel, one thing I had discovered: American business may thrive on grind-it-out competitors, depend upon bloody-fingered number crunchers, and love mud-in-your-eye daredevils—but it crumbles before the first glance of well-heeled indifference. In a game designed to squeeze blood out of stones, where careers are destroyed over tenths of a percentage point and grown men weep openly at the mere mention of diminished monthly capacities, indifference is looked upon as either a fool's bliss or the prerogative of the very rich. My fellow travelers merely wondered on which side of the tracks I belonged.

And since Henri had seen fit to pack me off to the most expensive tailor in town with explicit instructions to "redo" me—and hang the expense!—I looked, I knew, as convincingly affluent as anyone, no matter how unfamiliar and uncomfortable I was with the part. Since I—coiffeured, splashed, and arraigned in imported finery—was in no position to argue against the proposition that life is ultimately only a changing of rolls, I sat back comfortably, sipped my scotch, and played my part as well as I could. I smiled thinly, content in the private irony that whosoever mistook me for some game financier could not possibly be farther from the truth.

But then it always happened: I had to peek. Yeah, I had to glance across the aisle or up the row. I had to speculate. I just couldn't help wondering how many of them were masquerading as they flew, hiding the truth of their lives behind a welter of calculators and flying pens. Perhaps, I reasoned, the whole plane, the whole

AMERICAN RAIN

crazy world for that matter, was not filled with business people at all. Maybe they were just a bunch of ballplayers and sailors, artists and wallpaper hangers, or, like me, befuddled destiny seekers, dressed-up like business folk to polish the ruse. Perhaps they were dreaming their silver dreams while momentarily caught in an intractable web of responsibility. Who could say?

When we landed in Dallas, I ran for a phone and called Marcy. I felt guilty. In the weeks since I'd left her in Frederick, I had talked to her exactly once—at that a brief and harried midnight call from Los Angeles—although it had not been for a lack of trying. We just couldn't connect. She was out in the countryside painting; I was jetting cross country. I called and called but had only a fistful of pink message slips marked "Returned your call. Marcy Trimble" to show for it.

I was beginning to think the world, the sheer momentum of life, intended not only to pry us apart, but to enforce the separation as well. It was bewildering. Thus my heart soared when she answered the phone. "Hey," I called, "guess who?"

"My gosh!" she said, "I was starting to think I'd never hear from you again. Where are you calling from, Baltimore?"

"Hardly," I said, watching cowboy hats bob pass as the plane unloaded. "Try Dallas."

"Dallas!"

"I know," I said. "You don't have to say it."

"What are you doing, Donny? You haven't been to see me once. We don't even talk. You're just, well, flying all over the globe."

"I'll be home this weekend. Promise. As soon as the plane hits the ground, I'm throwing my junk in the Mercedes and . . ."

"What Mercedes?"

"My Mercedes. A company car. Part of the package, you know. Anyway, as soon as the plane hits the runway, I'm . . ."

"What happened to your old car?"

"You mean that old Ford?"

"Yeah," she said.

"Junked."

"But that old car had character," she protested. "You said so yourself. You don't belong in any Mercedes Benz. I don't like what I'm hearing."

"I'm fine," I said. "It was Henri's idea. Image is all. I'm still the same old me. Just much slicker. Got some thousand dollar suits, five hundred dollar shoes, and a watch that broke the bank. All image."

"Yeah, well, slick and you don't go together. I'm worried."

"Don't be," I said. "You'll see this weekend. I promise. I'll be there on Friday afternoon. Count on it. How's the art biz?"

"Oh . . . great. Really fruitful. How goes the great American Rain?"

I laughed and shook my head. "You wouldn't believe it," I said. "Business is such bullshit. All I do is go to meetings. Meetings for this, meetings for that. And nothing, I mean N-O-T-H-I-N-G, get's done. Marcy, you would not believe in a million years how much energy is expended, money spent, and time wasted in order to accomplish absolutely zip. It boggles the mind."

"Well, what are you doing in Dallas?" she asked.

"The computer people are here. I'm here so they can give me their ideas on greater storage capacity, greater networking capabilities, more robust interaction. . . . Hell, I don't know what any of it means. The bottom line is they wheel me around town for two days like some enormous big shot—meeting to meeting, restaurant to restaurant—until I smile and say something like 'Gentlemen, I like what I'm seeing. Give me more of the same. Much more.' and then I'm off. Two weeks later, we get a bill from them that would knock your socks to Hades. For doing nothing."

"Well, what's American Rain if not nothing?"

"True," I admitted. "I've thought of that. And it just makes it worse. Think of it, the accountant bills the lawyer for doing nothing, the lawyer bills us for doing nothing, and we pay it all out of our outrageous profits for doing absolutely nothing. Seems a little out of whack."

"A lot out of whack," she corrected, "but that's what the fat man always wanted, now isn't it."

"Whoa," I said, slapping my forehead. "I almost forgot. I didn't tell you the big news, did I?"

She giggled. "What? Tell me now. Is it good?"

"You'll die," I promised. "To begin with, seems 'The Brick' and OFF mutually decided it was in both of their best interests for her to step down as local chapter president and resign from the organization altogether. I think it was her panties hanging from the rearview mirror in the Rolls that finally did it. Linda Glicken had some sort of myocardial infarction when she saw them. Anyway, Molly had apparently already decided to get back into the music business before making the big split, so it was no big deal to her."

"The music business?"

"Yeah," I went on, "seems she strummed the guitar in the gal's glee club at Vassar or something. I heard her banging away the other day; she's not half bad."

"Well," Marcy said, "it's not so easy making a living playing chamber music these days."

"Scratch the chamber music," I corrected. "Country. Molly Brickowski wants to be a country western singer."

"Oh God! Give me strength," Marcy moaned. "Donny, you just can't be serious?"

"Wish I weren't, but that's the truth. She's gone out and bought a bunch of flannel shirts and tight blue jeans to wear, and she carries her guitar with her everywhere she goes. It's something to see."

"I'll bet," said Marcy. "How weird."

"It is that," I agreed, "but there's more."

"What?"

"Well, one day last week Molly came to the office unannounced to run the new song she'd been writing by Henri for a listen. Tell you the truth, Marcy, Henri's office is so big I had no idea what was going on in there. And I guess I'm to blame because I'm the one who let her in. Wouldn't you know, he had Kitty Fouchet in there, and they were into one of their *X* rated scenes. Molly went crazy. She chased Kitty out onto the street butt naked and whacked her with the guitar for good measure. Then she just broke down. It was sad. Molly cried and cried."

"Well, I've got absolutely no sympathy for her," Marcy exclaimed. "Just what in the world did she expect from him? You ask me, she had it coming."

"That's pretty rough," I said. "She didn't know anything about him. She took him at his word. I think she deserved better, and I said so."

"You did?"

"Yeah. I told Henri what a jerk he was."

"Did he care?" she asked.

"I don't know. Maybe. He sure as hell was upset!"

"What did he do?" she wanted to know.

"Ran right out onto the street after Molly. It was something to see, all these fat, naked, and semi-naked bodies running around downtown Baltimore. Caused quite a traffic jam."
She howled. "I'll bet."
"Anyway," I continued, "he promised he'd never do it again. Swore up and down to it. Told her Kitty was just an old friend and she had seduced him."
"Ha! Did she believe it?"
"Not for one second. But she did take him back. She loves him. Seriously. It may be crazy, it may be destined to failure, but it's the truth. And you know what?"
"OK, I'll bite. What?"
"I think he may love her, too."
"Come on!"
"No, I mean it. In his own twisted, distorted way, he loves her. I saw the look in his eyes when she ran out the door. It was pained, pure and simple."
"Well, I'll believe that when I see it," she said.
"You probably never will," I countered. "Love aside, I don't think he can control his appetite for more than forty, maybe fifty, seconds tops. That's always been his problem. He'll do it again and she'll walk. The only question is how soon."
Marcy laughed. "Then she can go and be a country music star. Who cares. When will I see you?"
"Friday. No question about it. Plane lands at three forty-five in the afternoon, and I'll be there by six. Be ready for a raging bull."
"I've got the cure."
"You are the cure."

The plane landed on Friday about fifteen minutes late. Not bad. I grabbed my luggage and headed for the long-term parking lot. All I had to do was swing by the house for a fresh change of clothes and I was on my way. I couldn't wait to see her.

I ran in the back door, in a hurry to get my things. Nobody around. The house was still. I started up the stairs to my room when I noticed a movement in the shadows. I stopped. "Who's there?" I asked.

"Sorry to bother you, Doctor," Myron Wilmer said, stepping into the light. "I have been calling for an appointment for weeks now, but I can never get through. Ever since our last phone conversation, I've tried, but you are always on your way to New York or some place distant. Have you gotten any of my messages?"

I was embarrassed. "Well, as a matter of fact I have, Dr. Wilmer," I said. "But I've been so busy I'm afraid I haven't had time to return a single one. I'm sorry."

"Well, your secretary told me you were coming in tonight, so I decided to simply take the bull by the horns and stop by. Hope you don't mind. I have a great deal to speak to you about."

"I do have an appointment scheduled in a couple of hours." I said, "But I suppose I can spare a few minutes now that you're here."

"Oh wonderful," he said. "I wanted to discuss with you the latest and most exciting discovery of my life. It has to do with the fundamental structure of time and matter and our relationship to the universe as a whole. You see, I have come to some rather startling understandings."

"You have, huh," I said, scratching my crotch. I was horny. I looked at my watch. "The fundamental structure of time and matter," I repeated. "Suppose this will take more than fifteen minutes?"

He stepped back as if struck. "There is that possibility," he said, lowering his head.

"All right, all right," I said, "don't get so morose. Just checking." I looked around. "OK, we can just go on into my old office and talk for awhile. Take your time, Doctor."

We sat down. "I suppose," he started out, "you have noticed the rather obvious absence of cross-country skis on my feet?"

I tilted my head. "Now that you mention it, I hadn't," I said. "You look so . . . well, almost normal with those silvery Hush Puppies on that I didn't even give it a second thought." I squinted and looked at him very closely. "As I recall, Myron, you said you were in possession of the biggest secret of all. Am I correct?"

"You are indeed, Dr. Mallory," he replied. "But let me digress."

I looked at my watch. Right about now, I thought to myself, she was probably finishing her bath and getting ready to slip into the sheerest, sexiest nightgown imaginable. I sighed. "The floor is yours, Doctor."

"As well you know," he said, crossing his legs, "there was a time when I was rather fearful of crashing through the flimsy material structure of this universe and disappearing into nothingness."

"I recall it quite clearly," I said.

"But of course," he said. "For some considerable period of time I labored under the incorrect conclusion that because the realm of matter is structured, in effect, of nothing at all at it's most primary levels, I, the discoverer of this fact, would crash through the veneer of this existence. That is, if not properly prepared and armed against this eventuality. This, I came to see, was a very limited and slanted view of things, a virtually backward conception of the truth."

"Go on."

"This business of losing my focus, for instance, I came to understand as not the beginning of the end I had previously considered it, but only a physical confirmation of my own lack of conviction. And what I realized over time, Herr Doctor, was that conviction, and not a lack of it, was the only thing that could move a body from one focus of realization to another."

"Focus of realization?"

"Yes. From one reality to another. From the material state to the immaterial."

"What you're saying, Myron, if I've got it right, is that you can't back your way into heaven."

He smiled a cockeyed smile. "Yes, precisely. And it was through reflecting upon the 'Sermon on Light' over a period of weeks that these realizations came to me. The part at the end, you remember, where it speaks of both religion and science as being imperfect pathways to the same truth. That had quite an effect upon me."

"How so?"

"Well, for years I have been a scientist. I wrote as a scientist, thought as a scientist, lived as a scientist. Yet ultimately, it had brought me to intellectual ruin. I was nowhere, wandering around the planet on a pair of skis, scared to death that each and every step I took might just be my last. The thing that did much to bring me around—and which I shared with you before—was the feeling the universe could not be completely described or addressed through the rational approach or scientific method. This was directly addressed in the 'Sermon on Light,' and enhanced exponentially by my experiences in the lab when, as I described over the telephone, I sensed the very mind of God drawing me close to a vision of majesty. That is the only way I can describe what I felt at those times, and I apologize if my unabashed sense of exhilaration produces in you strong feelings of embarrassment."

"Not at all," I said. "I can appreciate your feelings."

"Wonderful, Herr Doctor," he said. "Shall I continue?"

"By all means."

He rubbed his chin thoughtfully. "I have for most of my natural life been a man on the hunt, Dr. Mallory. That, after all, is what science is all about. It is a great, precise, and determined hunt for answers. For truth. But I realized at that moment I was no longer the fearless hunter of old. Oh, I still arranged the particle collisions, speculated on the density of dark matter in the universe, and so on. But in my heart, I had backed away from the most meaningful, the most compelling question of all. And I had done so without even knowing."

"Which was?" I asked.

"Which was, my good Doctor, the question of whether or not I would disappear into nothingness if I took off my skis. And then at the mere suggestion of the question, I understood the answer. It was simple. Of course not. And do you know why not?"

"I haven't a clue," I said.

"Because, Dr. Mallory, it is precisely as you suggested previously. One can not back his way into heaven. It is as simple as that. Likewise, one also cannot slip through the cracks of material insignificance into another focus of realization. It must be achieved!"

"Achieved in what manner?"

"Ah," he said, shaking a finger at my nose, "you have hit upon the crux of the issue. How indeed?" He smiled warmly. "Consider my situation. I was confronted with a perfectly testable hypothesis. If my reasoning was correct, I should be able to remove my skis and suffer no negative consequences whatsoever. And if I were wrong? . . ."

"Oblivionville," I said.

"Exactly, Herr Doctor. Of course, as a scientist I knew I had only one choice. But I can assure you, Mr. Mallory, as a human being I was considerably less than enthusiastic about the experiment. Controlled it was not. Imagine, if you can, my sense of dread at that moment. I can well attest to the fact the body does not always take for granted that which the mind holds to be true. I was, my friend, sweating bullets, as they say. Slowly, I removed each ski. I stood. My mind began to whirl. My focus deteriorated as never before." He stood and looked me in the eye. "Understand me, at that moment I realized absolutely that matter was nothing, that form was an illusion, and as I held that thought in my mind's eye, the floor instantly disappeared before me."

"Come on!"

"It's true, Doctor. The floor virtually evaporated like fog before the sun. There was nothing underfoot. Nothing! I tell you, fear gripped me like a vice. My knees shook. I wept, but still, somehow, I took that first step."

"God!" I said. "And? . . ."

"And I stepped above and across the abyss. Don't ask my how, but I did. One step led to another. Then another. My heart raced. I was standing on nothing, walking across a . . . vacuum. The pressure in my head was such I thought I might expire or explode. But still I stepped, now in a rush, now in a jangled romp, for the far wall."

I strained to hear what would come next. "Yes, yes? . . ."

"I made it. That's all. It was done. I collapsed in a chair and wept like a baby. I called for my mother, such was the frenzy of my emotions. My clothes were utterly soaked with sweat. My hair was matted and wet. I was a wreck. Then I remembered one of your splendid remedies and poured myself a double vodka martini. It was sharp and hot. It boiled through my tortured veins like sweet fire. I got down on my knees and blessed you and your entire family."

"Thank you."

"You're welcome." he said. He relaxed and sat back down. "The floor returned. My focus returned. It was then I understood."

"That you had been through the most incredible experience of all time?"

"No," he said. "The exact opposite, actually."

"What?"

"You see, what I did we all do every hour of every day. It's really no big deal. I merely saw it for what it was, and when I understood that, I understood how one achieves focus realization. Simple. When one has knowledge enough to see through the material fabrication, then one need only have the willingness to go. One isn't propelled by fear, such as gripped me, but desire. Doctor," he went on solemnly, "I understand something now I didn't know that day."

"Which is?"

"What I walked over was not the abyss, Donald, but the point of entry. The creator was waiting. Waiting for me. I can go. I can be a part of his mind. I need only the . . . the . . ."

"Balls?"

"Exactly," he said, slapping the table emphatically. "I need only the balls." He leaned toward me across the desk. "We are all capable of this. We are all capable of the grandest of transformations. The world is a shell. The will is supreme. Crazy talk from a physicist, eh?"

"Crazy talk from anyone," I said.

He smiled sheepishly. "Is that what you think?"

"I don't know what I think," I said. "I know you're telling the truth. What it means . . . ?"

He winked. "The day will come," he said. "I know it in my soul. I am a hunter, a scientist. The day will come when I will again visualize the matter away and then I will join the creator. My soul will fly. And then you will know."

I looked at him closely. "You seem to be handling all of this with considerable aplomb," I said.

He lit a cigarette. "Oh, really?" he replied. "I'm flattered. The fact is, I'm a wreck, torn now between the genetic desire to survive and the intellectual compulsion to know. I trip, fidget, and groan so regularly now I have forgotten how nice it was to be considered only mildly neurotic. There are times when even I think I'm going insane."

"You need a diversion," I said. "Like before. Something to take your mind off of the abstract."

"Like a pair of bodacious ta-ta's?" he inquired.

"Why not?"

He threw back his head and laughed. "This time I'm way ahead of you, Doctor," he said. "Remember Ms. Lawson from our polka catharsis?"

"Oh, yes. Ms. Lawson with the oh-so-tight leotards?"

"That's her! Well, Ms. Lawson and I have been vacationing together from time to time over the last number of weeks. I have found her companionship a very pleasant distraction indeed." He stopped and sat quietly for a long time, carefully composing his thoughts. "I must confess to you, Herr Doctor," he looked me earnestly in the eye, "my wonder at the sheer intensity of mental commitment required during the act of copulation. It is an extraordinarily one-dimensional endeavor, is it not?"

"Indeed."

"Unfortunately," he went on, "it is but a brief oasis for me amidst the desert-like terrain of my troubled mind. All too soon, the altered perception of reality and the unanswered questions begin to creep back into my thoughts, to inhabit my conscious meanderings, and soon thereafter I find myself tripping, fidgeting, and groaning anew. But I will conquer it, in time my friend. You will see."

We both stood. I thanked him for sharing his thoughts and experience with me and showed him to the door. He promised to stay in touch.

As he walked slowly down the steps toward his car, I had to wonder. Was he actually at the virtual edge of human thought and existence, a pioneer of extraordinary magnitude, or was he merely a lunatic, his mind gradually unraveling under the pressure of constantly trying to explain the unexplainable? As he shuffled his way down the last step and opened the door to his car, he turned and waved. Steam from his breath formed and slowly drifted away in the cold December breeze. I had to admit, I honestly had no idea.

17

"That's it?" I asked, motioning to the far wall. "You mean to tell me that's everything?"

She pulled the covers up around her nose. "You're such a Philistine," she answered dryly. "Yes, that's it, and quit hogging the covers. I'm cold."

"I find it very hard to believe you couldn't paint more than that, I continued, again motioning to the wall. "It's been months now."

She pulled her feet up and stuck them on my back. They were like two frozen bricks. "Yahaaa!" I yelled, leaping from the bed. I looked out the window. Winter in Frederick. A light snow dusted the roof tops and swirled down Church Street. Overhead, an unseen weather vane clanked angrily in the wind. I put my fingers on the icy windowpane as the old, twisted snake of a radiator gurgled then spit into the room. "Snow," I said.

"How much?"

"Not much," I replied. "Inch, maybe two. Come look."

"Are you crazy? It's cold out there."

A sudden shiver went through me. "You're right," I said, and jumped into the bathroom. I turned on the hot

water in the shower. Steam filled the chilly room. "Up and at'em!" I yelled. "Let's do it."
We showered and dressed. I felt new and clean. I pulled a sweater over my head and tucked my shirt into my jeans. "Feels good not to be wearing a suit and tie for a change," I said. "I'm hungry."
"What do you feel like?"
I sniffed the air. "Pancakes!" I declared. "Definitely pancakes."
"Sorry," she said. "I have cornflakes, yogurt, and fruit."
I moaned. "Well, let's go out then. There are twenty places near here. I'll die if I eat yogurt for breakfast on a day like today." We grabbed our coats.
In the snow, Frederick looked like a postcard. The tall, Federal style homes tightly packed along the street were elegant and well maintained. Even in winter, the town had a southern flavor. It was easy to imagine yourself in the deep south, Charleston or maybe Savannah. In the quiet snow, the buildings and sleepy side streets seemed timeless. If I closed my eyes, I could almost hear the sullen clop of Confederate cavalry on the pavement behind me returning from the debacle at Gettysburg, or perhaps headed west toward the mountain passes and beyond to Antietam Creek.
We hooked a right on Market Street and found a small restaurant. We sat near the window and ordered coffee. "I was only kidding about the art production," I said, dumping a few packets of sugar into my cup. "Seriously."
Her mouth puffed. "Art is not volume," she said. "It is patience and detail."
I tried my best smile. "Any sales?"
She gave me a sideways look. "A few."

I sipped the coffee and looked outside. "Well, that's real good," I said. "What did you sell?"

"This and that," she said. "I can't quite remember."

"Sure, OK," I said. "For ten years you've wanted nothing except to be a painter, but now you can't remember the first thing you ever sold. That's believable."

She laughed and looked away. "OK," she said. "It's coming back, all right? Yeah, now I remember."

". . . So?"

"So it was this sort of rural scene," she said.

"Well, what the heck's wrong with that?" I asked. "What kind of rural scene? The hills? The river?"

"A cow."

"Wha-da-ya mean, a cow? You mean a farm scene? A herd or something?"

She tilted her head nonchalantly. "No, I mean a cow, she said. "One cow. Bessie Blue, to be precise; painted on commission for the Steinkirks of New Windsor."

"On commission? Oh my!" I had to take a quick sip of coffee to keep from laughing. I regained my composure. "That's great," I said. "Big market there, Marcy. Why just the other day I was thumbing through the phone book looking for cow painters when . . ."

"Stop it," she ordered. "It beats selling nothing at all."

I put my hand on hers. "I'm sorry. You're right." I pulled my chair closer. "But I don't understand the hang-up. In Baltimore every square inch of wall space in your apartment was covered with paintings. You produced in some kind of frenzy."

"Well, it's coming here, too," she replied. "You just have to give it time. Art can't be pushed or forced, you know. It has to flow."

"Yeah, but that's exactly what I'm saying. Your flow has flown."

"Do you say things like that at your business meetings?" she asked. "I'm curious?"

"Quit changing the subject," I countered. "You're clever at it in that snooty little way of yours, but you can't catch me. The answer, for your information, is no. Now back to you."

The waitress came with our breakfast. She put a monster plate of pancakes and sausage in front of me. Marcy had more coffee and grapefruit juice. I frowned. "You have to eat better," I said. "It's no small wonder you can't get up the energy to work."

"I'm not roping steers," she said. "I'm a painter, remember? It's just that I haven't quite had the necessary vision so far."

"Vision my ass."

"It's true," she insisted. "What do you know about it?"

"I know bullshit when I hear it," I said between sausage munches.

She giggled. "OK," she said, "I give up. It has been slow. I admit it. It's just been one thing after another."

I took a gulp of coffee. "Like what?"

"Oh, like one day the furnace went kaput and on another the sewer backed up. Oh God, Donny, what a mess! I almost died. Anyway, it's just junk like that. And then, some of the local hotshots can't take a hint. You know, just a bunch of crap . . . But it will change. I'll be happy and productive here."

"Even if it kills you, huh?" I said.

She gave me a look. "It's not going to kill me. It's going to be beautiful, and you know it."

"Did you forget that you're talking to a guy who flies around the country for a company that makes money from rain? What the hell do I know?"

We finished breakfast and stepped back out onto the street. The snow had stopped. The sun was trying to break through. A bleak string of ominous clouds, darker than Bluebeard's scowl, hovered over the north edge of town. They were tumbling eastward at a rapid clip. "Snow squalls," I said.

She pulled up her collar. "Happiness, ultimate happiness, is directly linked to productivity and freedom," she insisted. "Art cannot occur outside of freedom either. It's all linked."

"You sound like a text," I said, kicking snow in front of me. "And a dogmatic one at that. Where did you ever here all that?"

"It occurred to me," she argued.

"Happiness is when you're happy," I offered. "Period. It doesn't require anything else. Some people are happy sitting on a log floating down a river, Marcy. Others are only happy when they're fulfilling their responsibilities. Happiness is personal and, probably the last thing on earth you can submit to formulation. Look at me, I'm happy when I'm with you. That's all it takes. Not money, not fast cars."

She looked at me for a few seconds. "I love you, too," she said, "but I will prove you wrong. You will see," she continued, but not convincingly. "Maybe I just need the spring."

I knew what she needed, but there was no sense in arguing. And at that moment it came to me as well that our lives, this love of ours, was lacking in it's most essential element. Love is heat, absolute necessity, a compulsion to be together, yet here I was the business drifter, allowing myself to be blown all over the country like a cloud on a whimsical wind while the thing I professed to cherish the most eluded my grasp a mere fifty miles away. And she was the same way. We were talk. All talk, and cheap talk at that. Like the flaccid characters on some made for television movie, connecting only at the edges, content to play at love just so long as it didn't interfere with the casual comfort of our everydays.

As we walked slowly and silently down the sidewalk arm in arm, I realized just how far we had to go. And I suspected she did too. Foolishness tends to be disquieting. In a sense it was a beginning.

Later that night, spent from hot, emotional sex, we lay curled together. "Where do we go from here?" I whispered, as the snow started to fall again, pattering the glass in the window gently.

For a long while she did not answer. Then she pulled closer and rested on my arm. "We'll just have to wait and see," she said. She lifted her chin. "Do you want me?"

"Yes," I said. "More than anything."

She nuzzled my arm. "Me, too."

"It won't work like this," I said.

She shook her head in agreement.

I rested my hand on her hip. She curled close. Soon we were asleep.

The next morning we were both suddenly shocked from sleep by a robust banging on the door below. I rolled over. "You expecting anyone?" I asked, rubbing the sleep from my eyes.

"No," she said.

I put on my jeans and she grabbed my shirt. We scooted down the stairs as the pounding continued unabated. Downstairs it was cold. The frigid air seeping in around the windows and doors of the twisted old structure settled overnight at it's lowest level. Marcy shivered. On the ground floor, the pounding was almost deafening. I stepped to the door. "Who is it?" I yelled.

"Henri Goldleaf Lafayette III!"

I opened the door and a rush of cold air and light snow followed him in. He rubbed his hands together. His face was red from the cold. "Exactly what sort of backwater burg is it," he asked disgustedly, "where they don't even have door bells to ring? Where fine gentlemen are left to freeze on the street in the frigid morning air without so much as a how-do-you-do from the inhabitants inside?"

"It's an old place," I replied. "This is the way it's always been. . . . Why are you here?"

He put a hand to his forehead and slumped into a nearby chair.

"Something awful has happened!" he cried.

"What?" I asked, going to him.

"I need a drink. First a drink, please."

I looked at Marcy. "You have anything here?"

"There's some beer in the fridge, I think," she replied. "And, oh yeah, half a bottle of old chianti in the cupboard."

Henri moaned and covered his eyes. "Old chianti? Beer? You have no cognac or brandy? Not even a nice, fruity beaujolais?"

"No," I said.

"Not even a crummy old California chardonay?"

"Take your pick," I ordered impatiently.

"Oh, I suppose the beer," he said, rubbing his chin thoughtfully. "But in a nice tall pilsner glass, with a cocktail napkin or two, if you please."

"I'm not pleased," I replied. "You can drink it out of the can just like rest of us."

His countenance drooped. He lifted his eyes toward heaven. "This, too, shall pass," he whispered.

I laughed. "Now what's the problem?"

His eyes focused. "A terrible misunderstanding. Donald and Marcy, an extraordinary mistake has taken place."

"Yeah?" I said.

"My dearest lemon lump discovered me this A.M. under the covers with Miss Kitty Fouchet in, shall we say, a rather compromising position."

"You were screwing?"

"No! Not by a long shot! Yet, like you, my tempting tamale jumped immediately to just that unfortunate conclusion. Don't ask me why."

"You weren't amorously entwined?" I asked. "You sure?"

"Absolutely, Donald," he answered. "We were merely in the pull-out bed in the library, albeit unclothed—I on top, she with her legs over my shoulders and wrapped around the back of my head, grunting wildly. This position, I will admit, upon first glance might appear to be one of joyous sexual reverie. But in reality, it was only an exercise I devised to help this dear friend and patient of mine stretch her back muscles in order to avoid certain spasms she sometimes falls prey to."

I looked sideways at Marcy. "That's your explanation?" I asked. "Is that what you told Molly?"

"But of course! It's the truth, Donald. I . . . I . . . I swear it."

"Then what happened?" I asked.

"Molly, for some reason, became enraged," he said, holding up his hands hopelessly. "She could see we were merely exercising, yet for some reason known only to her insisted we were at it again. No amount of logic could prevail upon her." He looked at me sadly. "She was very upset."

"Look, she caught you dead-to-rights, so you may as well admit it. What's the purpose of all this nonsense about exercise?"

"Nonsense?" he asked.

"Yeah," I went on. "Come clean. Tell the truth."

"The what?"

"The truth," I repeated. "Look, this line of yours has gotten you nowhere, so why not try the truth? It can't do any more damage than you have already done. Exercise," I scoffed, "do you really expect people to believe that?"

He looked down. "I didn't think it was bad for the spur of the moment," he said. "Could you have done better?"

"You're missing the point here, Henri. You always do. It's got nothing to do with cleverness and everything to do with honesty."

"How about that beer," he said.

I patted him on the shoulder. "I'll get it."

When I came back down he was sitting with his face in his hands, a stricken look plastered on his mug. "Cheer up," I said. "You'll get her back."

"Not unless I move to Tennessee."

"What's that supposed to mean?" Marcy asked.

"Well," he went on, pausing only to gulp at the beer, "she threw everything she owned into the Rolls and ordered Jules to drive her to the train station. I followed her down, of course, begging she reconsider all the way, but she would have none of it."

"Good," Marcy exclaimed.

"Once we arrived at the station, she purchased a ticket to Nashville. Can you imagine? Nashville, Tennessee, of all places. I'm sure the train must stop by a hospital somewhere along the way so they can surgically remove several of her front teeth so she'll fit in. Anyway, no amount of consternation, weeping, gnashing of teeth, or promises could make her stop. She slapped my face and boarded without so much as a thank you."

"A thank you?" Marcy said, almost convulsing. "Why you . . ."

"So," I broke in, "she's off to be a country western singer?"

"Apparently," Henri moaned. "The Grande Old something or other is all she could talk about." He shook his head miserably. "I can't get over it," he wailed, "my hot little mama, my sizzling señorita, is gone."

"You've got to learn to get a handle on it if you ever want her back," I said. "Your just too damn horny all the time."

He looked up, offended. "Is that what you think?" he asked, nose in the air. "I suppose you think I can't live a normal life, be faithful, be a one-woman man."

"Right," I said.

He looked shocked. "You really do consider me entirely out of control, don't you, Donald. Admit it! Why, I suspect you think that at this very moment I am ogling Marcy's long, sinewy, luscious legs?" He licked his lips. "The way her calves arch, for instance, or the fullness of her muscular thighs, the way they curve so enticingly up toward that skimpy shirt she is wearing? I suppose you think I would tilt my head like this just to get a peek at that steamy little fur . . ."

"Yes!" I yelled, as Marcy turned and ran furiously up the stairs, holding my shirt tight over her rear end for all she was worth. "Yes, I think that's exactly what you're thinking, exactly what you're doing right here, right now, you overripe pervert!"

He dabbed the sweat from his forehead with a handkerchief. "You're right, absolutely right," he admitted. "I am oversexed. I am out of control!" He wiped his face and put the handkerchief back in his pocket. "And here all along I just thought I was macho."

"You want her back?" I asked.

"Yes, oh yes. I would do anything."

"You're willing to do anything?" I repeated. "Is that what I'm hearing?"

"Yes! Yes! Anything at all!"

"Well, I have some ideas, but first you must be willing to cut down, to step back in a sense, to employ some restraint over this mindless, hell-bent-for-leather brand of gluttony. You must gain some measure of control over your appetites. Stop pursuing every drink; every culinary delight; and every attractive skirt—no matter how full in the breast, long of leg, or easy to bed. Do you think you can manage that?" I asked pointedly. "Do you think you can make just a start?"

He looked at me intently for a long while. Then he stood. He stepped forward. A fierce look crossed his face as if nothing could stop him. He put his hand on my shoulder. "No," he said, then sat back down.

18

"Morning, ya'll, morning now," said Clayton Crowntooth, removing his coat and handing it to Ms. Townsend.

"Well, well," I said, "Good morning to you, Senator. And to what do we owe the unexpected pleasure of your presence this early on a Monday morning?"

He winked. "Good news is what, Donny. Henri about?"

"Yes and no," I said. "He's here, but he's not worth talking to."

"What's he got there, Donny? Cold? Flu? Touch of the ol' rheumatiz?"

"I wish."

"Don't tell me the old pecker has gone and got himself the clap or some other kinda social disease?"

"Nothing medical, Senator," I explained. "Just the blues."

Crowntooth looked around our office carefully and winked again. "What the hell's he got to feel blue about? Making two billion dollars a year and living up here like the goddamn king of Egypt?"

"Love," I said. "The old hunk of lard has fallen in love. Molly Brickowski. You remember her, Buck."

"Sure I do," replied Buck. "Big voice. Boobs out to here."

"That's her. He's been pining away for days now."

Buck looked puzzled. "Hell, Donny, why don't he just go on and buy her if that's what he wants? He's sure got enough money. In fact, why don't he buy two or three of her if it suits him?"

I shook my head. "It's not that easy, Buck," I said. "You see, Henri ran her off with his constant infidelities. She packed her bags a few days ago and headed for Nashville. Wants to be a country western singer."

Clayton let out a whoop—"Yeeeehaaaa!"—and slapped Ms. Townsend's desk. "Don't that beat all! Heck, I wish her well. Don't know if she's got the voice for it, Donny, but she's sure got a first-class pair of tits. Tell me, where's that ol' slimy hound dog boss of yours now?"

"Come on," I said, taking the senator by the elbow, "I'll take you back."

We walked into my office. The senator whistled. I explained the different monitors and screens and put in a call to Henri. Reluctantly, he agreed to give us an audience. Crowntooth and I walked down the long hall between our two offices, and Alvon greeted us as the two huge mahogany doors to Henri's quarters swung open. We followed Alvon through the bar, down a short flight of stairs to an open lounge, up another flight of stairs, around the spa, and through gold-embossed doors to Henri's bedroom. There he lay, moaning, a wet towel covering his eyes.

"Hell's bells, Henri," cried Clayton, "you lookin' like you just found your sweetheart in bed with your best dog. T'aint nothing to be moping about now."

Henri peeled back the towel a bit so he could see. "I admit, Clayton," he said with an effort, "I've been feeling quite deflated as of late."

Crowntooth flapped his arms. "Well, inflate yourself then."

Henri attempted a smile. "Easier said than done, my good fellow. To what do we owe the pleasure?"

"To good news." replied Clayton. "You boys heard the morning scoop?"

"Not I," moped Henri.

"Yeah, I did," I said. "You mean the news about the stock market?"

"Hell no," said Buck. "About Senator Richmond Pell, senior senator from the fine state of Maryland?"

"Oh yeah, something about his being a rocket hero. I didn't catch it all."

"Rocket hero my ass," objected Buck. "That may be the official version, but ol' Buck Crowntooth's got the juicy truth. Seems our boy Richmond Pell, or shall I say the late Richmond Pell, done befell one awful accident. Kilt, deader than a door nail."

"He's dead?" I said, stepping forward. "I hadn't heard that. You call that good news?"

"Well, I guess it ain't too good for him, but it sure is good news for the lucky fella who comes to inherit the position, now ain't it?"

"Christ, Clayton," I objected, "the fellow's hardly hit the ground and you're in here talking politics already. It stinks."

Clayton put his hand on his chest. "Donny, ain't nobody's heart more broke than mine." he proclaimed. "That's God's own truth. Why, the first words out of my mouth were something like *awful* or *terrible*, if I do recall. But hell, boy, life goes on. That was a good twenty minutes ago."

"Let me get this straight," Henri interjected. "Richmond Pell got killed in a rocket accident this morning?"

"Last night, to be exact—at a top secret air force base somewhere in New Mexico. But get this, boys," he giggled, "the official version is he was there testing some sort of new fangled missile for the armed services. Didn't want any test pilots hurt, you see. A real hero." He winked. "But Uncle Bucky knows better."

"Well, what the hell happened?" asked Henri.

Clayton pulled up a chair and made himself comfortable. "Pell was on the take," he said. "Big time. Some of the GAO boys had uncovered major improprieties in a number of whopping big military contracts and everything pointed to Pell. The FBI was hot on his trail, and they had folks planted all over this here missile base to try and nab him. Word was out, you see, that a big pay off was going down. Well, the payment went down all right, but the FBI bungled the collar. Pell took off with an attache case full of thousand dollar bills. He ran this way. He ran that. Finally, he opened a door leading right out onto the gantry for one of these here fat experimental missiles. This is where it gets good. So, Pell unscrews the nose what-cha-call-it of the missile and stuffs the money in. Then he heads back to the launch area, where the FBI nabs him, but without the dough. No dough, no evidence, right boys? So they ain't a hootin' thing the FBI can do but let him go."

"That's incredible," I said.

"You ain't heard nothing yet," Buck continued. "So here's Pell, free as a bird, right? But instead of gettin' his sorry behind out of there as fast as his legs could carry him, our boy Richmond heads back to the missile gantry with a screwdriver later that afternoon. Trouble is, fellas, he don't know how close to launch it is. I'm a-talkin' 5—4—3—2. . . . Just as Pell gets the screws out and reaches in for his attache case—WHOOSH!—off goes this here experimental missile with our senator flapping away on top like that old Pooh bear on a honey limb. Held on to his money for dear life, he did. Probably could've fallen off and saved his sorry butt, but not ol' Richmond Pell. Defying gravity, defying *G*-forces out of this world, Pell goes a-sailing off into outer space. Must've been a *big* pay off, huh boys? Anyway, some air force flyboy is on report as saying he saw Pell about a mile up, giving him the finger, but I don't know."

"So the senator is dead," said Henri.

"And opportunity is born again," answered Buck.

"Hold on a second here," I said. "The reports I heard this morning were a whole lot different than what you just told us, Buck."

He rolled his eyes. "Well, listen up, tweedledum. Wha'd you expect them to do? The whole blessed thing turned into a fiasco. First the GAO bungled their investigation—should have picked up those kickbacks years ago—then the FBI blows the collar. Shoot, the Defense Department is embarrassed as all get out, and so's the President and Congress to boot. The truth would've hurt a lot of folks. Solution? Make Pell a hero, stamp the file *Top Secret*, and go have a nice lunch. End of incident. Except . . ."

"Except Pell has got to be replaced," I speculated aloud, "and that could be to our advantage—or not."

Clayton whistled. "Hey, you're catching on there, Sonny Boy." He turned to Henri. "And the political fact of life in this state ever since American Rain went down is everybody who's anybody is scared of Henri Goldleaf Lafayette III. Some of 'em don't even know why. They just know powerful people listen when you talk."

Henri eyes brightened. "Is that so?"

"You can bet your prize porker on'er," pledged Clayton. "Why, this morning someone from the governor's office called just to ask if I would run some names by you." Buck cackled. "They don't want to do anything that might rile you, pardner."

"So now I'm a power broker, eh Buck?" asked Henri.

"Yeah, I kinda like that. You got the list?"

"Nope," said Buck, "but I'll do you one better. Tomorrow at three, there will be a little get together, if you know what I mean. Some powerful folks, some good American folks are gonna' be there to toss this thing around a wee bit. We'll just figure out who's the best choice for all of us and ram the fella through."

"Democracy at work," I added dryly.

"Makes you proud, don't it," agreed Clayton.

"Well, I'll certainly be there, Bucko," Henri promised, thoughtfully rubbing his chin. "Power broker! I like the ring of that. Wouldn't miss it for the world," Henri grinned hugely and took Buck by the arm. "Can I show you around the new digs, Senator?"

"Lead on," Clayton replied.

As they walked away, I turned and went back to my office. I closed the door and smiled. When I figured they were both well out of earshot, I picked up the phone. "Ms. Townsend," I said softly, "would you please call David Winthrop for me."

Pastor Frickenfrayor strode into the lobby of American Rain looking lean, tan, and muscular. I put out my hand. "You're looking awfully fit, Pastor," I said. "I'm glad you called."

AMERICAN RAIN

He shook my hand and looked me in the eye. "Why, thank you, Doctor," he said. "I appreciate the compliment."

I took a guess. "Vacation?"

"In a sense, Donald," he said. "A working vacation. You see, I had the opportunity to join a group of my brethren who needed help in erecting a new church."

"A lot of work," I speculated. "Where about's?"

"Way out in the country," he said, "clear up by Hancock."

"Well, you certainly look the better for it."

He stopped short. "You know, I'd forgotten completely just how invigorating hard work can be," he said. "It was wonderful; the cold December air at dawn, the promise of warmth as the sun rose above the rolling hills, the sound of hammers ringing and echoing down the valley as the walls went up. It was an experience, all right."

"Sounds like it. I'm envious."

He glanced slowly around the foyer. "New quarters I see," he said. "Very . . . ah . . . big."

I laughed. "They are that. Come on back."

Entering my office, I sat behind my desk. The pastor went to the window and admired the view. Slowly he surveyed the new accommodations—humming as he did so, nodding here, smiling there. Finally, he sat down in front of me. "This location of yours is absolutely fantastic," he said. "It's," he went on, rolling his shoulders, ". . . *incomparable*. Yes, that's the word. Incomparable." He hesitated. "In fact, I would almost have to say—if I weren't so confident of your intelligence and sense of self—that I would have to wonder what in the world someone like you was doing here. But I don't have to worry about that. Do I?"

"I . . . I . . ." I stuttered.

He smiled warmly and crossed his legs. "Of course not. Now, Donald, I came down today to tell you about some important theological progress I made while I was working. You see, building the church brought me very close to something profound." He leaned back and took a deep breath. "Strange how some of the most meaningful ideas can come to you through the simplest, most common activities."

"For instance?"

"Well, let me tell you. We were laying the second floor joists one morning and the work was going well. There is a certain hum or rhythm to it, you know. Anyway, I took a short break and poured myself a cup of coffee from my thermos. I leaned casually against the foundation and watched the work progress, and as I did, I was overcome by the most intense feeling of power I'd ever know." He made a muscle with his biceps. "Not, mind you, this kind of strength, but rather a sense of almost infinite capability. It was everything coming together—the steady drum of the hammers, the smiles and assurance on everyone's face—that made it so. It was, I understood instantly, the power of human creativity, of all our uncharted possibilities, and it flowed through me with a brilliance I can hardly describe. I was so overcome I had to stop and walk away.

"So I went to the edge of the trees and sat down. But all the while, this awesome sensation prevailed. Let me describe it. It was like a white-hot glow was filling every pore of my body," he went on excitedly, eyes dancing. "It gave me an almost unbelievable feeling of confidence . . . then, and even more profoundly, a sense of connection."

He raised his hands solemnly. "I was connected to everything around me. I suddenly realized I was not separate and apart, even as I sat there by myself, but was as much a part of the process as the clouds or the trees around me. I suddenly knew that the stuff of the universe, this pulsing dance of energy and creativity too grand and awesome to measure, was furiously churning away in everything and everyone around me."

I took a long, slow sip of coffee. "Go on."

"Well, it was a profound and . . ." he paused, straining for the right words, "a . . . religious experience for me. Yes. You see, Donald, I understood without so much as a thought that I had, for lack of a better description, walked with God."

"You sound captivated," I observed. "I've never seen you like this before."

"It's because I understand things now I never knew before," he said emphatically. "The experience moved me as nothing else ever has. I went over it in my mind for days, but had only vague feelings and hazy premonitions to show for it. Nothing concrete. Yet I felt it's meaning was close at hand and that I could make sense of it eventually."

"So?"

"So one day I returned to the edge of the woods and sat. I cleared my head and tried again to conjure up a vision of that creative and vital universe I had felt so powerfully. Slowly, it came to me. And, gradually, I began to understand."

I leaned forward. "Well, spit it out!"

He laughed at my impatience. "I understood two things, Donald, both important, both connected. The first is that the Creator can only be approached through creation—and then only at a slant. That is, God can not be known directly, only metaphorically. Thus, we can hope only to understand what God is like, not what He is. I found him, you see, in the steady ring of the hammer. This, in turn, led to a powerful vision of the awesome creative dance of the universe going on around me. But who knows where you or others may find him?"

"I got you," I said. "Go on."

"The second thing I came to understand was simple. Once I felt the power of creation, saw clearly the spirit—again for lack of a better word—in the simple hammer I was holding, I knew beyond a doubt that building, sheer positive effort, was the work of God. To find Him, one need only struggle forward in a positive vein." He uncrossed his legs. "That's it," he said. "Except once I saw the interconnectedness of things and the sheer magnitude of creativity all around me—from the explosions of stars in the heavens, to the flowering of spring meadows—I understood how utterly futile a task it is to try and categorize and reduce it to biblical incantations or, for that matter, scholarly texts." He laughed happily. "It's all too indescribable."

"And easy to feel hopeless and lost in the confusion and immensity as well," I added.

He shook his head. "No," he said. "Quite the opposite."

"How so?"

"Because in all the heavens, from tree to tidal wave to timber wolf, only man gets to choose. The future is in our hands. We can create or destroy, Donald, build lives or tear them down. It is the spirit and will of man alone that in the end may determine the balance. We are not at all hopeless and lost, as was your concern, but grand to a degree hardly imaginable. God has given us much. But in the end, I fear, He will expect much in return."

I stood up and went to the window. I needed time to think. His words were impressive. But it was not his words that affected me. It was my sudden realization I had heard virtually the identical conclusion achieved before—from diverse, disconnected sources, and as a result of wildly contrasting approaches. I didn't know what to say. So I stood at the window and watched the city hum, suddenly unsure of everything. Thoughts of fear and wonder battled each other as I labored, unsuccessfully, to make sense of it all.

"I'm glad you could make it," I said, shaking David Winthrop's hand, my breath freezing then slowly dissipating in the dead, frigid air. "Have you ever seen so many expensive cars?"

He laughed and shrugged. "I'm glad you called me," he said. "Perhaps we can accomplish something here."

"I was hoping," I said, "that we might put your name up for senator."

He shrugged again. "Well, we can do that," he said, "but the chances of my being appointed are virtually nil. I am not a known commodity to the rich and powerful."

"You can never tell," I cautioned. "At the least, maybe we can influence the selection."

"Yes," he agreed, "I would imagine that we might be able to press for someone sympathetic to the needs of the city and its people. That, I think, is our only real hope here, Dr. Mallory."

I slapped him on the back. "Well, let's give it a shot," I said, and opened the door.

The Algonquian Club: very posh, private, and privileged. Men only. We were shown directly to the Poe Room where an assembly of about twenty men stood around chatting and sipping coffee. Henri, splendidly attired, milled from group to group along with Clayton Crowntooth. Everyone was happy to meet him, and displayed the utmost respect. David Winthrop and I grabbed a cup of coffee as the meeting was quickly brought to order.

R. C. Smythe tapped a glass with a spoon. "Why'nt ya'll just go ahead now and grab a seat, fellas, where ever you can find one. That's fine." David Winthrop and I leaned against the wall. Most everyone else sat. "As you know, gentlemen, we are here today because of the tragic and untimely death of a great and admired gentleman, space hero extraordinaire, the late Senator Richmond Pell." There was a round of snickers. "Now," R. C. continued, "I am certain all of us assembled here would like to see the senator's work continued, his memory honored, and all that crap, so I won't go on about it anymore. Suffice it to say he was a semicapable bastard who would have sold his mother for a dime. He also probably should have, from all accounts of his death, had a better handle on Newton's third law." Another round of sneers. "So let's replace him. Let's get a real American in there who understands the issues that real Americans carry close to their hearts."

"Like the corporate tax deductions on new company Cadillacs?" someone called from the back of the room.

"Exactly!" shouted R. C. "Issues that tear at your gut, that bring tears to your eyes. Like the deductibility of the three-martini lunch, for instance?"

"Yeah!"

"Or all those business meetings in the Bahamas the IRS has suddenly been taking such a hard look at," R. C. went on. "We need someone, boys, who will see the world our way. The right way. The way a real American sees the world. Someone who is willing to play ball."

"That's right!"

"Absolutely!"

The men were standing and shouting. They were in a froth. R. C. was pulling the right strings, I noticed—their purse strings. He continued, "No more of this namby pamby, Casper Milktoast, talk of decency and fairness, huh fellas?"

"No more!"

"Boooooooo!"

"From now on it's going to be a return to the hard-hitting, no-holds-barred, money-grubbing values of our forefathers!"

"Hoooooray!"

"Gentlemen, gentlemen," R. C. went on, rubbing the sweat from his brow, "please, return to your seats. I assure you, your enthusiasm and support are very much appreciated. But we have a lot of work to accomplish. Now, I have here a list of names of American Americans who I think we should consider as Pell's replacement. Do I hear any suggestions?"

"Roland Medwick," someone shouted.

"Too liberal," Clayton said.

"Truman Campbell," somebody else shouted.

"Too poor," R. C. objected.

I held up my hand. "David Winthrop!" I yelled.

Everyone turned and looked at me. "Yeah, that's right," I said, defensively. "David Winthrop, the gentleman to my right."

R. C. pouted. "I see no David Winthrop on my list, Donald," he said sharply.

"What the hell's your list got to do with it?" I asked.

His eyes bulged. "My list, Donald, just happens to be compiled monthly by Americans for an American America as a litmus test of preferability."

"Hooey," I said. "Mr. Winthrop is an educated and capable man. He runs a business, heads up a very successful community program, and cares deeply about the people of our state. He would be a fine senator."

There was much grumbling. "Look, son," said Clayton Crowntooth, "I get the feeling sometimes you just don't understand. I got's the feeling that when I look up the word *naive* in the dictionary, ol' Web is a gonna' say: 'Donald Mallory.' Catch on, boy? This here is America. Ain't got nothing to do with who will do a good job. Hell, it's about seeing eye to eye, about scratching each other's backs. Right, R. C.?"

"Exactly, Clayton," snapped R. C. "Now let's just move on with the proceedings here and get back to some kind of reality. Any other ideas boys?"

David Winthrop touched my sleeve. "Nice try," he said with a wink, "but it's like I said, better to try and exert some influence on the decision and get somewhere, then to try and run away with the whole shebang and come up bone dry. Something is always better than nothing."

"Maybe you're right," I admitted. "I didn't have much of a shot. Not without some serious backing."

"Let's just wait and see what happens," he suggested.

The meeting dragged on for hours. We got nowhere. Every candidate was objectionable to someone. Too liberal, too tall. Too soft on crime, too educated. It droned on. We went through R. C.'s list twice, but with no breakthrough. Tempers were wearing thin. Finally David Winthrop strode to the center of the room. "I have an idea," he said.

"Well, I . . . I . . ." R. C. stuttered.

"I would like to place into nomination, if I may," David continued boldly, "the name of a fine and eminently renowned philanthropist whom I have had the pleasure of working with over the last number of months. He is not only a successful businessman, but an extraordinarily well educated individual as well. His influence in these halls, I can tell from mere observation, is considerable and yet his heart has always been open to the poor and less fortunate of the city. His appointment would be a boon, I believe, for all concerned citizens. I am, of course, referring to none other than the revered, Henri Goldleaf Lafayette III."

Backfire! The pose I had maintained on Henri's behalf had just come back in my face like a large lemon pie: a shocking, sticky, and very big mess. But nothing could be done. Almost at once, the entire group rose with the nomination in unison as if it were an act of divine intuition.

"Fantastic! Fantastic!" beamed R. C. Smythe. "An American American if ever there was one. Can't believe I didn't think of it before. Outstanding choice, Mr. Winthrop."

"The governor will be delighted to support the honorable Henri Goldleaf Lafayette III!" the state representative called above the ruckus.

And so on, down the line. They slapped him on the back, wished him well as the next senator from the state of Maryland, and popped cigars into one another's mouths.

Henri swelled with the praise like an overfilled balloon. His eyes glowed. He was transfixed. I had never seen him so pleased with himself, so infatuated. He shook every hand, delighted in every comment. He would do it without even thinking, I knew. He would step off the edge, and he would wind up sorry.

I leaned back against the wall. It would never work. But in a room full of unabashed, freewheeling support, I was the only one who knew it. The death defying, high wire act Henri called living would never survive a world of flash bulbs and inquiry rooms. At least for long. Part of me was sad, part relieved. It would all come crashing down with a very loud bang, and the only questions left to ask now were when it would happen and how bad it would hurt?

19

"Oh, I'mmm a yankee doodle dandy, a . . ."

"Stop it!" I yelled at Henri as he twirled around the dining room, a pancake on his head.

". . . yankee doodle do or die. . . . A real . . ."

"Give it a rest already, will you!"

". . . life nephew of my Uncle Sam, born on the . . ."

My nostrils flared. I bared my fangs, but nothing would stop him. So as he strutted past jovially, I grabbed the pancake from the top of his head and squished it between my fingers. "Enough!" I yelled, throwing the mangled pancake high in the air. It fell with a thump on the dining room table amid the breakfast dishes."

"Hey!" he cried, "what do you think you're doing?"

"Trying to restore some sense of sanity and balance to this residence," I said. "For weeks now, you've been driving me crazy with all this Uncle Sam reverie. You seem to think you're impervious to the normal procedures Congress employs to check out it's appointees. Well, you're not!"

"And you're nothing but a killjoy," he protested, "throwing water on every new and nifty scheme I hatch.

And now you've gone and tossed my top hat into the eggs Benedict!"

"Will you get a grip, please!" I demanded. "This is not going to be all fun and games."

"Yes it will," he argued. "You heard it yourself, I own half the state. Why, they wept when my name was placed into nomination. By the way, who was that guy anyway?"

"David Winthrop," I said, "and they weren't weeping for you. They were weeping from sheer exhaustion. No one can listen to R. C. Smythe for more than fifteen minutes without breaking down."

"David Winthrop, huh," he repeated. "Do I own him?"

"No," I answered, "he's a community activist."

"Oh how dreary," he said. "Poor chum. Perhaps we should do something for him."

"Something nice?" I asked, not quite sure I'd heard him straight.

"Well, something . . . cheap."

I thought quickly. "How about something that would be good for him, much better for you, and cost nothing at all."

"Now that's the spirit!" he applauded. "What did you have in mind?"

"Simple," I said. "Go to the governor and tell him you want two men listed as appointees; a first and second choice. You, of course, are first and since, like you say, you're a shoo-in anyway, the second place is nothing but window dressing. But it would make the overall appointment look better—what with a minority in consideration—and down the line, it could help you."

"How?"

"Look," I said, "the first time you're appointed, but the second time you have to be elected. What makes you think you can win anything in a popular contest without popular support?"

"Ah, now I get it," he said. "But what does he get out of it?"

"Visibility," I answered. "Prestige. His business picks up, he has more clout as a local leader. He gets the glow, but you get the go. Two years from now you may have a local heavyweight in your corner."

He slapped the table. "Donny," he exclaimed, "you can be terrific when you put your mind to it. That sounds like a plan to me."

Just then Alvon showed Clayton Crowntooth into the dining room. "Morning gentlemen, morning," Buck called, "lovely day, ain't it? Why I believe spring may be just around the corner."

"You may be right, Senator," I said, "to what do we owe the visit?"

"Update is what," he responded. "Everything seems to be going real smooth in the senator-making biz," he said. "The guv is about to name Henri and it should be clear sailing from there."

"One small change, Clayton." Henri interjected. "The splendid chap who nominated me . . . Winthrop."

"Yeah . . . ?"

". . . should be named on the ticket as well."

Crowntooth rubbed his chin thoughtfully, glanced my way, then looked back at Henri. "'Tain't no ticket," Henri," he said. "It's a damn appointment."

Henri explained our reasoning: the minority rub, the future considerations.

"Hmmm," Buck crooned, "now I see the logic in'er. Like greasing up the old spit ball. By golly, you boys is out thinking the pros, ain't yuz. OK, I'll alert the guv. Think he'll like it. That minority stuff always plays well downtown."

"Buck," I said, "tell the guv to play up Winthrop. You know, his education and credentials and all. This should all appear absolutely on the up and up. Otherwise, he could look like just a token, and everyone would see through that. Could backfire."

Buck put his arm around my shoulder. "Henri," he proclaimed, "I believe our boy, Donny here, has finally come of age."

Henri nodded approvingly. "The lad could be diabolical if he just put his mind to it, Senator. "I've always seen the potential in him."

"Indeed, indeed," Buck intoned, "and, oh yeah, just one more thing."

"What's that?" I asked.

"The FBI will be a-knocking on your door real soon."

"The wha . . . ?" asked Henri, eyes starting to bulge.

"Yeah, the FBI," Clayton repeated. "I put them on the case. We need a good solid background check on you. Standard operating procedure. But, hey, not to worry. They will just check out your past in detail. You know, the education, business background, money ties, etc. Just to make sure it's all legit."

Henri looked like a corpse.

Clayton's eyes narrowed. "It is all legit . . . ain't it?"

I coughed. "Ah . . . yeah. The, ah, sheepskins are all real. Aren't they, Henri?"

Henri sucked air through his lips like a vacuum in reverse, then exhaled it in a burst. "Y-y-ye-s-s."

Clayton threw his arms in the air happily. "Well, hell, then there ain't a thing in the world to worry about. It will all work out right as rain, and we'll be doing business together for a long time. 'Course," he went on matter-of-factly, "if it don't turn out right, I'll have to disavow having ever known either of you and leave you to rot in hell, if you get my drift?"

"Delicately put," Henri said. "Yes, I catch your meaning."

Clayton waved goodbye cheerfully and departed. The door slammed.

I picked up a pancake from the table and put it on Henri's head. "Let's hear a chorus or two now."

Agent Truman Spencer looked at Henri with an odd sort of gleam in his eye. "So you're Henri Goldleaf Lafayette III," he said, a thin smile on his lips. He motioned to a thick file on his desk. "I have compiled a fairly comprehensive report concerning you," he said. He sat back. "That's a very nice suit you're wearing."

"Handmade," said Henri. "Cost a bundle."

"I know," said the agent. "I spoke to your tailor."

Henri gave me a sideways glance and rolled his eyes. "I trust your investigation finds me well-*suited* then for the position of Senator of the United States."

Spencer was young, lean, all business. He rolled his shoulders. "I don't determine whether you're well-*suited* or not," he said. "I just get the facts."

Henri tried to bluff him. "So you are aware, I surmise, that I have lived my life as a virtual paragon of virtue? My honesty, charity, and good deeds are legendary."

The agent reached for the file and flipped it open. "Let's see," he said, "honesty, Huh? Hmm, yeah. Here we go, first paragraph." He pulled out a page and started to read slowly. "Henri Goldleaf Lafayette III, a.k.a. Maxwell Taylor, a.k.a. Leonard Stewart, a.k.a. . . ."

Henri swallowed hard. "I have," he admitted, "as a result of my charitable activities, had to assume an alias from time to time so as not to become overwhelmed by the demands of my public. I can certainly understand how it may appear somewhat compromising to a trained investigator such as yourself, Agent Spencer, but I really don't think I should be stigmatized simply because I have an open and compassionate heart. Do you?"

The agent nodded in agreement. "Not at all," he said. "However evidence of your alleged 'compassionate heart' is hard to come by, Monsieur Lafayette."

Henri feigned great indignation. "My entire life is a testament to charity!" he argued, nose thrust in the air. "I warn you, I shan't be trifled with like this, Agent Spencer. And what's more, I do not think it fair to cast dispersions upon my life's work when your investigation—if you can even call it that—is so obviously inept. Next you'll be questioning my character."

Spencer giggled. "Character, huh? Yeah, let me take a look here," he went on, thumbing through the pages. "I believe there is something here that touches on that topic. Yup, got it. Wanna hear?"

Henri folded his arms across his chest and looked coldly across the room.

"Why not," I said.

"Here goes," said the agent, taking a quick sip of water. "Public drunkenness: Baltimore 1956, '61, '63. Disturbing the peace: Baltimore, New Orleans, Chicago. Jury tampering: Detroit 1974. Indecent exposure: New York, Miami, Baltimore, and Dallas. Trafficking in stolen goods: New Haven, 1963. Hand gun violations: Philadelphia, Newark, Fort Wayne. Receiving stolen goods: Raleigh, 1959. Resisting arrest: Pittsburgh, Canton, Wichita Falls. Petty larceny: San Francisco, Boston, Albany. Passing bad checks: Newark, Columbus, and too many other cities to mention. Counterfeiting: Chicago and New York. Grand larceny: Atlanta, 1974. Mail fraud, wire fraud, insurance fraud, just plain old fraud: Baltimore, New York, and Washington. Assault: Cleveland, 1957 . . . Shall I go on?"

"No," I said.

Henri spun on his seat. "Oh, oh," he said, throwing out his hands, "so I suppose you grew up the perfect little man, huh, Agent Spencer. Never got your hand caught in the cookie jar? Never went even the slightest bit wild? So I sowed a few wild oats before settling down to become a model citizen. Boys will be boys, right, Agent Spencer? 'Least I wasn't destructive."

"No?" answered Truman Spencer. "Milwaukee, 1969: you drove a stolen corvette through a shopping plaza at 111 mph, destroying eleven automobiles, demolishing three telephone poles, and devastating fourteen retail stores—for an estimated total damage of $1,534,679.98."

Henri laughed and waved the whole thing off. "But the parking pattern was most confusing and . . ." he said.

The agent flipped the page again. "Dallas, 1961: you drove a herd of approximately 214 Holstein cows up Mockingbird Lane at rush hour causing an estimated twenty-three automobile accidents. You also destroyed eleven residences, six fire hydrants, nineteen plate glass windows, and caused eight fist fights. Approximate damage: $951,722.55 and four broken noses."

"Listen," Henri said, "how was I to know they couldn't take a joke down there? Texans get so hot and bothered, you know?"

Spencer frowned and turned yet another page. "Baltimore, 1956: the residence of one Mariane Mallory . . ."

"Hey, that's my mother!" I said.

"After a brief domestic argument with your sister," the agent continued, "you removed from her home by chain saw the entire second floor stairwell, six wood doors, two interior walls, four windows, five joists, and eleven rafters before passing out in the flower bed. For this, you spent two months, three days, and eleven hours in detox."

"YOU JERK!" I screamed at him. "That was my house!"

"Donny," he said, "your mother could be so prissy at times. It was just a little misunderstanding is all. So she didn't like what I did. So I did a little interior decorating and the results were not what she had envisioned. OK, I admit it. But since when is poor taste a sin?"

"You are a sick man!" I said.

Henri shook his head violently. "Need I remind you that I am a psychiatrist and, as such, happen to be an expert on sick behavior."

"You are that," I said.

"About those degrees," said the agent, "I know they are all bogus, obtained through blackmail and extortion. Your Center for Psychiatric Retribution was a total fraud before you grossly misrepresented the entire thing and sold it to the eminent trial attorney, Ian Stanforth, for twenty times it's actual value—vengeance for which, by the way, he has sworn on a stack of Bibles to wring from your hide."

Henri tossed a hand cavalierly in the air. "He can't touch me," he said. "Besides, he's just another fool who doesn't understand business."

"Well, perhaps I am as well," said Agent Spencer.

"How's that?" asked Henri.

"American Rain," Spencer replied. "That is the name, is it not?"

Henri stiffened. "Why, yes, of course. Why do you ask?"

The agent stood for the first time. He began pacing. "This is really you, isn't it?"

"Why, I haven't the vaguest idea what in the world you are talking about, young man," Henri replied, wide eyed.

Spencer stopped and propped a foot up on his chair. He leaned forward. "I think I understand what you're up to. It's nice. It's tight. I've watched the money come in and go out. I have the cash runs and all your transaction records. Did you know that?"

Henri smiled casually—on the hot seat, he was giving a world class performance. "Well, then you know it is an absolutely legitimate business employed by the United States of America as a environmental consulting firm."

Spencer stared at Henri for a few moments, then resumed his pacing. "By act of Congress, funds for your firm were established and shortly thereafter, you went into business. This I have documented. Of course, the wisdom with which Congress carries out it's duties is none of my business, still . . ."

"That is exactly right, young man," Henri interjected. "You're a professional, right? Well, I would appreciate your sticking to your job and not speculating wildly about my business friends and connections."

Spencer stopped and stared pointedly at Henri. "I never speculate, Monsieur Lafayette," he said. "I have no idea why Congress decided to pay you outrageous sums of money every time it rains, but I can guarantee you this: I will find out. I'll go over every transaction, every check and every telephone call if I have to. But I'll find out. And if there is a violation of federal law, I promise I will squeeze you like a grape, Henri Lafayette—or whatever you're calling yourself by then"

"Guess again, flatfoot," laughed Henri contentiously, "once you send your report to whoever you report to as a munchkin in this little magic world of yours, your

263

work will be finished. Over. Finito. Your threats are idle. You will be a non-factor."

"Henri!" I pleaded.

He waved my fears aside. "It's the truth, Donny. He's on a fishing expedition. If he had something—which he doesn't because there isn't anything—he would have dropped the net by now."

Spencer bowed slightly. "Absolutely correct, Monsieur Lafayette. How foolish of me to have prodded you. You are a pro; I should have known better. What you say is correct. My investigation is over, for all intents and purposes. So I will have to take whatever solace I can from the fact your appointment to the Senate will, no doubt, be torpedoed by this report."

"I was going to withdraw my name anyway," Henri fired back with a sneer. "So all your gumshoeing will have no effect on me at all." He smiled. "All your work down the drain, eh, Agent Spencer?"

"Down the drain indeed," replied Truman Spencer. ". . . Unless, of course . . ."

Henri shifted uneasily. "Unless what?"

"Well, unless this report should somehow find it's way into the hands of the press," he continued. "A leak perhaps. You know, Monsieur Lafayette, there are a good many people in this country who would love to know that the government is paying you millions of dollars every time it rains. It would embarrass any number of people, I'm sure. Political dynamite is what I have here. I can imagine quite easily the congressional scandal that would ensue should such a report appear in the press. The hearings, the subpoenas, the interrogations. Everyone will be diving for cover. But you will be out there all alone with no place to hide. Now, won't you?"

"You're a professional," Henri objected nervously. "You would not stoop to such a contemptible tactic." The agent shrugged. "Maybe," he said, "maybe not."

"Molllyyyyy!" Henri cried into the receiver, "at least speak to me, at least come to the phone. Spring is in the air; the birds are singing. My heart is breaking. Do you hear me, BREAKING!" I want your BOD!"

"You said you were going to maintain your composure," I hissed. "You said, you would keep it strictly platonic."

He wiped the sweat from his brow. "I can't help it," he cried. "I'm possessed."

"You're a nitwit," I said. "Here, give me the receiver." I took the phone. "Molly," I said, "Don Mallory here. Henri wants to say that he is sorry he treated you badly, that he will never do it again.

". . . Go on," she said.

"He has practiced all morning. He is sincere. Really. He just got a little . . . well . . ."

". . . Out of control?"

"Yes, a little out of control," I confirmed.

"But that's his entire problem, isn't it?" she asked.

Henri rubbed his cheeks furiously. "Wha'd she say?" he demanded to know. "Come on, wha'd she say?"

I pushed him away and put the receiver against my chest. "Sit down, you idiot," I admonished. "This is exactly the type of behavior that scares her."

"After all," she continued, "I gave him a second chance, but he couldn't control himself for even a few days. I just don't know."

265

Henri began convulsing. He jumped up on one of the kitchen chairs and started doodling his lips. "Beee-a-beee-a-beee-a-bee."

"Well, he's really got himself back together now," I insisted, trying to keep the sound of his vibrating smackers off the line. "You'd hardly recognize him, Molly."

"Well," she went on, "I had read he was going to be a senator or something now. He'll have no time for me. And I don't want to be just another woman."

Henri's eyes bulged enormously. His face reddened. "What do you mean, scares her?" he asked.

I cupped my hand over the receiver. "Get down off of that chair, you maniac," I said. "You deserve nothing! Nothing, . . . Molly" I went on quickly, "well, he bowed out of that situation a couple of days ago. Didn't you know? Yeah, just wasn't for him."

"Well, no, Donald. I didn't know that," she said. "That could make a difference."

Henri slumped down off of the chair and rolled onto the floor. He began slowly rocking, then rolling back and forth across the kitchen floor. His fat, sweaty body made a succession of rhythmic, sticky sounds on the linoleum as he completed each revolution.

"Really! Gee, that's great, Molly." I said, as Henri rolled directly into my chair and almost sent me flying. I kicked him several times about the hips until he backed up and rolled off toward the dishwasher. "I'm sure you will be pleased with the new Henri," I said. "He's really down to earth."

"Well, this is what I'll do," she said. "He may come to visit me in Nashville for a few days. How's that?"

Just then Clayton Crowntooth walked into the kitchen with a copy of the morning paper tucked under his arm. "Mornin' fellas," he called.

"Hello, Buck," I said. "Help yourself to the java. . . . Well, that sounds like it might work, Molly."

Clayton poured himself a mug of coffee and sat at the table. He studied the scene for a few seconds then looked at me quizzically. "Hey, Donny, what's Henri making those sick, syrupy kinda' noises down there on the linoleum for?" he asked.

I covered the receiver once more. "'Cause he's rolling back and forth across the floor in anticipation of seeing his lady love, Buck," I replied. Then into the phone: "He seems very excited at the prospect, Molly."

"Well, that just flat out makes sense, now don't it," said Buck, sipping his coffee calmly as Henri whacked into the cabinets repeatedly.

"Perhaps he could help out with the gang here," she said. "I've come a long way, you know. I'll be recording my first cut next week."

"Wow, super," I said. "Could you hold on a second, Molly?" I put her line on hold, grabbed a ripe apple from a bowl on the table, whipped it across the room, and whacked Henri on the back of the head.

"Nice shot," said Buck, clapping appreciatively.

"Thanks," I replied. "Henri!" I hissed, "Molly says you can come visit her in Nashville. Maybe you can even help her out during her first recording session. That's a big breakthrough. What do you say?"

He looked up. "I wouldn't go to Tennessee for all the freaking tea in China," he said. "It's a city citizened by nothing but biological throw backs, backwater clods, hammerheads, and mutants. Why, I would have to have one entire hemisphere of my brain removed just to be able to order breakfast."

"He loves the idea, Molly!" I yelled.

"Noooooo!" Henri protested.

"Oh, wonderful," Molly exclaimed. "When should I expect him?"

"I'm not going and that's final!" Henri fairly spat.

Buck threw the copy of the morning paper he had been carrying on the kitchen floor. "You may want to think about that trip again, Henri," he said.

Henri stopped rolling and sat up. He held up the front page. In huge bold letter it read:

CONGRESS CRIES FOUL!!!

And then below that in somewhat less sensational print:

Local Mogul Sought for Questioning

Henri jumped to his feet and grabbed the paper. "Agent Spencer has struck!" he cried. "Alvon, pack my bags at once." He shook his head forlornly. "We're off to the fair city of Nashville, Tennessee," he said. "Pack me plenty of rhinestones, stirrups, and a nice jar or two of coon oil, my good man. It appears I may be gone for awhile."

20

"Get that stinking guitar out of my face, will ya!" I yelled, trying to look around the instrument as Henri packed in a fury. "I'm trying to concentrate on the television here for God's sake." I hit the button that controlled the volume.

"Let me see," said Henri, stepping back to survey his suitcase, "coon skin cap, six-string guitar, three snake skins, one bar of possum soap, and a jug of rot-gut whiskey. They'll love me in Nashville, huh, Donny?"

"Can you shut up a second?" I asked. "This reporter just said something about American Rain."

"Ah, don't pay any attention to it," Henri called over his shoulder. "They been barking up every other tree since we hit the newsstands yesterday. I'm tired of listening."

"Shhhh!" I said. "This is something else."

The reporter was interviewing a tall, regal, elderly gentleman. "Could you tell us what's going on, Counselor?" the reporter asked.

"I have filed a class action suit in federal court this afternoon on behalf of my clients, the Rollins family, and the entire population of the United States, Ted," the elderly man replied.

"What are you asking for, Counselor?"

"I want damages in excess of one hundred billion dollars, Ted. The human carnage that has been wrought by this fiend, Henri Lafayette, or whatever he calls himself, on the citizens of our country has been, in my book, virtually incalculable."

Henri pivoted quickly to face the screen. He blanched. "Ian Stanforth," he exclaimed, "my arch enemy! My God, what's he up to?"

"Why don't you shut up and listen," I suggested.

The reporter continued. "Mr. Stanforth, there seems to be some legal ambiguity contained in your suit, if I understand the action you have taken. Isn't it farfetched to hold someone, or some organization, responsible for the rainfall? Isn't this suit just a lot of wishful thinking?"

"Not at all, Ted. The suit is not ambiguous in the least. It is a clearheaded and straightforward extension of the commonplace tort of products liability," Ian Stanforth responded with a fatherly smile.

"Jeeez," I said, "this guy's good."

"How do you mean, Mr. Stanforth?"

"Well, Ted, the court has accepted for years the notion that a manufacturer of a product is strictly liable for any injuries caused by a defect in that product. Now, I am not arguing that American Rain and the villainous Henri Lafayette manufactured rain in the strict sense—merely that the acceptance of such large sums of taxpayer money whenever a precipitation event occurs blurs the distinction between manufacturer and consultant to a point of triviality. In essence, Ted, my argument before the court is that the distinction at this point becomes meaningless and, as such, the strict law of products liability should apply in this instance as well. American Rain accepted such outrageous amounts of federal funds that I believe the court should find it responsible for rainfall and all precipitational damage anywhere in the United States without further deliberation or delay."

"The flood last month in Florida?" asked Ted. "The acid rain across the entire nation. Across most of the globe?"

Ian Stanforth stood at attention. "Exactly, Ted."

The camera zoomed in on Ted. "This monster lawsuit filed just this afternoon by one of the most prominent members of the city's bar is but the latest development in the strange, unfolding drama of American Rain since the story broke yesterday. Questions still abound. Questions for lawmakers, for voters, but most of all for—as the eloquent Mr. Stanforth referred to him—the villainous Mr. Henri Goldleaf Lafayette III, who cannot be reached for comment. From the federal courthouse, Ted Barnett reporting."

I slapped the side of my face. "One hundred *billion* dollars!" I said.

"This guy means business."

"Stanforth is a fool," Henri insisted. "He's just trying to get back at me for pulling the clinic caper on him."

I stared at him. "Looks like a pretty good job of it to me," I said. "The court just might buy that strict liability routine. Sillier decisions have been made, you know."

"I know. Believe me, I know. I'm a lawyer, remember?"

Later that night, I rode with him to the airport. He seemed strangely animated for someone who had just been sued for almost half the gross national product. He was tapping his toe on the floorboard and humming vague melodies out of the corner of his mouth. "What gives?" I asked.

He stopped humming. "What do you mean?"

"How can you act so carefree when everything you've worked for is crashing down around you? You told me yourself—Ian Stanforth is a tiger looking for a kill. Yet you pass off his one hundred billion dollar lawsuit as if it were a parking ticket."

"Kid," he said, "I learned a long time ago never to worry about diddly. Worrying won't get you anywhere. Sure, Stanforth's a good attorney. But that's all he is. He can be foiled. Oh, he may win. He may even win a lot. But he won't get to me, and that's what he's really after."

We walked to the departure gate, and I wished him a good trip. He was as excited as I had ever seen him, talking about Molly, wisecracking about Nashville. He was like a schoolboy in love. And here I thought I knew him.

He threw his coat over his arm when they announced the flight, then laughed at me. "You knew we were playing a high stakes game all along, Donny."

"Yeah," I said.

"Well, you know what they say: Keep your feet moving and never, ever look back 'cause someone could be gaining on you."

"Yeah, great," I said. "And did you hear the one about the guy who jumps off the Empire State Building and on the way down, say at the tenth floor, passes a window washer?"

"No," he said. "Tell me quick."

"So the window washer turns and asks the guy as he's sailing past, 'How's it going?'"

". . . And?"

"And the guy says, 'so far, so good.'"

He smiled. "Well, Donny," he said, "we'll just have to see, now won't we. We'll just have to see."

The following morning I woke early and sniffed the morning air; something had changed. I couldn't tell what, but something was definitely different. I shaved and showered, a vague sense of dread in the back of my mind. The house was very quiet. It was Saturday, so I had given all the help the day off, seeing as how Henri was out of town. I went downstairs and looked at the kitchen clock. Seven-thirty.

I fixed a pot of coffee and, as it began to perk, sauntered down the hallway to the front door. I stepped outside and looked for the morning paper, but I couldn't find it anywhere in the grass. Then suddenly it hit me. There were leaves on the trees and young flowers popping out of the beds along the fence line. Spring had come, had bloomed for gosh sake, and I hadn't even noticed. The grass smelled rich, the clouds blew by lightly overhead. April. Where had I been?

I shoved my hands into my pockets and ambled down the front walk. I looked for the paper boy, but he was nowhere in sight. Nearby, the forsythia and dogwoods were nearing full bloom. They smelled clean and wonderful in the soft morning air. I went back inside, fetched myself a cup of coffee, put on a sweater, and went back out. I was intoxicated. Perhaps it was just the peace and quiet, and the suddenly relaxed pace, but I didn't think so. I thought it was more.

I heard the clank of the paper boy's bike as he rounded the corner. I walked out to meet him. He smiled and pulled up slowly to where I stood. He had a baseball hat on his head and looked about ten. "Nice day," I said.

"Yeah." He handed me the paper. "See the game?" he asked.

"What game?"

He looked at me as if I were crazy. "The *O*'s!" he exploded.

"The *O*'s, huh," I repeated, half embarrassed. "Who'd they play?"

"Kansas City," he answered. "Opening day. Ever hear of it?"

I couldn't believe I'd missed an opening day. I was shocked. "You're kidding," I said. "Who won?"

"We did, Mister," He regarded me suspiciously. "Come on, Mister, where you been?"

Good question. And one for which I lacked a ready answer. "How much I owe you?" I asked, dodging the issue.

He checked his cards. "Twenty-five bucks, Mister. You and that fat friend of yours, . . . what's his name?"

"Lafayette."

"Yeah, whatever," he went on. "Well, he keeps telling me he's going to take care of me next week. I can't keep carrying you deadbeats like this, you know."

"I know," I said.

I went back inside and got enough money to pay the kid. I tipped him ten and said I was sorry. A mix-up I called it.

He counted it carefully and put the wad in his pocket. "Did the fat dude think he was going to beat me out of it?" he asked sarcastically.

"No, I don't think so, he . . ."

"'Cause I'da sued him. Small claims court, Mister. I know all about it. I'da closed him down."

"Christ, kid." I moaned, "Get outa here will ya"

I went back inside, poured myself another cup of coffee, and scanned the front page. There was a story about American Rain on the front page, but I passed over it. Later, I thought. I turned to the sports page and read about the Orioles. I studied the box score and glanced at the batting averages. That kid wouldn't out do me again. I heard the front door open and a voice call "Hello?"

It was Marcy. I sprang from the table and sprinted down the hall. When she saw me coming, she jumped into my arms. We hugged and kissed. I think it was the most natural, uninhibited moment we had ever had. She laughed like a little girl. "God!" I said, "It's good to see you. Where have you been? I tried to call."

"Oh, I figured," she replied. "I've been up in the hills on my grandmother's farm."

"How long?"

"Just a few days."

"Why?"

"To work."

"Let's forget work," I took her by the hand. "Let's make love."

Later she made breakfast as we talked in the kitchen. The April sun filled the room. I felt clean and alive, real again in some distinct way. Her simple movements, the sounds and smells of breakfast cooking made me feel good. "Any luck?" I asked.

". . . Some."

"Just some?"

"For right now," she said. "It will work. Don't worry."

"OK," I said.

"And besides," she went on, "sounds to me like you and Henri have about as much as you can handle on your own hands without worrying about me."

I whistled. "You said a mouthful."

She put a plate of eggs in front me and pulled up a chair. Her eyes sparkled merrily. "So what's the scoop?" she asked. "Bacon?"

"Yes, please. Well, Henri has fled for Nashville in the hopes of laying low for a few days."

"I read no one could find him."

"Well, no one's looking too damn hard, Marcy, because we've been right here all along and there hasn't been a single knock on the door."

"This house isn't in his name," she explained. "It's in yours, remember?"

"Yeah, I guess that's right. Well, anyway, the FBI leaked their report on Henri to the press after he committed to becoming a senator. It's been all downhill from there. Ian Stanforth has sued him on behalf of the entire population of the United States for one hundred billion dollars, and Congress is hot on his trail as well. I got a feeling American Rain is dead as a shot duck. But you know what?"

"What?"

"I don't think he gives a hoot."

"Be serious!" she cried.

I put up my right hand. "As I live and breathe, I swear it's the truth. I took him to the airport the other night and all he cared about—I could tell—was going to see Molly. The money didn't faze him at all."

"Grow up, Donny."

I tilted my head. "I was there, Marcy. I saw it. People do change, you know."

"Even if I saw it with my own eyes, I don't think I'd believe it, Donny."

"Well, we'll find out one way or another pretty soon," I said. "All of this heat is going to cause some serious problems."

Just then the phone rang. Reluctantly I answered. "Yeah?"

It was Henri. "Donny!" he cried. He sounded desperate.

AMERICAN RAIN

"Calm down. What's the problem?"

"You seen the morning paper?"

"Well, sorta" I said. "But not the whole thing."

"Look at it, pinhead! For Christ's sake! I'm being taken down by the jerks in that Congress of ours, and you're up there playing with yourself."

I grabbed the paper and looked at the front page. "This thing here about American Rain? Let's see, it says Congress is about to cut off all further funding and seek a freeze on current accounts until a complete audit has been made of all funds and a full explanation offered to the American people . . . Ah, oh."

"'Ah oh,' he says," chided Henri. "You know now what we have to do? What any honorable, prudent person would do in the same situation."

"Wait a second here," I said, not exactly believing my ears. "You mean admit to everything, throw open the doors to public examination, and trust in the American public's enormous capacity for forgiveness?"

He almost gagged. "Hell no! Have you lost your mind altogether? I mean move every single dime as fast as we can to Switzerland and liquidate everything else. Destroy the books, fire all the employees, torch the office."

"Wait a second here," I responded. "Just hold on a minute. You expect me to do all of that? You're out of your mind. I'll move the dough; the rest is up to you. But, hey, we don't even have any Swiss accounts . . ."

"I'm working on that," he said. "But Crowntooth says we don't have much time. Early Monday at the latest."

"Well, then we're finished," I said. "There ain't no way."

"Cram that negative yap," he insisted. "I still got plenty of folks on the payroll. And you know what they say: Where there's a bill, there's a way. Plus don't forget, until Monday A.M., I'm still loaded."

"Call me when you have an account number," I said, "and I'll see what I can get started from this end."

He hung up.

Marcy smiled. "Changed, huh?"

I tried all weekend, but it was no use. I reached several bank presidents, but none would make a move. The GAO was already on the scene along with the FBI, and although there was no official hold on the accounts, the banks and other financial institutions were terrified to do anything out of the ordinary. They wouldn't move a plug nickel, let alone a few hundred million.

First thing Monday morning, I tried again, but this time got the official sentence. Until further notice, all our accounts were frozen by order of Congress under supervision of the FBI. That was it. American Rain was finished. A short but sweet life.

I turned off the monitors in my office and let the staff go. We didn't even have enough cash around to meet the payroll. We were wiped out. I should have been happy, relieved at least, but I wasn't. I was miserable.

Marcy was with me. She stood at the window and looked out over the city. "It's beautiful from here," she murmured. "See the way the light hits the marketplace down there, the sharpness of the angles, the richness of the color?"

I went to her. "You know," I admitted, "I'd never noticed that before."

She held me close. "You care about him and that's OK. I think it's crazy, but I understand. You know what?"

"What?"

"I feel like painting again."

I smiled and looked out over the city. It's funny, I thought, how you never really know just what you think or feel—what you are, for that matter—until something unexpected comes along and makes you really look at yourself. The results can be strange and unexpected. I hugged her. "I don't honestly know what I feel right now," I said. "But I do know this—it's not good."

21

Later that morning, David Winthrop dropped by the office. I was packing my things. He stood by the window and observed casually over his shoulder: "Representative government is an odd and oft-times exciting thing, is it not, Dr. Mallory? One thing on paper, something else altogether in practice." He and Marcy were enjoying the view.

"Judging from my own experience over the last few months," I replied, "it would seem to be nothing but a whirlwind of petty, niggling, deceitful, competing interests," I said. "And that's when it's working, which is not too often."

I returned to my desk and continued packing. He followed me back. Marcy remained behind at the window.

He chuckled. "Well, from my somewhat limited experience, I would have to say you describe it very well. And the upshot of all this is I hardly know whether to thank you profusely or curse you to your grave for helping me gain this appointment to the Senate."

I laughed. "That much fun, eh?"

He sat down and crossed his legs. "Well, it's just the governor gave me such a robust buildup prior to Dr. Lafayette's present . . . ah . . . difficulties that I fear it may be near impossible to ever live up to it. I'm afraid my constituents are expecting some sort of knight in shining armor. That I am not."

I tossed the picture of my mother and father into the open attache case. Then the pen and pencil set. "You'll be effective," I said. "You know how to get things done. Some people never figure that out."

"Oh sure," he replied, fiddling nervously with his fingers, "I can run a modest hardware store or a small, neighborhood organization. I can do wonders when I'm entirely in charge, when the methods are simple, and the goals specific. The community group had such ridiculously meager resources, in fact, that we had to limit our objectives to things we knew we could do. Understand what I'm saying? We never messed with anything grand or intricate because we knew before we started it would be hopeless. We had no resources. But in the Senate . . . ?"

Marcy turned to face us. "You have all the resources you could ever imagine, but you don't know where to start."

He threw his hands in the air. "Exactly!"

"I understand," she said. "It's just like having all the time in the world to do something. For some reason, it just never gets done."

David Winthrop clapped his hands. "That's the truth. Enormous money, power, and resources can render you virtually impotent. I would never have believed it if I hadn't experienced it myself."

I stopped packing. "Come again?"

He stood and began to pace. "Look, enormous resources do not mean unlimited resources. Yet everyone

I talk to expects their problems and priorities to be addressed and—let's face it, folks—not every problem can be solved by the government, even if we had the resources. And we don't!"

I understood what he was driving at. "So you wind up having to move funds from achievable programs to wish lists just to suit the politics of the day." I folded away my extra tie. "Soon the funds are spread so thin nothing gets accomplished. All you do is end up stroking some sensitive egos—which you quickly learn to do—because if you don't, you get oh-so-quickly buried in the unctuous din of orchestrated outrage."

He stopped in his tracks. "Yes, Dr. Mallory," he said. "Why, there have been times when I have honestly wondered if the people I was talking to weren't far more interested in making sure all the available resources were dished out in some perfectly representative mix than in actually accomplishing anything."

"So you tell somebody to kiss off," Marcy suggested. "God knows, it needs to be done."

"I wish I could, but that's easier said than done. It's frustrating because it's almost as if they don't want me to work. I think they'd prefer I pose at working instead. Just give them a steady diet of this witless vision of constant movement and energy that passes for political action these days and everyone will be perfectly satisfied. I'm not sure . . ."

"Oh I don't know," Marcy interrupted. "I don't really think it's all so new. I think it's just the same old thing, the difference between leadership and pandering." She smiled coyly. "And you're not one to pander, Mr Winthrop. Are you?"

"No, I'm not. You're right, of course. It's really very simple. It's the difference between knowing and doing. And it all boils down to confidence, doesn't it? The confidence to do what I've talked about doing for years." He put his hands in his pockets. "But it should be fun no matter what, eh, folks?" He turned to me. "And what about you and Dr. Lafayette, Dr. Mallory? These newspaper articles I've seen are very disturbing. What in the world is going on?"

I slumped into my chair. "They're all true," I said. "Every word of it."

"My God," he exclaimed, leaning forward eagerly, "you mean to tell me that you and Dr. Lafayette actually created this . . . this machine, this money engine that created cash from rainfall?"

"Yes."

"Wow!

I threw the last few items from my desk into the case and snapped it shut. "It was his baby, all right, but I helped him every step of the way. I knew what I was doing. I'll take my share of the blame."

"Blame! What blame?" He laughed uproariously. "From what I've read, the whole thing was legal. At least in a strict sense. I may not agree entirely with your priorities, Dr. Mallory, but this scheme of yours does have a certain internal elegance to it. Money from rain." He laughed again. "Why, just to conjure up such an intrigue staggers the imagination. But to pull it *off* . . ."

I laughed out loud for the first time in days and it felt wonderful. I slapped the desk. "You know, you're right. That fat bastard, Henri Lafayette, is a piece of work, isn't he? Look around. For what it's worth, what we achieved here was some sort of capitalistic ideal. Money from rain. I doubt it will ever be done again."

David Winthrop eyed the batteries of monitors and switches that stared at us mutely from all sides, the rich leather, the mahogany. "Certainly not with quite the panache," he agreed.

283

I looked at Marcy. "Well, where do we go from here?"

"How about lunch?" David invited before she could summon an answer. "We can go and pretend to forget our difficulties for an hour or so."

"Sounds good," I said.

"I'm starved," agreed Marcy.

We slipped out the back door of American Rain in order to avoid any snooping reporters and took the elevator to the ground floor. Outside it was clear and blue. A warm breeze played on the side streets, rippling the water in the harbor. The sunshine was invigorating. We decided to walk down to the water and find an outdoor cafe.

The inner harbor was crowded with smiling people. It was a beautiful day to be out and alive. We found a restaurant near the water and sat on the patio in the sun. We ordered drinks and toasted success (whatever that was). The gin worked to relax me slightly. When David excused himself to go make a phone call, I glanced at Marcy. She looked beautiful in the first blush of spring warmth, her hair gently tossing in the breeze. "Going back?" I asked her.

". . . I guess," she replied.

"Why? You're not getting anywhere."

"Who said that?" she asked stiffly.

"You did. All that about too much time to accomplish anything."

Her eyes flashed. "That wasn't about me."

"Like hell it wasn't."

Just then David returned. "Sorry, folks," he said, "but I'm afraid I'm going to have to run. The new office and all, you know. I do apologize, and lunch is on me."

"Forget it," I said.

"Dr. Mallory," he was suddenly very serious, "I want you to know that there may be some rough sledding ahead for you and Dr. Lafayette. I'm new at all of this, but the scuttlebutt I get on the Hill is some powerful people have been embarrassed by this entire American Rain episode. They'll be looking to come down very hard on someone in the hopes of saving face. I want you to know I will do anything within my power to help you both. You helped us when no one else would and that counts for a lot with me."

"Thanks. I guess we'll just have to wait and see."

We exchanged goodbyes and he left. Lunch came. We ate slowly and watched the flags ripple on the ships nearby. We made small talk.

Finally she placed her fork on the edge of her plate and looked at me. "I'm scared for you."

I shrugged my shoulders.

"Don't just do that," she said angrily. "You can't just sit there. This could be serious, Donny. You heard what he said."

"Well, I don't think they're after me as much as they are Henri," I responded, thinking hard. "After all, I'm just an employee."

She rolled her eyes sarcastically. "Yeah, well, suppose they don't see it that way? You're vice president, aren't you?" she asked pointedly. "You are the one flying around making all the deals, right? You speak for the company. I mean, it's not as if you were up there sweeping the floors at night."

I swallowed hard. "Yeah, but the whole thing is a double-edged sword, Marcy. That's what I'm counting on."

"How so?"

"Half the governmental big shots who are shooting their mouths off to the press have a lot to lose if Henri gets up before a congressional hearing and starts singing. He paid off so many of them that squeezing him too hard is going to make them bleed as well. And don't think they don't know it. That's why I suspect the whole thing is going to be a lot more thunder than it is lightning."

"You hope," she snapped. "You'd just better pray that someone Henri didn't bribe doesn't try to ride his way to prominence over the political corpses of his colleagues. Someone clean could make the whole lot of them look awfully sorry. It could happen, you know."

"Anything could happen," I agreed. I moved closer to her. "I'll admit I'm scared. Principally because of how stupid I was."

She touched my arm gently. "Oh, Donny, you were just trying to help. You're a soft touch is all."

"Not just that," I said.

"What?"

"Us."

She looked down. "I feel awful," she whispered.

I was surprised. "Why?"

She shook her head. "Because it's my fault. We could have been together. It could have been different, except I had to . . ."

"No," I objected, "don't go blaming yourself. Look, something profound has finally dawned on me over the past few weeks. It's so clear and simple I swear an idiot could have seen it, but I didn't."

"What?"

"I love you," I told her. "You are all that really matters to me. Everything else is trivial. Will you marry me?"

She squeezed my arm. "Yes!"

"When?"

"I don't know," she said, fumbling for a tissue to wipe her eyes. "I mean, whenever you want."

I threw my head back and laughed. I felt fantastic. "I do love you. Look at us, we're both the same."

She smiled. "It's just that I wanted so much. I've always wanted too much, I guess. I want to paint, be free, in love, and in Frederick."

I hugged her. "And it just don't work that way, Honey. We're both the same. We tried to press love into an odd space, a hole in a puzzle it was never meant to fill. Love is something you just have to go with—a hot, rushing blast of wind that yanks you right off the ground and sends you soaring. From high above, everything else looks small and totally beside the point. Love becomes everything, all heat and compulsion."

"But we tried to dress it up in tailored clothes," I went on, "teach it manners, and make it wait politely on the veranda for us while we went about our business. Won't work. We kept hammering away at our lives, trying to make them conform to some preconceived pattern like, oh . . . I don't know, Marxists or zealots of some stripe, furious and bewildered at a world which refuses to bend. Marcy, I see people like that around me all the time. I just never realized I was one of them."

Just then the waiter approached our table. He handed me a small, folded note. "From the gentleman at the far table," he said, pointing beyond the terrace.

I looked up to see Dr. Myron Wilmer sitting across the way. He saluted crisply with a pair of sunglasses. "Oh no," I moaned.

"What?" Marcy said, touching my sleeve lightly.

I unfolded the note:

> A moment of your time?
> M. Wilmer

I crumpled it into a ball. "Dr. Wilmer," I said to Marcy, nodding toward his table. I frowned. "The guy has a virtual instinct for bad timing. I told you about him."

"The physicist?"

"The nut." I patted her hand. "I'll just be a second."

I stood and motioned toward the patio rail. He met me with a highball glass in his hand. "So sorry about the intrusion," he apologized. "I always seem to be doing that, don't I? But then, that is the real nature of the universe is it not, Dr. Mallory? Randomness, collisions, and all sorts of unexpected intrusions."

"Don't worry about it," I answered curtly. "What's up?"

"Well, it has been virtually impossible to reach you lately, what with all this American Rain nonsense going on, and I did want to let you know I'm gaining enormously in confidence." He held up a hand. "I know, I know," he went on quickly, "you don't have to say it. You think I'm crazy. But I want you to be informed. After all, you have the inside track on my entire story. And when a world renowned atomic physicists disappears one day from the face of the earth without even a trace, there will be some hard questions asked, I'm sure. I'm counting on you to supply an answer or two. To give my side."

I glanced back at Marcy and gave her a little wave. "Yeah, sure, OK," I said.

"Well, I can see I've caught you at a bad time," he said and turned to walk away.

I grabbed him quickly by the arm. "No, that's all right. Go on."

"If you insist. It seems I'm very much nearing my time."

"Time for what?"

"Why, to soar!" he cried. "To move from one focus of realization to another." He tapped his foot. "Aren't you listening?"

"Oh, yeah, yeah," I said, stuffing my hands into my pockets, "that's right."

He took a sip from his drink, set himself firmly before me again, and continued. "The other day, Friday to be precise, I was overcome by the most intense feeling of wonder and serenity imaginable, Dr. Mallory. I could actually feel myself slipping away, and this time it was not at all frightening like before. It was actually exciting and, well, pleasurable beyond measure. But I pulled back. You see, for a number of reasons, I'm not quite ready to go just yet. Soon though."

"That's real good," I quickly replied, anxious to avoid another dose of Wilmer's metaphysical gibberish and get back to Marcy. "Give me a call when you get there."

He chuckled. "Still the doubting Thomas, I see," he said. "That's all right, of course. I would be too if the shoe were on the other foot. Anyway, Ms. Lawson and I will be vacationing for a few weeks away from the area and I wanted you to know."

"Why?"

"Just in case."

"In case you beat it for the other side?" I asked.

"Yes, exactly." He stuffed another note into my pocket. "That's the address and phone number for her sister's beach house in Atlantic City. My notes, diaries, and mathematical conjectures will all be left there to your attention. I intend to keep working right up to the end. Please promise me you will come get them."

"Fine, yeah," I said, then added more softly so no one else could hear, "when you disappear from the planet in a little white puff, I'll drive up and get your stuff. I promise."

"Fine, fine," he said, slapping me on the back. "Can I buy you and your lady a drink?"

"We're OK. So you're going up to the beach for a little sun and relaxation to calm the nerves?"

"No. I can't stand the beach and the sun. The timeless sea, the endless pounding of the surf, the countless particles of sand all scream infinity at me with a capital 'I' and tend to bring me down emotionally to low ebb. Actually, I'm going for the gambling, booze, and sex."

"Well, enjoy yourself," I said, "and look me up when you get back."

"I'll do that," he replied, suddenly serious. "And if I don't make it back, remember two things: I went with the stars in my eyes, and you promised."

"I'll remember," I assured him.

We shook hands, and I went back to Marcy.

"Well?" she asked curiously.

"He thinks he may be heading off to another focus of realization soon," I explained, trying hard not to break out laughing. "Wants me to pick up his notes and tidy up after he's gone."

She shook her head in sympathy. "Oh, God. Poor guy."

"Anyway," I continued, putting my arm around her, "if I recall correctly, we were talking about us just before we were so rudely interrupted."

"Is your offer still good?"

"You bet it is."

She kissed me gently. "Well, so is the answer then."

"So, want to set a date?"

"I don't know," she replied. "Everything is so up in the air, you know?"

"What do you mean, up in the air?"

"You said yourself you were scared. Who know's where all this American Rain stuff is leading. You could be in real trouble, Donny."

"Oh, come on," I scoffed.

"No, I'm serious," she insisted. "You just blow everything off, but you don't know. Those people can be vicious, and you're just the kind of person they'd like to pin it all on. Don't forget, you're the one who said Henri has a talent for landing on his feet. But you have a talent for falling flat on your face."

"That's ridiculous!"

"I'm not so sure. Look, I just worry about you— because you won't. Who knows, someday maybe a bunch of police officers like those big men over there," she said, pointing to a group of cops, "will come looking for you. Then how smart will you feel?"

"Oh, Marcy! You've lost all perspective here. The police, like those guys coming this way, are not in the business of bothering honest citizens out for a simple bite to eat. You see," I went on knowingly, "ours is a nation of laws, not of men. And in a nation of laws, things like that do not happen. They can't happen. They are probably just . . ."

The officers circled our table. A very large lieutenant stepped forward. "Mr. Donald Mallory?"

"Ye-ye-yes," I stuttered.

"Come along with us please."

"Wh-wh-why?"

He grew impatient. "Just come along with us please."

I pointed to Marcy. "I-I-I'm here with . . ."

"We'll see that the lady gets home. Sir?"

I stood slowly. "D-d-do you have some sort of warrant or other?" I asked.

"Just come along now, Mr. Mallory. Don't be foolish and resist. We're just obeying our orders."

Marcy was in shock. She started to cry.

I swallowed hard. "Well, I guess if I have to."

"You have to," the lieutenant replied sternly.

Two large officers stepped forward and grabbed me by the elbows.

"Donny!" Marcy screamed.

They led me slowly out of the restaurant as stunned onlookers gaped open-mouthed at our procession. "I . . . I . . . I . . ." I stammered, as Marcy's cry rang again and again in my ears.

22

"You!" I screamed, "you did this?"

I had been dragged to a motel room off the beltway near Towson. Henri was sitting on the bed, munching away on a large cheese tray he had carefully positioned across his outstretched legs. He took a long pull on a glass of wine. "Calm *down*," he said. "Don't go acting all hysterical."

"Hysterical!" I yelled. "You have these goons virtually *kidnap* me from my lover's side, haul me across town to some cheap lay-for-pay motel, and I'm supposed to be happy as a clam? Here I didn't know if I was going to be shot and stuffed into the trunk of a late model Chevrolet or what, and you're sitting on the bed stuffing your face, gulping wine, and telling me not to be hysterical. You have your gall."

He wrapped his lips around an enormous slice of Gouda, devoured it in five chews, and swallowed the lump with a horrible slurping noise. "I've been accused of worse," he said. "Besides, they were under strict orders not to break any bones."

"Oh, that's gratifying!" I said. "And Marcy?"

"She's fine. They took her back to the house."

I put my hands on my hips. "Well, just what the hell is this all about? Why did you drag me here?"

"The winds of discontent are swirling about me."

"The winds of discontent have been swirling about you like a hurricane since you were sixteen," I said. "What's new?"

He laughed, cut himself a slab of Swiss, and continued. "That's true," he admitted, "but these winds blow from a profoundly more sinister source. In short, lunkhead, I'm presently concerned that my ass might just be grass in these climes."

"So why the motel and the goons?"

"For the time being, this will serve as our bunker. Nobody knows I'm in town or of my present whereabouts and I'd like to keep it that way just as long as possible. I'm also trying to find out who's with me and who's not. Apparently the local police still are. And you?"

"Of course," I said. "I'm in it just as deep as you, you know."

"We'll see," he said. "Anyway, Crowntooth is due here shortly. We need to put all our ducks in a row if we're going to salvage this thing. How much money do we have?"

"Millions," I said, "but we can't touch a dime of it. The question is how much money do we have access to. And the answer to that is zero."

"They shut us down completely?"

"Tight as a drum," I said. "I tried over the weekend to get someone to move some cash for us, but the heat was really on and nobody would touch it."

"There's still some," he said.

"Where?" I asked. "None that I've seen or invested."

"That's right, numbskull. I had some iced a long time ago. Just in case."

"Where?"

"Never mind. It's there. The green from the sale of the practice to Ian Stanforth. It's salted away. A little over two million."

"So what's the plan?"

"Same plan as always," he said. "We'll buy our way out."

"I got you," I said. "So that's why Crowntooth is on his way."

"Bingo."

Buck Crowntooth tapped lightly on the motel room door. The large lieutenant identified him through the peep hole, then opened up. Buck, sporting large sunglasses and low hung fedora, entered the room. He glanced around, then slowly removed his camouflage. "This here's wonderfully American," he said. "Like the movies or in the books, you know, fellas? Wonderful. American! Wha-da-ya-say there, Henri?"

"A pleasure as always, Senator."

"Vacationing I see."

"In a sense," said Henri. "Care for some imported cheese?"

"Love to," said Crowntooth, stabbing a piece of cheese with a toothpick and leaning back in a chair. "So what's up, boys?"

Henri set the tray aside and stood up. "It would appear from a brief glimpse of the papers, Buck, that American Rain has hit a small, shall we say, snag."

Clayton finished his cheese, smacked his lips, and looked cautiously at Henri. "You could say that, Henri. Yes, I believe that would be entirely accurate."

"And, of course," Henri continued, "if I should happen to befall a scandalous fate at the hands of Congress, you would not be far behind."

"Oh?" Buck said, curiously. "How do you figure?"

295

"Well, Buck, it certainly isn't difficult to envision my breaking down completely under the pressure of a congressional investigation or, worse yet, a full-scale hearing. Under those circumstances, it would be entirely likely that I would spill my guts to the American public about all the graft I'd been involved in. You know, all the payouts, the payoffs, and the influence peddling . . . Now, let me think. You're in there somewhere, aren't you, Buck?"

"Not at all, Henri!" Clayton protested. "Why, it's damn near indefensible just bringing my name up in the same sentence with those other naughty words you used. I'm offended!"

"Well, there you go," Henri said, shaking his head. "My memory has been so traumatized by the events of the last couple of days, I'm afraid I'm working on only a few cylinders, Buck. I'd probably just have to open all my records to the committee and let them draw their own conclusions. That way innocent folks like yourself would be spared any undue embarrassment."

Buck's eyes grew very large. "I couldn't let that happen to you, Henri. You're just too good a friend. And you, too, Donald. Why, I wouldn't be able to sleep at night knowing fine Americans like yourselves were being victimized by a pack of political hooligans. No! It's just entirely undemocratic and I won't stand for it! Call me wild, call me idealistic, call me nothing but a crazy old defender of the underdog, but I, Clayton "Buck" Crowntooth, will fight for you boys right up to my last dying breath. I'll throw my aged carcass in front of horses hooves if I have to, fight them physically with my bare knuckles up and down the stairways of Congress, proclaim with my last breath of freedom's sweet air your innocence, my friends!"

"What's the price tag?" asked Henri.

"Three million."

"Three million," Henri gasped. "That's fucking extortion. Out of the question."

"I'm sad to hear that," answered Buck. "And here I was all set to do the right thing, to man freedom's battlements once again. Won't you reconsider?"

"I ain't got three million," spat Henri. "Make it two."

Buck put his hand over his heart. "If it was up to me, Henri, I'd gladly give it to you for two million, but I'm afraid it's not. There are others to consider. You just have to realize that decency of the stripe you're trying to acquire comes at a pretty steep price."

"Steep is right," Henri replied. "Two and a half and you got yourself a deal."

"No can do."

"What is this crap?" howled Henri. "Two and three-quarters, and that's it. Take it or leave it, Buck!"

"I'll take it then," said Buck, smiling warmly. He slapped Henri on the back. "You're a fine man, Henri," he said. "A fine and noble American. Now where's the dough?"

"I got it, I got it already, Buck!" wailed Henri, "but it ain't here right now."

"Oh, Bucky doesn't like to hear that, Henri. Timetable?"

"Forty-eight hours. Sixty, tops. I just gotta move some things around is all."

Buck frowned. "Time is very short on this, boys. Only because the two of you are such good friends of mine and known to be of upstanding character will I take it upon myself to prevail upon the powers-that-be to accept your offer. Forty-eight hours, Henri. Not one second more."

"That's very decent of you, Clayton," snapped Henri.

"No thanks necessary, Henri. I believe in decency."

I showed Buck to the door. "You'll be hearing from us," I said. I turned and slumped against the wall. "You said you have only a little over two million," I said. "So where do we get the rest?"

Henri fidgeted nervously. "Call Kiddo Kenny London," he said. "We got to think."

"Wiped out!" exclaimed Kiddo Kenny. "What do you mean, wiped out?"

I explained the situation.

"And my cut? What's my percentage?"

Henri raced across the room, knocked Kiddo to the floor, and commenced choking him to death as Kenny gargled and spat vainly in protest.

"Grab a hold here!" I screamed to the large lieutenant, and together we managed to drag Kiddo free of Henri as the two struggled furiously on the carpet.

"S-s-so, what you're saying," stuttered Kiddo, yanking his collar open for air, "is that my bank account is dog meat."

Henri was sweating and drooling excessively. He looked like a lunatic. "Listen to this guy," he screamed, pointing to Kiddo. "I'm out billions, about to be drug before a congressional committee, and this ingrate is whining about his freaking bank account. Kill him! Kill him, Donny!"

"Just shut up," I snapped. I went to Kiddo Kenny and helped him to his feet. I dusted him off. "Kiddo, I have to say this. You are without question the most unbelievably one dimensional human being I have encountered. Tell me," I asked, "what did you see when Henri was close to murdering you just then? Did your life flash before your eyes?"

"Yeah, kinda," he replied, straightening his suit. "I seen the big board in New York go blinking out very slowly and I . . ."

"*I*," I said loudly, "is your problem, Kenny. It's nothing but I this and I that. Try and get this through your head: We're all in trouble. Get it? All!"

"OK, OK," Kenny intoned, massaging his neck, "I get the picture, Donny baby. Our cash flow snapshot is momentarily blue."

"Yah!" Henri wailed. Then he leaped to his feet, grabbed a lamp from the night stand, and lofted it overhead like a truncheon. "I'll add a little black to that blue for you, Kenny. How'd you like me to introduce this lamp to your brainpan, you stinking maggot!"

"Put it down," I screamed at him. "That won't accomplish a blessed thing. We have to try and put our heads together, not split them wide open."

"I really resent the names you called me, Henri," whined Kenny.

"Look," I said, "the two of you can just calm down. OK? Kenny, I'm going to come straight to the point. We need to borrow some cash from you for a week or two. Say, a million."

"Nothing," replied Kiddo Kenny.

Henri turned scarlet. His face furrowed. He pointed at Kenny. "Wha-da-ya mean *nothing*, dead meat?"

"I mean I got *nothing* for ya, thunder thighs," shouted Kiddo, little eyes beading menacingly. He cupped his hands around his mouth and spelled it out. "N-O-T-H-I-N-G!"

I put my hand on Henri's chest to hold him off and tried reasoning with him. "Kenny," I said, "think. You've made millions off us. We're just asking for a loan to see us through a little lean period here."

"You don't understand too good, Donny baby," he answered. "I got nothing to give you."

"What the hell is that supposed to mean?" snapped Henri.

"All my green was in your accounts," Kenny said. "When they shut you down, they shut me down, too."

"What are you talking about?" I demanded

"Well, you guys had that computerized system which was unbeatable. Day and night, night and day—bing, bang, bong—the thing never stopped cranking out winners. At first I tried, but it was useless. So why try? Why bust your buns for a better margin when the machine did everything from zip to zap better than me every time—and in seconds on top of that. Hell, I quit trying months ago. I just left my money in with yours, let it ride on automatic pilot, and headed for the golf course. Didn't you know?"

I threw my hands into the air. "Well, that's that," I said, turning to Henri. "Got any ideas?"

He slowly lowered the lamp and placed it back on the night stand. "So what's hot, Kenny?" he asked. "Huh? What looks good?"

Kenny shrugged vacantly. "Beats me," he said. "Hell, I ain't looked at the board in months. No reason to."

Henri's lips puckered as if he had sucked on a particularly ornery lemon. "You mean to tell me I have been paying you that obscene percentage of yours for doing absolutely nothing? Millions for GOLF! For practicing little wedge shots!"

"Hey!" cried Kenny, "It ain't like I was stealing or something. It's mine, you know. That's right. I'm part of the process, see? I get my cut because I'm there, because that's the way it works."

"When this is over, London," Henri threatened wildly, "when I got the time to do it right, I'm gonna' feed your face to the paper shredder, make linguine with your sorry puss, and then personally feed it to the vultures."

"Ah, stick it, Dumbo!"

"Arghhhhhhh!"

"All right!" I yelled, "this is getting us nowhere. We have to think. We need to come up with something that will work. Kiddo, do you have that little lap-top computer of yours?"

"Yeah, but I don't know how current any of it . . ."

"Just get it out!" Henri wailed.

Kenny set his small computer on the edge of the bed. "I really don't trust too much of the gunk that's in here," he said, cranking it up. "It ain't been updated in quite awhile."

"Forget the stocks then," I said. "Is anything in there current?"

Kenny shrugged.

Suddenly a light went off in my head. "Hey!" I exclaimed, "how about that horse? . . . What was his name?"

Henri looked at me questioningly. "You mean House of Cards?"

"Yeah."

Henri scowled. "That's pushing our luck, don't you think?"

"Got a better idea?" I asked.

"Three times in a row is just too much to ask," Henri argued. "It's pushing good luck to the limits." He turned to Kiddo. "What do you think, London?"

Kenny squinched up his face. "I don't know," he said. "He ain't a bad mount, I'll have to admit. He runs well, and we won't have to post outrageous odds this time around to pull our butts out of the fire."

I was excited. "Where's he running?"

301

"Well," Kenny said, "we're lucky because I still been dabbling in the ponies, so the computer is up to snuff in that department. Let me see." He began popping the keys and little green lines started peppering up all across the screen. "Here we go. House of Cards should be running at Monmouth Race Track tomorrow and later in the week. Fella by the name of Schubert is scheduled to be the jock."

I rubbed my hands together. "That horse has been damned good to us, Henri."

"Yeah, but I feel bad about him this time for some reason."

Kenny hit a few more buttons. "OK," he said as a string of numbers blipped to life across the screen, "here it is. House of Cards is running in the fourth race tomorrow at Monmouth all right. Odds? . . . Ah, here it comes. Two to one."

Henri peered carefully over Kenny's shoulder. "Who's he running against?"

Kiddo pushed a few more buttons. Blips came and went. "Here's the field, Henri: Gin Man, Shucker's Blues, Ernie's Lady, Savage Salvage . . ."

Henri clapped. "They're all broken-down nags," he said, beaming from ear to ear. "Not a one of 'em can run. This is easy pickings." He turned to me. "Donny," he said, "I got to hand it to you, this time you hit the nail on the head."

"Hot damn!" I shouted. "Let's do it!"

"Kiddo," Henri said, "let's lay it clean, OK? Two mil to win?"

Kenny spun around to face us. "Big problem."

"What?" I asked.

Kenny frowned and shook his head. "Ain't a book on the planet would touch our money right now," he explained. "The Feds would be all over them in seconds and they know it. We're hot stuff, boys. We're the kiss of death."

"How 'bout the phone?" Henri suggested.

"Not a prayer. I'm dog meat," Kenny continued, "you're dog meat, and so's the kid. No, the bet's gotta' be laid in person and by someone no one knows. Somebody who's absolutely clean."

"Oh no!" Henri wailed. "I don't know anyone who's clean. Never have! You, Kenny?"

"Not a chance," Kenny admitted. "Not to mention someone who can get to New Jersey in twenty-four hours."

"Wait a second," I said, "I think I may know someone."

Henri lit up like a Fourth of July sparkler. "You do? Someone clean, Donny? Someone we can trust with two million clams?"

"Kinda," I said. "And he's probably in New Jersey right now."

"Oh great!" cried Henri. "Wonderful! Who is it?"

"Dr. Myron Wilmer."

The look that wrenched Henri's face could best be described as one of absolute agony. His nostrils flared and his ears began to waggle. Sweat covered his face, his eyes rolled back into his head, and he flopped backward onto the bed like death itself.

"What? What?" cried Kiddo Kenny. "Wha'd I miss here?"

"Dr. Myron Wilmer," I repeated.

Henri quickly propped himself back up on one elbow. "Do you mean to tell me you would entrust our wellbeing to that schizophrenic sack of Swiss cheese? Are you *completely* out of your mind?"

"What's wrong with this sucker?" asked Kenny.

"Look, all right," I said, "so he's not entirely certain that he actually exists. At least here, see, in this dimension. But I know he can handle this."

Kenny looked sideways at Henri.

I tossed a hand in the air. "OK," I said. "Go ahead, laugh all you want. But do either of you have another name? He's down there right now, by the way. In Atlantic City. He's our only chance, as I see it—like him or not."

Henri sat up and sighed. "Tell me," he asked, "does he know how to lay a bet down?"

"Of course not," I replied. "But what's the big deal? Kiddo can give him written instructions, and we can set the whole thing up by phone from this end. We'll just use his name."

Kenny stroked his chin thoughtfully. "Might work," he observed. "We lay the groundwork and all the stiff does is deliver the coin and keep his yap shut. Just may fly."

Henri covered his face and whimpered like a baby. "So it's come to this," he moaned. "My entire fortune, a life's work, now rides on a fuzz ball like Myron Wilmer." He beseeched his Lord. "Oh God in heaven," he cried, "why are you so cruel? What has your boy done to deserve such a nimble backhand?" He shook his head mournfully from side to side. "I don't like it at all," he said, "but if we got to, we got to." He looked at me. "How do we get a hold of this lunatic?"

I dug into my pocket. "Got his number right here" I said. "Let's give it a whirl."

I reached for the phone and dialed the number. Ms. Lawson answered. I tried to sound officious. "Dr. Donald Mallory calling for Dr. Myron Wilmer." In a moment, he came to the phone.

"Well, Dr. Mallory, my condition remains unchanged at present," he said, "but thank you so much for your concern."

"My what?"

"Concern . . . your."

"Oh . . . y-yeah," I stuttered. "That's good to hear. Yeah, wow, what a relief."

"Things will be when they will be," he intoned philosophically.

"Ain't that the truth," I replied. "Ah, listen, Doc, since you're feeling so spry, I was sort of wondering if you could do me a small favor?"

"Well, I don't see why not. Some quantum calculations?"

"Not exactly," I said. "More along the lines of laying down a bet on the ponies over at Monmouth."

"My gracious!" he exclaimed. "I've never done that before. You mean with money?"

Henri placed both hands around his own throat, stuck out his tongue, and feigned a horrible death.

I covered the receiver with my hand. "Quit that!" I hissed. "Let's at least give this a fair chance." I returned to Wilmer. "Ah, yeah, Doc. Quite a bit of money, in fact."

"Sounds neat," he said, "but I'm afraid I don't know how."

"That's OK," I answered. "We can walk you through it. Believe me, Myron, it's as easy as pie. We'll tell you where to go, who to see, and what to say."

"Well, I don't see why not. When, Dr. Mallory?"

"Tomorrow. Early. A man will meet you at your place and take you to the track. His name is Kenneth London. He will have the money and explain every little detail to you. Piece of cake, Doc."

"Kenneth London," he repeated. "Fine, I've got that. How much money, by the way?"

"Two million dollars," I said, trying not to let my voice crack.

. . . He whistled. "OK, sounds like fun."

Henri shook his head and wiped tears from his eyes. "That's it," he moaned. "We're finished."

"Talk to you later, Doc."

"Bye-bye."

I hung up.

Henri leaped to his feet and grabbed Kiddo Kenny by the lapels. "Get a train ticket now," he demanded. "Don't go home, don't change your clothes, and don't open those stinking fat lips of yours to anyone until this is over. Understand? Write everything out for this nitwit," he continued. "Hear me? Leave nothing to chance. Take him down to the track and stick an electronic beeper on him so you can track him if he gets lost or tries to high-tail it outa' there with our bread. Check?"

"Check," said Kiddo.

"OK." Henri held out his fist. Kenny put his fist on top and I followed suit. "It's fourth and ninety-nine, gents," he said with feeling, "and we're going for the bomb."

23

I awoke early the next morning to the sound of birds. The window was open and the first splash of sunlight on the far wall caught my eye. I sat up. In all the excitement, I had completely forgotten about Marcy. Bolting out of the bed, I decided to make some coffee and give her a call before the pace of the coming day took over. I carefully tiptoed past Henri's room, crept down the stairs, and quietly made a pot of coffee. Then I sat patiently at the kitchen table as it began to perk.

Henri had slipped into the house in the early morning hours after meeting Kiddo Kenny at Penn Station with the money. I had no idea where he had gotten it, only that he had been gone about two hours, and he had gone somewhere north of town to get it. He saw London off on the train for New York and then returned by cab. Apparently, he had paid the cabby several blocks away, then snuck in the back door after carefully negotiating a number of neighboring backyards. He now slept peacefully upstairs, snoring like a gorilla.

I expected Kenny would call sometime before noon. After that, I guessed, pandemonium would reign. The race was scheduled for two in the afternoon. By then, Henri's blood pressure would be headed for the star system Andromeda. Since a towel capable of absorbing his noxious fumes and abundant perspiration had not yet graced the inventor's table, it would be, I knew, a sticky situation.

When the coffee was done, I poured myself a cup, sipped it for a moment or two, and tried to come alive. The day had a sense of the surreal to it. I needed something concrete. So I grabbed the phone and tried Marcy's number in Frederick.

"Hello?" she answered tiredly on the sixth ring.

"Hey," I said.

"Donny!" she cried. "Where *are* you?"

"Sorry," I replied. "Should have called. I'm at the house. I'm fine."

"Oh Lord, I was so scared. I thought you were in jail or . . . worse."

"It was Henri. Can you believe it? He had me picked up."

"That creep. Why?"

"To see if the police were still on his team. Plus," I continued, "he has to lay low. Agents, cops, reporters, and bankers are looking for him everywhere. Anyway, it looks like things will come to a head this afternoon."

"Why?"

I quickly explained the situation. "So if the horse comes in, we'll all be off the hook."

"And if it doesn't?" she wanted to know.

"We're sunk. But one way or the other, I'll be up to see you tonight. We're still on, aren't we?"

"You bet."

No sooner had I hung up the receiver than the phone rang. I grabbed it on the first ring. "Hello."

"Yes or no?" It was a man's voice.

"What do you mean, yes or no?" I asked, perplexed.

"Yes or no?"

"Who is this?" I demanded angrily.
"Buck Crowntooth. Yes or no?"
"Yes or no what, Buck?"
"You got the money or don't you?"
I looked menacingly at the receiver. I felt like slamming it into the wall and denting his hearing for the next few months, but I didn't dare—too much to lose.
"Not yet, Senator," I replied, holding my tongue. "Why don't you call back around three or four this afternoon. We should have an answer for you then. Can you handle that?"
"Do bears suck honey?"
"Goodbye," I said.
Henri arose at eleven. He drank coffee and lounged around gloomily in his pajamas until the phone rang. It was almost noon. I scurried down the hall and picked it up. "Yes?" I said.
It was Kiddo Kenny. "Mary had a little lamb . . ."
"Yeah?" I replied. "So what's up Kenny?"
"Mary had a little lamb . . ." he repeated, this time more urgently.
Henri came to my side. "That London?" he asked.
"Yeah."
"You need the coded phrase," he continued. "Tell him, 'whose fleece was white as snow,' and he will answer."
"I'm not saying that," I objected. "It's ridiculous."
"Say it," Henri pleaded. "It's all been arranged."
"No! I'm not going to say that. It's stupid."
Henri grabbed the phone. "Hold on, Kenny!" he yelled into the receiver, "we'll be right with you."
"Now look, Don," he pleaded, "you got to say whose fleece was white as snow. You got to!"
"Ain't got to."

Henri put the phone to his ear again. "It's OK, Kenny," he said, "Donny knows the coded phrase. Just go ahead."

"I ain't squawking till I hear it," Kenny replied.

Henri looked at me menacingly. "He ain't gonna talk till he hears it. Now, tell him!"

"You tell him!" I shot back.

"No, you!"

"You!"

Henri ripped the phone from my fingers and slowly raised it to his ear. ". . . whose fleece was white as snow." he said. Then he shoved the phone into my face.

I answered. "Yeah."

"This is Kenneth London."

I turned to Henri. "It's Kenny."

Henri balled up a fist and shook it at my nose.

"What you got for us, Kenny?" I asked.

"Just checking in. Everything is cool. I met our operative at zero nine hundred hours and made the necessary exchange. We drove his late model Plymouth to the track and had coffee across the street. He understands his mission. Everything is written down for him. No margin for error. The bet is going down at thirteen hundred hours as scheduled in the parking lot with a book by the name of Guido something-or-other. Word is, he's reliable."

"Sounds good, Kenny. We'll be listening to the race. Keep us informed. Any slip-ups, let us know right away."

"Over and out," he said. "Say it, Donny," he insisted. "Over and out."

"No, Kenny. I'm not saying over and out."

"You said it! You just said it!" he screamed.

"You said over and out," Henri confirmed, clapping happily. "He tricked you. Kenny tricked you, all right. I told you the guy's a genius."

"Oh brother," I moaned, slamming down the phone. The race was scheduled for two. There was no television and no local radio. It was broadcast only on a small New Jersey station that we couldn't pick up. We tried the car radio—nothing. The super expensive digital receiver. Nothing. Finally Henri pulled out a vintage 1961 Japanese transistor radio from a dusty sack in the basement and gave it a whirl. We got something fuzzy. "That might be it," I said, fiddling with the knobs. But it would come in and go out, chaotically oscillating between barely audible and nothing at all.

"Wait here," Henri said, racing for the closet. He pulled out a pair of slacks, threw them on the bed, and began twisting the wire hanger this way and that. When he had it broken in half and bent into roughly an antenna-like shape, he shoved the broken end into the appropriate hole in the radio. Masterfully, he lodged it in place with a large, wet wad of bubble gum. "There," he said, stepping back and smiling at his craftsmanship, "give her a try."

I turned it on again and we got the track loud and clear. "Amazing," I conceded.

Ten minutes to post time. We couldn't eat. We sat in the library and propped the radio up on a stack of books. Henri stared nervously at his watch. I turned the radio on.

Again, a high-pitched, nasal voice: ". . . day at Monmouth Race Track this afternoon. The track is in excellent condition for this next race, the famed Jersey Futura, featuring a number of fine horses brought in from across the country. Jack, your thoughts . . ."

"Get on with it!" I bellowed, anxious as all get out.

"Shhhh," Henri said, "I want to hear."

". . . any number of horses that could take this thing, Martin, including the Maryland bred House of Cards who ran so well at Pimlico and up at Belmont earlier this year. Although, personally I like . . ."

"Who cares what this muffin head thinks?" shouted Henri. "Let's get on with the main event."

"It'll come," I said. "And soon enough."

". . . and Gin Man, Martin, is always strong on the pole."

"Right you are, Jack. I see now they're loading the horses into the starting gate, so we are just about ready for the fourth race today, the famed Jersey Futura. Your final pick, Jack?"

"Locomotion, Martin, unless House of Cards can get out early. That horse closes strong, but I don't think Locomotion will give him the chance. Should be a great one, Martin."

"Well, there you have it, folks. We'll be back with the race in just a moment. And now this from our sponsors . . ."

I rubbed my hands together. My heart was pounding. "Well, here we go. Think Kenny got the bet down?"

"He'd call if something had blown," said Henri. "We're in."

I turned the radio up. "Martin Lewis and Jack Brown back to you from Monmouth Race Track, scene of the famed Jersey Futura. The horses are all in the gate, and we're getting the sign. *They're off!* It's Gin Man in the early lead followed by Shucker's Blues, House of Cards, Savage Salvage, Locomotion . . ."

"We're OK," I whispered under my breath.

Henri stood and began to pace. "If we're in the top three at the final turn, it's ours. Damn horse closes like a machine."

AMERICAN RAIN

". . . as we round the first turn, it's still Gin Man, followed immediately now by House of Cards, Shucker's Blues . . ."

"Yeah!" I yelled, clapping once loudly. "Get it!"

". . . and Locomotion moving up strongly on the outside."

Henri began to sweat. He marched to the window, spun, and marched back to the center of the room. "My life's on the line here," he moaned. "My whole life's on the freaking line!"

". . . as they round the far turn, it's Gin Man holding valiantly to the lead as House of Cards comes at him strongly. Behind them both and moving to the rail is Locomotion running free and well now. Shucker's Blues is a length back and starting to fade. Ernie's Lady is on the rail, foll . . . by . . . e . . . o . . . EEEEEE . . . Shucke . . . EEEEE . . ."

"What's that?" Henri asked, turning to the radio.

I sat up quickly. "We're losing it," I said, fiddling furiously with the knobs. "It's fading for some reason."

". . . House o . . . ca . . . EEEEEE . . . comotio . . . Shuck . . ."

"Do something!" Henri pleaded.

"I'm trying!" I said, yanking the hanger this way and that. But nothing worked. I thought quickly. "Let's move it," I cried, picking the radio up and racing into the kitchen. I placed it on the window ledge over the sink, attached the antenna to the screen, and turned it on. ". . . and in the back stretch it's House of Cards running magnificently . . . by a charging . . . EEEEEE . . . EEEEE . . . tion . . . EEEE"

"That's a little better!" Henri coached.

I lurched at the radio, and just as I did, the reception improved dramatically.

313

"That's it!" Henri yelled. "Stand right there, don't move."

I froze.

"What a race, Jack! These two horses are way ahead of the pack now, Locomotion and House of Cards, running a two-horse race, having at each other for all they're worth. As they turn and come at us, it's House of Cards and Locomotion neck and neck, mud flying, people cheering wildly. What a sight! What a race!"

Suddenly, my nose itched terribly. I tried to think it away, but it just got worse. It became a monster itch. I struggled and struggled, but I wasn't man enough. I reached and itched it vigorously.

". . . and as they . . . EEEEEE . . . EEEEE . . ."

"What are you doing?" Henri shrieked. "Look what you've done."

I tried to regain my position again, but in moving too quickly, I lost my balance and stepped forward two—or was it three?—steps.

"Come *on*!" Henri yelled. "That's not where you were."

"I'm trying!" I screamed, stepping here and there, desperately trying to relocate myself. In my frenzy, I slipped, hit the table with my leg, and nearly broke my neck.

". . . as they round the club house turn, it's still House of Cards and Locomotion—flying around the track, neck and neck, in one of the greatest races this announcer has ever called. . . . It's . . ."

"Don't move!" Henri ordered. "We've got it back."

"You can't be serious!" I screamed at him. My leg was twisted behind me at an impossible angle. I could hardly stand.

"Hold it! Just hold it a few more seconds!"

I bit my lip.

AMERICAN RAIN

"... House of Cards and Locomotion. No, Locomotion and House of Cards . . . As they near the wire . . ."

I fell. I couldn't help it.

". . . EEEEEE . . . EEEEEE . . . EE . . ."

"NOOO!" Henri yelled. Get up! Get up!"

I struggled to my feet, grabbed the refrigerator by the handle and the door swung open wildly, sending me swirling across the floor.

". . . House of Cards!!!"

"What did he say?" I yelled.

Henri grabbed the radio. "WHAT?"

". . . House of Cards has edged the valiant Locomotion here today at Monmouth in one of the greatest races ever. Yes, race fans . . ."

Henri turned to me and, in one motion, threw the radio thirty feet into the library. "We WON!!! We did it!"

I jumped six feet into the air. "Yahhhhhh!"

We danced around the kitchen like mad men. We threw utensils. We smashed heads of lettuce and tossed them like confetti. It was bliss—sheer- undiluted, high-octane bliss.

"Wine!" Henri screamed. "Let's celebrate with one of my finest!"

"Why not," I agreed, laughing and crying.

We downed a bottle of wine, and followed that with another of champagne. We were ecstatic. We couldn't stop laughing.

"I'm gonna' buy that damned horse," Henri proclaimed, pouring champagne over his head "and build it a palace. That's right. With pastures and all the mares he could ever want. He'll live well, I promise you that."

We were still going strong about an hour after the race when the phone finally rang. "Yee yahh!" I yelled, laughing merrily, "that would be our boy Kenny." I sashayed over to the wall and yanked the receiver off the hook. "Who's fleece was white as snow," I said, giggling.

There was no answer.

". . .Who's fleece was white as snow," I repeated, this time more seriously.

Still no answer.

"Kenny?"

"Yeah."

"What gives?"

"I . . . ah . . ." he stuttered.

I sobered up fast. "Kenny!" I demanded, "you did get the bet in, didn't you!"

"Yeah. . . . I got it in."

I let out a sigh of relief. "And you got it? You collected, didn't you?"

". . . ah . . . yeah . . . we collected, all right."

I looked at Henri and winked. "He collected," I said. "He's got the dough! So when are you getting back, Kenny? After all, we need to—ha, ha—flow the cash ASAP."

". . . There's a hitch," he said.

I experienced a sudden sinking feeling. It was apparent something was very wrong. I shook my head and motioned to Henri.

He took the phone and cocked it so we could both hear. "Where's the freaking money, London?" he asked. "And where's that fruit bag, Wilmer?"

". . . Gone," Kenny replied very softly, almost whispering.

Henri and I shuffled our feet anxiously. "Gone!" Henri yelled. "Just what the hell do you mean, gone?"

". . . I seen something . . ." Kenny said. "I . . . I . . ."

"What?" demanded Henri. "Where's Wilmer? Did you make the exchange?"

"No."

Henri slammed the table with his palm. Whomp! "Did he give you the slip or something? I'll fry that two bit physicist, I swear. Where did he duck you?"

"In the lobby of The Charlton Hotel."

"Wha'd he use, the elevator?" Henri asked. "The back door?"

"No," Kenny replied. "Was nothing like that. It was like, one second he was there, the next he wasn't. Gone, that's all. He just . . . disappeared."

The word *disappeared* hit me like a sledge hammer. "Oh my God!" I started to hyperventilate. Taking hold of the chair to keep from falling, I took very deep breaths and slowly regained some composure. "D-d-disappeared," I stuttered. "As in completely?"

Henri looked at me questioningly, and then in a split second he understood. His mouth flew open. "Noooo!" he wailed. "You don't think . . ."

I placed the palms of my hands carefully on the sides of my head and rubbed my temples slowly. "Let's just stay calm here," I cautioned. "Let's remain sane." I took the phone from Henri. "Kenny, tell me exactly what happened."

"I don't know, Donny" he answered honestly. "We were supposed to meet in the lobby of the Charlton Hotel. By the telephones. I was there."

"And?"

"And then I seen him. He came into the lobby, right through the front door, and I thought, wow, what a cinch. He had the attache case in his hand and he waved it at me. The money was inside. I know, 'cause he called from the track and told me he had it. Anyway, he comes trooping on in . . ."

"You sure it was him?" I interrupted.

"Bermuda shorts, hush puppies, Hawaiian shirt, Mickey Mouse sunglasses."

I groaned. "Yeah, that's our boy, all right. Go on."

"So he comes on into the lobby and spots me. And just as he does, this look kinda hits his face."

"What kinda look?" I demanded.

"I'm not sure," Kenny said. "You know, like rapture or something. Like he'd hit the lottery or the daily double. Happy, but more than just happy."

"Got you. Then?"

"He comes walking right at me then stops. Right there in the center of the lobby. People start to back away from him 'cause he looks kinda weird, what with this look and all. I say, 'Doc, you got the beans? You got the bongos? Doc . . .' But all of a sudden he starts looking around the lobby like he can't see me or something. 'Kenneth,' he says, 'I hear you . . .' and he's looking all around the place with this twisted smile on his mug. 'Doc!' I yell, 'right here by the fire extinguisher. It's me, Kenny. You got the dough?' He holds up the attache case. 'Yes, Kenneth,' he says, 'but I can't seem to . . .' And then it happened."

"What?"

"He just started to like . . . fade."

"No!" Henri howled.

"Oh yeah," Kenny continued. "He was there and then, poof, he wasn't. Just like that. I-I-I ain't never seen . . ."

"You're crazy, London," Henri screamed. "You're in cahoots with that . . ."

"NO!" Kenny protested. "Ask anyone. People were running and screaming. I wasn't the only one who saw it, Henri. The bell boy fainted and the hotel manager called the cops. People were going nuts. I ain't never . . ."

"The *money*, Kenny!" Henri yelled desperately. "Please, tell me what happened to my *money*."

"Gone. Disappeared right along with the Doc. He tried to toss it. He did. But he just couldn't manage. He was holding it up to me when . . . poof."

"Oh . . . my . . . God," I moaned. "He's actually gone and done it. And here I thought he was nothing but a crank. Now he's gone off to another focus of realization, or whatever he called it. He told me all along, I just wouldn't believe him."

Henri grabbed me by the shirt and lifted me up. "Are you trying to tell me that God has lifted my four big boys?"

I shrugged. "Yeah, I guess. Why not? That's as good an explanation as any, I suppose."

Just then the other phone line rang. I brushed Henri aside, put London on hold, and answered.

"Yes or no?" It was Crowntooth.

"Would you mind holding for just a second, Buck?" I asked.

I pushed the buttons. "Kenny," I said, "are you absolutely sure of what you saw? Are you positive the dough is history?"

"I'm sure."

"OK. Take care," I hung up.

Henri broke into a blubbery whimper. "What's God want my money for?" he whined. He wandered back and forth aimlessly. "It's not as if he needs it, right? I mean, what's going on?"

Before I could answer, he became suddenly enraged. He hurled his drink across the room and charged down the hallway. He threw open the front door and leaped out onto the stoop. He pointed threateningly at the sky and shouted. "Give me back my money! Now! You hear me?" When nothing happened, he fell to his knees and began rocking back and forth. Then he tried again. "I had you figured for a cut. I swear it! What, did you think, I'd welch? No way. I had you down for a fat percentage, God, I swear. I-I-I'll take a lie detector test. Yeah, I'll . . ."

"You're losing it," I observed. "Listen to yourself, already."

"No, no, I'm serious," he protested. "I'll take a . . ."

I shook my head negatively. "God don't care about some lie detector test," I argued. "You're reaching."

"But I . . ."

I put my arm around his shoulder. "Forget it," I said, "it's no use. It's gone. Wilmer is gone and the money is gone with him. Forever. And now it's all over." He stretched out on the front stoop and wept.

I went back inside and picked up the phone. "Yes or no?" Crowntooth repeated.

"No," I said.

Click.

24

Senator Winston Boggs stroked his silver mustache and glared at Henri dramatically. "Never before, sir," he declared contemptuously, "have I encountered conduct of such a despicable nature." He pointed theatrically, slowly allowing the entire room to drink in the gesture before continuing. "You, sir, are a cur, a pox on this wonderful and decent land of ours. Never have I witnessed such uncommon greed, such deceit and arrogance in one man. I stand before you in utter shock, appalled now by the mere mention of your name. My colleagues and I are . . ."

". . . at an absolute loss for words," interrupted Senator Lester Hooton. "Stunned, speechless, aphonic, and mute is what I am. Shocked dumb, inarticulate, unable to put this entire thing into words." He glowered at Henri. "You have robbed me, Dr. Lafayette, of something far greater than coin. For you have robbed both me and my countrymen as well, you villain, of our innocence!"

"But no one has been shocked more than I," shouted Senator Eileen Spindle. "The lives that have been ruined by this man, why the sheer bestiality of his . . ."

"Nor I . . ."

"May I say . . ."

"Order! Order!" Clayton Crowntooth shouted, as he pounded the gavel in an attempt to bring the hearing under control.

It was our first day before the special congressional committee called to look into the American Rain scandal, and the senators before us circled like blood-frenzied sharks, the sweet scent of piety driving them all into uncontrollable spasms of self-serving hyperbole.

"Can we try and keep this thing movin' along and not go on about our feelings so much, folks?" Buck Crowntooth asked. "Elsewise, we's gonna' be here all night."

"I for one would be pleased to stay all night," countered Winston Boggs, "if it would serve the people's interest to do so. Why, I would stay for a week, sleep on the floor, starve if it were necessary, just to remain true to the oaths I have given my constituents and the great and noble voters of this country. No greater gift . . ."

"Not only would I be pleased to stay," Lester Hootin broke in, "but I would consider it offensive to leave without carrying out to our last gasping breath the duty with which this committee has been so honorably charged. Why, I'm reminded of a . . ."

"Folks!" Clayton Crowntooth demanded, "do I have to remind you all that the topic of the day is Dr. Lafayette and his consulting firm, American Rain. Let's address the topic, if at all possible, and not go on about our strongly held beliefs, no matter how sincere our convictions." He turned to Winston Boggs. "I believe that Senator Boggs was set to outline the charges against Dr. Lafayette."

Winston Boggs raised his eyebrows. "Indeed, I am," he stated, forcefully grabbing a piece of paper in front of him and whipping it across the table. Slowly he raised his eyes to the awaiting crowd. "I have here in my possession a lengthy list of sinister speculations, insidious insinuations, and downright suggestive suppositions, my friends, the mere accumulation of which lends great credence to a clear presumption of guilt against Dr. Lafayette for the unmentioned charges levied against him." He hesitated for a moment, allowing the merit of his statements to take effect, then continued. "But so strong is the case I bring before you today," he droned on, "that it will convince all in attendance of the vile nature of Henri Lafayette. For I come to you not only armed with damning speculation, insinuation, and supposition, but with real, honest-to-goodness *rumors* as well!"

"Rumors!" Lester Hootin cried. "My God man, you have actual *rumors*?"

Winston Boggs smiled. The chamber was buzzing. "I do indeed," he acknowledged.

Clayton Crowntooth frowned. "This is most serious," he admitted. "If you have in your possession actual rumors against this individual, I would ask that you bring'em on out in the open, Senator, so's we can all judge for ourselves."

"I intend to, Mr. Chairman," Winston Boggs replied, "but first I move the committee consider assassinating the witness's character at this juncture in the hearing."

Crowntooth rubbed his chin and turned to the other members of the committee. "There's a motion before us to assassinate Dr. Lafayette's character before moving on to the rumors at hand. All in favor say 'Aye,' those against 'Nay.'

The vote was over in a second. "The 'Ayes' have it," said Clayton. "The floor is still yours, Senator Boggs."

The senator smiled imperiously. "Do you deny, Dr. Lafayette, that you drink to excess? Do you deny cavorting with known madames of the night, breaking marriage vows, being seen with gamblers and horsemen of questionable repute? Do you deny . . ."

". . . spending an inordinate number of hours in the university library?" interrupted Lester Hootin. "Why, Dr. Lafayette? Was it because you were studying to be a Marxist or because you are a Marxist even as we speak? Admit it, Doctor! Admit that . . ."

". . . you hated your mother!" screamed Eileen Spindle. "Go on, deny it, you cavalier, capitalistic, Type A personality!"

"I have evidence the man is a homosexual!" a senator from the end of the row howled.

"Well, I have evidence the man maintains a harem of over six hundred concubines!" another countered.

"Deny, Sir, if you can," continued Winston Boggs, "the fact that you drank beer your freshman year in college."

"There is some suggestion," Eileen Spindle went on, removing her glasses, "that you cheated on at least one examination in the sixth grade. Do you care to elaborate?"

"All right!" Clayton Crowntooth interjected, "I believe the aforementioned character assassination has been effectively carried out. I would suggest we move on to the more serious matter of these rumors Senator Boggs was talking about. Now, I would . . ."

"I'm not quite finished," argued Winston Boggs, nose in the air, "and I will not yield the floor until I am." He spun about and faced Henri accusingly again. "Do you deny that you are a ruthless, unprincipled, lowdown, egg-sucking, communist loving, capitalistic, yellow-bellied . . ."

Henri changed position with a sudden grace and ease of movement I would not have thought him capable of.

In one quick action, he grabbed a book off of the table in front of us, leaped to his feet, and threw a perfect strike, drilling Winston Boggs directly in the forehead and sending him head-over-heels backwards onto the floor. The act was so unanticipated and carried out with such dazzling marksmanship that for a second no one in the entire room knew what to do. The senators sat motionless and stared in wonder at Henri as Boggs lay dazed and incommunicative on the carpet at their feet.

But then Eileen Spindle seized the moment and let out a blood curdling screech. "Ahhhhh! An unprecedented act of aggression has just taken place in these hallowed chambers," she cried, "and we can not let it go unpunished!"

The committee's political ire was aroused. "Impeach Lafayette!" Lester Hootin wailed. And then they all rose in a wave against Henri.

"Excommunicate him!"
"Censure! Censure!"
"Hang the lout!"
"Exile the cur!"

"Now hold on here, folks," Buck Crowntooth pleaded. "Let's conduct this investigation with just a tinge of decorum. Now what do you say?"

"The witness is an undemocratic beast," protested Eileen Spindle. "Why, just look what he has done to poor Senator Boggs who was only exercising his first amendment rights. Tell me, Mr. Chairman," she continued, "if there is any good that can be spoken of this awful man?"

All eyes were on Clayton Crowntooth. Clearly the committee was in the mood for a lynching, and only something of substance could stop them. Buck looked up and down the seated row of senators, at Henri, then back at the committee again. He did not want the hysteria to go too far, for he knew if it got entirely out of hand, the investigation would eventually lead to his door. Still, he was hard pressed to think of anything good to say about Henri. He gritted his teeth, then glanced down at Winston Boggs who groaned mournfully as he slowly regained consciousness. He pointed. "That was one hell of a shot!" he declared happily. "Now y'all got to admit, the man can throw a book with the best of 'em."

Eileen Spindle screwed up her face.

"Boooo!" Lester Hootin said. The others fell in line.

"Hisss!"

"Nooo!"

"All right," Clayton said, surrendering to the blood lust. "Y'all have it your way. Sue me for thinking the fella has one whale of an arm."

Eileen Spindle's eyes glowed red. The senators closed in for the kill. In the audience, reporters wrote furiously, trying to keep up. Then a man stood up behind us. Everything came to a stop. "Yes?" said Eileen Spindle. I turned to see who it was.

"David Winthrop," he said, "Senator from Maryland. And I have something good to say about Dr. Lafayette. In fact," he went on with a smile, "I have quite a few good things to say about him."

Eileen Spindle frowned. "You do, huh?"

"Indeed, I do," he went on. "I know of many people who owe their very lives and health to Dr. Lafayette's kind generosity. He is an open and giving man. I know first hand. You see . . ." he went on, explaining in great detail the impact of Henri's charity, speaking eloquently on behalf of his kindness and compassion. David Winthrop went on and on. The clock ticked. Lunch neared. Senators started glancing at their watches. The air slowly went out of the hang Henri balloon. Eileen

Spindle started doodling on her pad. When David Winthrop finally finished, most people were yawning.

"Well now, there you go," said Clayton Crowntooth, slapping the table top. "Fella over there thinks the witness is a fine ol' body. Now me, I wouldn't know, but our colleague does sound convincing. I move to adjourn the proceedings."

"Never!" countered Lester Hootin. "For today maybe, but not indefinitely. This matter is far too important to the American people to let it drop. Justice, Mr. Chairman, must prevail."

Buck was outnumbered and he knew it. "OK," he said, "till next Monday. Vote."

The vote carried. Henri jumped to his feet and hurried out of the chambers, passing the waiting press who shouted and elbowed one another for a chance to question him. But he ignored their questions. He barged through their groping ranks and burst into the hallway at full steam. I was on his heels, pushing the reporters aside, dodging flashbulbs all the way. It was madness. In the hall, we hesitated one moment. Then a door opened down the hallway to our left. Crowntooth whistled for us. We ran for our lives, and the door slammed behind us with a whack.

"Can't talk long," Buck said, huffing and puffing, frowning miserably. "Look fellas," he went on, "I tried my best out there, but gosh they are after you something fierce. That Winthrop fella saved your sorry behind today, but they will think of a way to have him occupied next time and you'll be on your own. They all got their snoops out, you know, and by next Monday, who knows what they'll come up with."

"If they get into the real stuff," I advised, "like the fake degrees, the fake practice, and the fake everything else, you'll smell like bacon frying in there by the time they're finished with you, Henri. We simply have to sidetrack this somehow."

"I'm starting to feel like Custer," Henri replied, wiping the sweat from his forehead.

Buck shook his head. "You should have it so good," he said. "You'll wish you were Custer by the time they are finished with you. He went fast, you know."

"What do you suggest, Buck?" Henri's shoulders drooping forlornly.

"Damned if I know, boys," Clayton answered. "But make it good and make it fast. These committee scumbuckets are playing for keeps. Too bad you couldn't come up with the cash."

"Yeah," Henri said, throwing his coat over his arm and putting on a large pair of sunglasses. "Happy trails, Buck."

"Happy trails, Henri."

We ducked out a side entrance.

Jules drove us back to the house. He took a bizarre route through Washington at close to one hundred miles an hour just to make sure no one followed. When we got home, we both went to the library for a drink. I had a double. Everything seemed to be in a state of utter collapse. I couldn't get over how fast it all happened.

I turned on the television. The evening news. The anchor smiled knowingly. He was grey, tanned, and regal. He was perfect. He turned slowly to a screen behind him. "And now," he said solemnly, "for the latest on the strange and still unfolding story of American Rain. Ted Barnett is on the steps of the Capital Building in Washington, D.C., with an update. Ted?"

"Well, that's right, John," said Ted, listening intently to his earplug. "Strange and still unfolding to say the least." The camera zoomed in on Ted's face. "A rough day started early this morning for the now notorious Dr. Henri Goldleaf Lafayette III in one of the most bizarre, hostile, and combative hearings this reporter has ever witnessed. Amid wild allegations of misconduct hurled from virtually every corner, Dr. Lafayette maintained a composed, almost bored, attitude throughout most of the proceedings."

The camera then cut to an artist's rendering of Henri, sitting like a stone, then quickly to another of Winston Boggs screaming at the top of his lungs, angry flecks of sweat buzzing around his lathered face like indignant bees as furious senators hurled accusation after accusation at the ponderous shrink.

"John, Lafayette remained absolutely dispassionate for hours until suddenly, incredibly, and with no warning whatsoever, he jumped to his feet, fingered a large brown book (cut away to an artist's rendition of a large brown book), and tossed it halfway across the room, striking Winston Boggs directly between the eyes and knocking the senator unconscious onto the floor. (Cut away to a close-up of the soles of two black shoes, one pointing this way, one pointing that.)

"Ted, that is truly unbelievable," said John, the anchor. "Has anything like this ever happened before?"

"Not to my knowledge," replied Ted Barnett. "At least not such a spectacular shot, John. The gallery was truly stunned by the precision of Dr. Lafayette's aim."

The anchor tugged at his earplug. "Yes, he's obviously a very talented fellow. And I understand there is more."

"Indeed. Quite a bit more, John." (Cut away to film of Molly Brickowski in tight denim jeans banging a guitar and singing on the capital steps.) "Despite all the controversy swirling around Dr. Lafayette," continued Ted Barnett, "he is not without his supporters. Today up and coming recording artist Molly 'B' staged a sing-in in support of the doctor, regaling the small but vocal crowd with her new release, a make over of the Tammy Wynette smash, 'Stand by Your Man.' It was an emotionally charged performance, John. The crowd really got into it."

"I'll bet. But there have been some rather sinister reports," the anchor continued, "concerning Dr. Lafayette. For instance, Ted, we are given to understand that the noted nuclear physicist, Dr. Myron Wilmer, was one of Dr. Lafayette's patients. Do you feel there is any connection between American Rain and the doctor's sudden and unexplained disappearance?"

"No telling, John. My sources on the Hill tell me the FBI will be looking into just that possibility. This story just keeps growing in dimension. Who can tell where it will lead?"

John's brow furrowed. "Of course, there has been some speculation that Dr. Lafayette is in actuality some sort of enemy agent sent here to drain our resources and destroy our best minds. Any thoughts?"

"Well, that's certainly occurred to some very influential people, John. But who can tell at this juncture?"

"Right. Now, I understand you have an interview for us, Ted."

"Yes. I have here Counselor—could you just step this way—Ian Stanforth, the famed trial attorney from Baltimore, for his impressions on the day's hearing. Counselor?"

"Thank you, Ted. Well, I certainly felt that Mr. Lafayette took quite a beating this afternoon, and he emerged the obvious loser from the hearing room. I thought he displayed for all to see his true, violent, antisocial colors out there on the floor."

"That opinion wouldn't be tainted at all by the fact you have lodged a one hundred billion dollar law suit against Dr. Lafayette, would it, Counselor?" asked Ted.

"Not in the least," Stanforth replied without hesitation. "My assessment is one hundred percent objective."

"And how about the committees' overall approach to the witness? They seemed just a bit on the offensive. Any comments?"

"I thought the committee members conducted themselves with style and intelligence," Stanforth said. Of course, now that the opening volleys have been fired, so to speak, I would expect that the questioning of the witness might become a bit more . . . factual in nature."

"Factual, Counselor?"

"Yes, factual. You know, Ted, facts, evidence. That sort of thing."

"So you feel that facts ought to be introduced into the proceedings?"

"Oh . . . a few, Ted."

"And how would you categorize the future for Dr. Lafayette, Mr. Stanforth?"

"Grim indeed. The man's past is nothing if not a testament to promiscuity, corruption, venality, and greed. Soon it will all hit the fan."

Ted turned to face the camera thoughtfully. "Well, there you have it: an insider's analysis. We now await round two of Dr. Lafayette verses the people. From the capital building, Ted Barnett reporting."

I turned the television off and looked at Henri. His face drooped miserably. "Curtains," he said.

"No, we can't take this lying down," I protested. "We've got to dream up a good plan is all."

He shook his head no. "I'm fresh out," he said. Then he took his drink and slowly dragged himself out of the room.

I stuffed my hands down into my pockets and turned around. Kiddo Kenny London was standing by the window, staring raptly into the heavens. I hadn't seen him come in. "Kenny," I said, "where'd you come from?"

He turned to me. "Oh. . . . Hi, Donny."

"What's up?" I said, looking towards the window and skyward despite myself.

He stared at me for a long while without saying a word. He was not the Kenny London I remembered. "I have no idea anymore," he said. "Do you?"

25

I sat back down and put my feet up. "Kenny," I said, "why do you keep looking out the window?"

"Because I never done it before, Donny," he replied. "See what I'm saying? I mean, I looked but I never really saw." He rubbed his face and pointed suddenly to the sky. "You know, there's something out there," he said, mysteriously. "Something... different, something ... I never thought about before." He smiled a lopsided smile. "Where did Doc Wilmer go, Donny?"

I frowned. "I really don't know, Kiddo. But he knew he was going. He knew he was close. He told me so."

Kenny understood. "All my life, I ain't never thought of nothing but bread. Francs, marks, dollars, pounds sterling, diamonds, gold, stocks—you name it. When I was just a kid, Donny, six or seven maybe, I used to steal crabs off the trucks down on Lombard Street and sell them to the crab houses uptown for a buck. I hustled papers in the winter, snow cones and pit-beef in the summer. Always, I got a cut. Always. Then one day this guy disappears right in front of my face. You know? Poof! And now I can't get it out of my head." He dug down in his pocket and pulled out his gold money clip. He held it up to me. "There's more to life than this, Donny. You hear me?"

"I hear you."

He threw the money down on the desk and whacked the wall with the palm of his hand. "There's more to everything than this stuff, too," he said, staring at the wall. "I seen it, Don. I seen it with my own eyes. God, th-t-the guy just flat vanished, for Christ's sake. Wh-what we see here, Donny—the nice cars, the ponies, the ladies—is not all there is. There's something more here as well . . . something unseen."

"Kenny," I commiserated, "I'm as stumped as you are. I can't figure it. He said he was heading off to another focus of realization—to join the Creator. At first I thought the guy was a nut—you know, unraveling. But then this. . . . Well, now I reckon he made it."

Just then there was a knock on the door. I turned quickly. "Yes."

Pastor Frickenfrayor stuck his head in. "Got a minute?"

I smiled. "Sure, come on in, Pastor."

He looked as trim and fit as ever. His blue eyes shined. "Just wanted to say goodbye," he said. "I've founded myself a new . . . well, church I guess, and I'm off to do God's work."

"Great," I acknowledged. "Where about's you headed? And who's in it with you?"

"Well, so far, it's just me, son," he responded, "and I'm headed wherever I'm needed."

"Sounds good," I said. "You packing your new Bible?"

He shook his head. "Nope, no Bible." He pointed to his neck. "I threw away the collar in favor of this here set of overalls, and that new Bible of mine for a good claw hammer. I'm throwing away fancy words for simple deeds. I'm journeying forth to build, Donald."

"Build what?"

"Whatever needs building. God knows, there's plenty to be done. Just look out the window. People in need of safe places for their toddlers, old folks needing a hand with their roofs and fences. Whole darn country is falling apart. Why, you hardly have to walk two steps before bumping into something that needs mending. I imagine I'll be busy for the rest of my life all right, but each night when I lie down to rest, the world will be one fence or roof better off." He held up his hammer. "I feel the power, Donald. I am the power."

"Hallelujah!" I shouted.

He laughed. "Forgive my enthusiasm, but when you feel the power of the life force surging in your arms, well, it's difficult not to be swept away. I call it the Church of Good Works. Want to join?"

"Not me," I said, "I'm getting married."

"Getting married," the pastor repeated happily, "well, good for you. The world needs all sorts of builders, son. Some to build boats, some books, some families. It's all the same. When you hold your children in your arms, you'll know what I mean. I'll be in touch. Until then . . ."

I shook his hand. "Good luck."

"Pastor!" Kiddo Kenny called.

He stopped in his tracks. "Yes?"

Kenny stepped forward. "I heard what you said there—about your new church, I mean."

"Yes?"

"Pastor," I said, "you remember Kiddo Kenny London, don't you?"

"Of course," said the pastor. "Mr. London, I hardly recognized you. You seem a bit . . . well, beleaguered."

335

"This new church," Kenny pressed on, "is it taking on new members?"

"Indeed it is, Mr. London," answered Frickenfrayor. "Is there some chance that you may be interested?"

"Yeah . . . yeah, maybe," Kenny said, stroking his chin. "This life force thing . . . What is it? Like, can you catch it or what?"

The pastor smiled and put his hand on Kenny's shoulder. "Kenneth," he said, "I believe you may have already caught it." He winked and held up his new claw hammer. "Can you use one of these?"

Kenny grabbed the hammer and swung it back and forth. "As good as the next guy, I guess. I got some dough, you know. Not much, but some. We'll need it for grub and nails. Wha-da-ya say, Pastor?"

Frickenfrayor put his hand solemnly on Kenny's head. "You're in!"

Kenny looked up. "That's it?"

The pastor nodded. "Not too fancy, but it'll do."

"Sounds like a done deal," I observed.

"Yes," agreed the pastor, beaming at Kenny. "We have but one commandment, you know: To improve the world each day, board by board, nail by nail."

"I can handle that," Kenny declared. "And how about this life force gig? Can you cut me a slice of that action, Pastor?"

Frickenfrayor laughed. "You cut that one yourself, Kenneth!"

I shook my head in disbelief. "Stay in touch now, will you?"

"You bet," they both promised.

I walked them out to the front stoop and waved goodbye as they trooped happily down the walk to the street. I couldn't get over it. Myron Wilmer vanished into nothingness, the indomitable Henri seemingly

AMERICAN RAIN

broken and beaten upstairs, and now Pastor Frickenfrayor and Kiddo Kenny London in overalls, hammers in hand, marching off to nail America back together again. It was as if the world had been turned upside down. What next?

I had never before encountered Bruno Diamond but, as he stepped into my office, I knew him at once from Henri's vivid descriptions. He was unmistakable: six foot seven, two hundred and fifty pounds, the jutting jaw, Neanderthal brow, a blazing scar across one cheek—but most of all, those *eyes*. The dazzling, uncontrollable glint of those insane eyes flicking excitedly around the room. All that size, strength, and lunacy packed into one man: it was frightening. His presence spelled nothing but trouble. The question was—for whom?

"Good day," I said with measured calm, standing to greet him. "Can I help you somehow?"

He assumed a sort of amused posture, mouth dropping just slightly and a half-smile winding across his lips as if I had just demonstrated some remarkable display of wit. He said nothing.

I felt a distinct tightening in my chest. The man's arms looked like two huge hams. It was painfully apparent he could crush me in less than a second. "May I be of some service?" I almost pleaded.

He cocked his head just slightly to one side like a confused dog. The smile disappeared. "We got business," he said finally.

I swallowed hard. "Oh . . ." I said, trying very hard not to cry. "I . . . don't really recall. What sort of business?"

337

He shrugged. Again those glinty, crazy eyes.

Just as I started to feel the sweat coursing down my legs into my socks, Henri came flying into the room. I had never been so happy to see him. "Bruno!" he called in salutation, "Squish any bugs lately?"

Bruno smiled a cockeyed, this-far-from-the-loony-bin smile. "Naaaawwww, Henri," he said. "But maybe today, huh." He picked up a glass paperweight from my desk and slowly pulverized it between two monster hands. Then he giggled.

Henri clapped as the paperweight gradually formed a small pile of dust on the carpet. "Well done, Bruno!" he exclaimed. Then he turned to me. "I've decided to import a little muscle."

"That's reasonably evident. What, may I ask . . . for?"

He screwed up his face. "I'll let you know in due course," he replied. "Plenty of time for that."

I felt uneasy. "What do you have in mind, Henri? I hope it's nothing violent."

They looked at each other and burst out laughing. I squirmed. Then the phone rang. I grabbed it quickly. "Yeah?"

It was Buck Crowntooth. "Donald, I'm afraid the evil forces of righteousness are again circling for attack. You boys hatched any sort of plan yet?"

I handed the phone over to Henri. "It's for you."

Henri listened to Buck for awhile, then spoke very softly. "Buck, I do indeed have a plan. It's a good one. It should solve everything and leave you and all of your fine associates in good stead. I humbly apologize for any discomfort my actions may have inflicted upon you. I will not be around much longer to be a bother to anyone."

"Not around?" I said. "What's that mean?"

AMERICAN RAIN

"Yes, Buck, I will take care of everything. Adieu. . . . Adieu." Henri hung up.

"Just what in the hell is going on here?" I asked, hands on hips.

Henri's shoulders drooped noticeably. "You'll see," he replied weakly. "Now, let's get going."

"Going where?" I demanded. "I'm not going anywhere. I'm waiting for a call from Marcy."

He stepped forward and grabbed one of my elbows. Bruno took the other. Henri shook his head. "There's no time. It's all over."

"What do you mean all over?" I asked, squirming in their grip.

They pushed me toward the door. "We have to get on the move," Henri answered.

It was useless fighting. Bruno's grip was like a vice. "All right! All right! Just tell me where we're going."

"Downtown." Henri said. "And that's all I can say."

Jules brought the Rolls around and they shoved me into the front seat. I was scared to death. My heart was pounding. I had never seen Henri so tight-lipped and pensive. I couldn't believe he would ever do me any harm, but still. . . . "What's going down?" I asked anxiously.

Henri fidgeted in the back seat. "You'll see." Diamond smiled that erratic, erie smile of his and said nothing at all. We pulled away from the curb.

It certainly seemed as though I was being set up for something, but I couldn't imagine what. Then suddenly it hit me. THE INSURANCE MONEY! Henri had taken out that huge policy on me, and it was his last shot at big bucks. But he wouldn't! *Would he?*

I turned quickly and faced them both. "I want to know the plan right now! Come on, spit it out!"

Henri smiled and pointed to Jules. I turned and looked questioningly at the confused chauffeur, and, as I did, I heard Bruno Diamond slid quickly across the seat behind me. Before I could react, he grabbed me from behind. I felt the enormous strength of his arms and shoulders concentrated on my neck, and smelled the sharp, distinctive odor of chloroform filling my nostrils.

I tried to struggle. It was impossible. My whole being was nothing more than a tiny voice far back in my skull screaming, pleading, for my body to do something. But it just wouldn't listen. The last thing I remember was the brightly polished mahogany dash glistening in the sunlight. Consciously—but only for a second—I realized I was losing consciousness. Then there was nothing.

26

I awoke on the wings of a cloud, floating high above the water like a gull. The sun filled the sky. I had been tumbling in the wind, only faintly aware of the glistening surface of the water below as I desperately soared across the heavens. I was being chased by demons of indefinable intent. For how long this had been going on I did not know. Perhaps years. My throat was dry.

For quite some time, I was content to just lie on my cloud. I weighed nothing. I was spirit. Then gradually, my legs returned. Then my arms. In time, I heard above the water's din the heavy, rhythmic rasp of my own lungs. I was flesh again. Far away, there was a window. I struggled to see. Outside it was blue. A puff of cloud crossed my vision and tumbled out of sight. I sat up.

I felt my arms and legs. I rubbed my face. I was alive. Looking around, I was in a room I did not recognize. My head was very light and I could remember little. I lay back down for a moment then struggled up onto my elbow and swung my legs to the floor. The room began to spin hideously and I grabbed the bedpost to right myself. In time, the spinning subsided and I ventured out across the floor.

My limbs were rubbery and weak. With effort, I made it to a small table and held onto a chair. From there, I looked about. There were two twin beds and a small kitchen area. There was a television and, off to my left, a bathroom. Out the window, I could see a brilliant blue sky and a large body of water. Gentle waves broke on an empty beach nearby. I reached for an ashtray on the table and removed a packet of matches. Its cover read—The Sundowner Motel.

The sound of the surf drew me outside. In the parking lot, only a few cars lazed in the sun. There was no one around. I made my way across the hot asphalt to the beach. Far away, a dog barked. I realized as my feet burned that I only had a pair of slacks on. The sun felt good on my back.

Weaving down the beach to a small clump of pines, I removed my slacks and hobbled into the surf. The water was cold, delicious to the touch. I kneeled down to wash my face and arms. I tossed some on my head before standing up. The waves were gentle and the water calm. It was the Chesapeake Bay—where exactly I did not know, but I judged from the empty beaches and the green runs of pine that I was on the Eastern Shore of Maryland or maybe southern Virginia. A few yards up the beach, two crabs eyed me attentively. I took a deep breath and dove in.

The cold water hit me like an explosion. My chest heaved, my lungs raged, and I surged across the water's surface, stroke after heavy stroke, until blood bubbled in my limbs and a wonderful clarity returned. I swam maybe fifty yards out, turned, then started in. By the time I climbed onto the beach, my name had come back to me. Then it all came back—and with it, the vital, gnawing realization I was absolutely starved. I hurriedly returned to the room.

AMERICAN RAIN

In an instant, I was scared, confused, and angry. But most of all, I was hungry. I went to the little kitchen and ripped open the cabinets. Nothing. Under the counter, there was a small refrigerator. I found a can of Coke and some ice. I filled a glass with ice, poured the coke slowly, and consumed it in a frenzy, but there was no food anywhere. Out the door, a small restaurant attached to the motel office beckoned to me. Its red neon sign blinked open. I almost wept. I had never been so profoundly hungry.

I ripped open the closet door and found a suitcase. I needed money. I tore the suitcase apart and flung the contents across the bed. No wallet or cash. I spun around. On the nightstand by the bed was my wallet. I ran and grabbed it. Several twenty dollar bills fell to the floor. Almost weeping with joy, I scooped them up, tossed on a shirt and shoes, and flew out the door.

Above the restaurant entrance, a small air conditioning unit was purring. A trickle of water ran down the wall. I opened the door and went into the bright room. Somewhere unseen, a grill was cackling—the pungent aroma of burgers, bacon, and potatoes filling the air. I slid onto a stool at the counter. The waitress seemed friendly, but hesitated. Several men, contractors or fisherman I gathered, turned slowly and eyed me as well.

I felt uncomfortable. I looked across the counter and spotted my image in the mirror across the way. I was shocked. My face was covered with a considerable beard—two, maybe three days growth—and my face seemed pale and shallow. My hair was a mess. The waitress grabbed her pad and approached me slowly. "Whatcha havin', Hon?"

I looked the menu over quickly. "Steak, eggs, potatoes, pancakes. And bring me some orange juice, too. Two glasses, filled with ice."

She raised an eyebrow. "Hungry, I'd say." Then she added, smiling, "So, you finally decided to come up for air. You writers must be some kinda crazy breed."

I looked at her for a long while. I had no idea what she was talking about. Finally, I just smiled back. "Guess so."

The men farther down the counter shook their heads, laughed among themselves, and went back to their food.

When the food came, I ate like a beast. I licked the fork, ran bread across the emptied plate to sop up every last drop. I polished off both glasses of juice then burped contentedly.

My stomach full, I looked up and down the counter again. A few of the men had gone. Others continued eating, paying me no attention. But at the far end of the counter, an older fellow caught my eye. Quickly, he looked away. Then back again. He was staring. I looked back the other way and pretended not to care. But in the mirror, I could see him staring still, occasionally glancing at the newspaper he held in his hands. I called for the check.

The waitress came. "So, when do you expect to be done?"

". . . Excuse me?"

"With the book, silly. The big guy said you was writing a book. About the bay, crabs and such. So when's it going to be done?"

". . . The big guy?"

"Yeah, you know. The fella with those nutty eyes and the scar."

Bruno Diamond, I thought. "What else did he tell you?"

"Oh, nothing much. Just that you was busy as all get out and not to bother you or nothing cause you was very intense when you was working. We was all excited, seeing as how we don't have this kinda' thing go on much here in Crisfield." I nodded and glanced quickly in the mirror. The old guy was still staring. So that was where I was, Crisfield, Maryland. So when did you see him last?"

She laughed and looked at me as if I were crazy. "Last night, I guess. Boy, I guess you really are intense when you work not to notice that big sucker. He's hard to miss."

I faked a laugh and paid what I owed. I threw in a couple of bucks for a tip. Checking the mirror as I started to leave, I saw the old guy showing the newspaper to someone else. Then he pointed my way. The other guy shrugged. I left quickly.

Outside, there were newspaper dispensers by the motel entrance. I strolled over and looked for the *Baltimore Sun*, finding it at the end of the line. I dug out a quarter and slipped it in the slot. What I saw on the front page froze me in my tracks. There was a picture of Henri and another of me. The shot was old, from my teaching days, but me nevertheless. The headline read:

AMERICAN RAIN VICTIMS STILL UNACCOUNTED FOR

Harbor Search Continues

I quickly folded the paper under my arm and ran for my room. Throwing open the door, I jumped inside, slammed the door, locked it, and drew the curtains together. My heart was beating wildly. Slowly, carefully, I walked to the bed and sat down. I pulled out the paper and read on:

BALTIMORE—In the murky waters of Baltimore's usually placid inner harbor the search continues for the bodies of the two principal players in the now famed American Rain scandal that recently rocked the nation's capital. Members of the city's underwater search and rescue team have been combing the muddy water since late Monday evening when the Rolls Royce owned by Henri Goldleaf Lafayette III careened out of control and hurtled into the water. Eyewitness accounts confirmed the fact that Dr. Lafayette and Donald Mallory were the sole occupants of the vehicle at the time of the crash. The Rolls, recovered later that evening, is being held by the city police in conjunction with the FBI. Unconfirmed reports indicate that a tie rod in the vehicle's front suspension may have been hacksawed prior to the accident. Foul play has not been ruled out.

Agent Truman Spencer of the FBI is coordinating the investigative efforts and has been unavailable for official comment. He has, however, indicated unofficially that he doubts the incident was accidental. "Lafayette has a record as long as my arm," he was overheard confiding to another unidentified agent. "He's a conman's con. He's perfectly capable of pulling this sort of thing off and I don't believe for a moment that he or his sidekick, Mallory, are dead.

I rubbed my face and stood up. I paced back and forth across the motel room. "Holy cow!" I said. My throat was dry again. I filled a glass with ice, added water, and sat back down. I grabbed the paper and picked up where I had left off:

> Speculation concerning the accident has been both volatile and wild. Some, such as Agent Spencer and the noted attorney, Ian Stanforth, call the incident nothing short of an obvious ruse, while others, notably Senator Clayton Crowntooth, have characterized it as ". . . a sure-as-shootin' American tragedy and a witch hunt to boot." Senator Crowntooth has called for an end to what he calls "this here defiling of the dead whose mouths are too dern choked with water to rise in reply." He has gone on to characterize the ongoing investigation as "the work of the devil and some unscrupulous politicians." Support for Senator Crowntooth's position seems to be growing in Congress as well as across the land where Dr. Lafayette has fast become a folk hero of sorts. After release, for instance, of a national poll taken by CBS news yesterday indicating that seventy-seven percent of the population polled favored Dr. Lafayette to the congressmen and women who seemed to be publicly pillorying him, eighty-three percent of the congressional representatives available for comment switched their positions on the matter in favor of Dr. Lafayette.
>
> Whether Dr. Lafayette is a "con-man's con," as suggested by Agent Spencer, or "a dyed-in-the-wool American who served his country well as a precipitation consultant and died bravely in the line of duty," as was declared in a teary, emotional speech on Tuesday morning by Senator Crowntooth, may never be known for

sure. For the bodies of the two may never be recovered. Hope is growing dimmer by the hour. Lieutenant Geoffrey of the city's search and rescue team has stated that "hope of finding anything out there in that muck is next to nil. A body could get lodged up under these peers and never be found, or, worse, float on out into the bay as food for every scavenger in and around the area."

The search efforts, in all likelihood, will be called off within the next twelve hours if no new information comes to the fore concerning Dr. Lafayette and his young "genius" assistant, Donald Mallory. In all probability, the truth of American Rain and these two shadowy figures went into the murky waters of the Chesapeake Bay when their Rolls Royce took that cold, dark plunge three days ago. And there it will probably remain.

I put the paper down and took a deep breath. So that was it: scam! The insurance money was no doubt behind it. But that failed to explain where I was, how I got here, or what I was to do next. And what about Marcy? I had to reach her as soon as possible to let her know I was all right. My brain perked. I jumped from the chair and went to the nightstand by the bed. I grabbed the phone from the hook and started to dial, but the line was dead. I banged the receiver down several times, but it made no difference. Then I noticed a note behind the phone. It was in Henri's distinctive, muddled handwriting. I snatched it up and started reading:

Dear Featherweight,

By the time you get around to reading this, you will have put in a good snooze and hopefully be clear headed enough to grasp the strategy of my actions. That I chose to keep you uninformed of my plot and it's immediate aftermath was only a common-sense reaction to your impenetrable honesty which, no doubt, would have torpedoed us all somewhere along the line. If you find that somehow degrading, well, tough luck!

As you read this I want you to understand that I am gone. It is not what I had planned, but the only course of action left open to me. I had dragged our lives off the cliff and only you among us, I knew, was young enough to put one back together again. Bruno was good enough to drive you down to Crisfield and keep you drugged for a few days. The effects should wear off quickly.

Unfortunately, because of the tightness of our logistics, we were not able to inform your family or Marcy that the news of our deaths was—as far as you were concerned, at least—untrue. You may want to call them when the heat dies down. I have arranged for both of our obituaries to appear in Friday's paper. As for my obituary . . . well, your dear friend and financial guru is no more.

I had Bruno cash in your accounts—which remained untouched—and have packed away the cash in the lining of your suitcase. It is not a fortune by any stretch of the imagination, but it should tide you over for the duration. The monies secured from the insurance policy I had the foresight to take out on your life I have directed in my will to go to Ian Stanforth—in order to settle his absurd lawsuit against me. It isn't much but at this point in time I don't believe he has much of a choice. In passing, I will appear gracious and Stanforth will just have to choke on it. Once the lawsuit is history, the dust should settle and in a year or so, I believe you should be able to return to your normal life.

Donald, I have chosen the high road for once, but I want you to remember me always as the freewheeling bastard I was. I have followed my heart now to the big sky, to live for love, and to walk among the stars.

Adieu.
Your Idol,

Henri Goldleaf Lafayette III

I crumpled the note in my hands and wept. The big idiot had done it. He had gone down with the Rolls after all. Here I thought he was going to kill me, and all along, the opposite was true. It was all his twisted, demented idea of saving me. Tears rolled down my cheeks. I couldn't move.

I sat on the edge of the bed and cried for over an hour. I couldn't stop. Finally, I dragged myself away from the bed and washed my face. I had to pull myself together and call Marcy. I gathered some change and looked out the window. There was a phone booth at the end of the parking lot.

I opened the door and the afternoon sun hit me in the face like a hammer. I found it difficult to walk. Henri was gone, I kept thinking. Henri was dead. I struggled across the lot, and suddenly, about halfway across, I stopped, immobilized. Then I began to shake. I was dead, too! Not perhaps in body, but for all intent and purposes, I was just as dead as Henri. I had vanished from the face of the earth just as completely as Doc Wilmer had. My obituary would be in the morning paper. Everything I had ever been, had ever struggled to be, was gone. The thought went through me like an electric shock. I was nothing.

I didn't know what to do. I dropped the change back into my pocket and straggled to the beach. How could I call Marcy? What would I tell her? What could I offer her?

I walked along the edge of the pines until I found a secluded spot not far from the water's edge. I sat, gazing out over the bay, and was suddenly angry. I had been robbed! My identity had been whisked out from under my feet like a rug from under a circus clown and now I, like that befuddled clown, sat stunned and sore on my can, wondering where to turn.

I could think of nothing. So I sat and watched the small waves lap playfully at the beach like a cat's tongue. I fiddled with the sand. I sat for an hour or so until something simple finally dawned on me: I wasn't dead. My worldly identity had been snatched away, but I—my body, thoughts, and will—was still intact. What after all was I, I wondered? Was I merely the accumulated notions of the world, the collective . . . whatever of past accomplishments? Because if that was all I was, then surely I would die when my obituary ran in the morning paper. Because the world I had allowed to define me would consider me so. But if I was more, if, for instance, I was me—an entity separate from the world's opinion—then the death of the name Don Mallory wouldn't matter in the least.

I smiled. I had set out in search of my destiny with a vision of distance in my mind. Somewhere out there, I had thought, I would find my fate, across some river, or over the next mountain. But now I knew the truth. Destiny is not where you go, but what you become. And the things you become, those thoughts and feelings that knit together to both change and create you, cannot be scraped away like barnacles from a ship's bottom after journey's end. You and they become one. I stood and dug back into my pocket for some change. I headed for the phone.

"Marcy!" I cried when she answered.

There was a long hesitation. ". . . Donny?"

"Yeah, it's me," I assured her. "I'm OK."

She started to cry.

I held the receiver tightly, pleading with you, "Don't cry, Honey. It was all just one of Henri's stupid deals."

"Why didn't you *call* me?" she demanded.

"I was out of it." I explained the situation as best as I could. "Bruno Diamond had me drugged for a few days. I just now came to."

"Oh Donny," she moaned, "I'm so tired. I'm just worn out. I couldn't eat or sleep at all. All I could do was cry. Oh God, I'm a mess."

"I'm sorry."

She grew serious. "Donny, the FBI has been here looking for you. So have the police, congressional investigators, bank investigators. . . . Gosh, they're turning over every rock, searching for you and Henri."

"Well, I'm in Crisfield at a motel," I said, trying hard to hold my voice steady. "Henri's dead."

She started. "He is?"

"I have a note from him. He really did go down with the Rolls."

"Oh no," she said, barely above a whisper. She took a deep breath. "I always thought this thing would come crashing down one day. I just didn't know how hard it would land."

"I know."

"Oh Donny," she wept, "I'm just so glad you're alive. I hated myself for not being with you, for all the wasted time."

"Are we still getting married?" I asked her.

I could hear her smile over the wire. "Just let anyone try and stop us."

I sighed. "Marcy, I don't have much of anything to offer you now. No car, no job, no future. I don't even have my name anymore. Don Mallory is dead and buried. All I've got is me."

"That's all I want." There was no hesitation in her voice at all. "Those things don't matter to me. They've just been getting in the way."

My heart leaped. "I'm going to have to get out of Dodge for awhile. Let things cool down. I suppose anywhere that's not here will do, but I've got no car, no means . . ."

"Where are you exactly."

I told her.

"Fine. I'll leave first thing in the morning. I'll pack tonight and be there by noon tomorrow. That OK?"

"Damn right." I paused a moment. ". . . Are you sure about this?"

"I'm sure. Donny, I love you."

I hugged the phone. "I love you, too."

That night I slept fitfully. The bay was stormy; the sullen surf heaved about ominously like a moody actress. Flashes of distant lightning momentarily lit the motel room wall and the sound of faraway thunder rumbled across the water in black, angry waves.

About midnight, I got up and put on my pants. Down the road, I found a convenience store that was just closing. I bought a six-pack of cold beer and walked back to my room. After turning the air conditioner off, I opened the window. A cool breeze filled the curtains as I sat nearby sipping a can of beer and feeling somehow completely lost—yet absolutely at peace. It was an odd sensation. When I closed my eyes, I felt almost as if I could fly right out of myself—so tenuous anymore were my ties to my former life. I wondered if that was how Doc Wilmer felt when he disappeared. I opened my eyes quickly and pulled away. I grabbed another beer.

About 2:00 A.M., the phone rang. I jumped from the chair, spilling beer on the floor. I had fallen asleep and was groggy. I stumbled around and found the phone. "Hello?"

"I have a person-to-person call for Mr. Donald Mallory from Cherokee Spike Tobakeechew," the operator said.

"Who?" I answered, rubbing my eyes.

She repeated herself.

"But I don't know any Cherokee Spike Tobakeechew," I said, about to tell her the whole thing was a big mistake. Then a voice on the other end demanded in a perfect southwestern drawl, "Teck the dern cawl, idjit."

"Henri!" I yelled. "I'll take it, operator. I'll accept the call."

". . . 'Tain't no Henri. 'Tis Cherokee Spike a callin', boy. Say it!"

"Forget it," I said. "Come on, Max."

"Was hailing you, boy?"

"'Was hailing' me, bullshit. I thought you were dead, you stinking, gelatinous bastard. Why'd you leave me that note? Why'd you pull this shit on me?"

"'Twas the oney thang couldo."

"Yeah, like hell," I snorted. I grabbed his note from the nightstand. "What's this poetic crap about choosing the high road, following your heart to the big sky, and living among the stars?"

"'Tain't no crap, boy. I done rode out highway seven to these here Wyoming prairies cause'n my little gal, Molly B's, done wrastled herself up a ranch. Yer ol' Cherokee Spike's riding herd on little doggies and a singing ranchin' songs these days, idjit. I done lit out fo' the territories! Whadju thank, I kilt myself?"

I looked down at the note in my hands. "Yeah."

"Buffalo balls, boy! Ain't I learnt you no better than to go off a thinking fool thoughts like that what you just described? I lef' the note case'n the federalies stumbled upon yer sorry behind, see. Meanwhiles, I stole off to become a ranchin' man."

I laughed out loud. "You, a rancher?"

"There is sure more to livin', idjit, than that city life of your'n. Why, out here a body can stretch out and breathe. I learnt me a thing or two about pan fried beans, a good dawg, and a fine woman to boot. You could do worse, boy."

"The horse that could carry you ain't been born yet, Max." I scoffed.

"I do my ranchin' from a jeep, dude. This out here's what you call yer real life."

"Real life?"

"Real life."

"Well, Cherokee Spike, I'm certainly glad you called. Hope the FBI doesn't get a hold of you out there."

355

"They already come a calling, Lookin for some dern eastern lawyer fella named Lafayette er something, but they didn't find hide nary hair of'em out here. Just an ol' God-fearin', bronco-bustin', hard-drinkin' ranch hand name of Cherokee Spike."

"Well, God bless you, Cherokee Spike," I said. "Keep the sun out of your eyes and the injuns off your butt."

"I'll do that, boy. And someday . . . well, I'll a be in touch."

I hung up, laughing.

Henri's new identity just clinched something for me: Destiny is not where we go, but what we become. And what we become is nothing more than that which we work to be. I like to think it was for the better, but for better or worse, Henri was now Cherokee Spike. I turned and looked in the mirror. But who was I?

27

At first I wasn't nervous. At first I figured she had just gotten a late start or maybe stopped for gas. But as the minutes ticked away, I began to fidget. She'd had second thoughts, I fretted. Or maybe the FBI had come again. Maybe her phone had been tapped! What an idiot I had been to call her in the first place!

I packed my things and tried to relax. It was barely noon. And she was always late, I thought, wasn't she? So what's to sweat? But I could sit by myself no longer, so I strolled across the parking lot to the motel restaurant. I sat at the counter where I could see the road and ordered a glass of ice tea.

"Book all done?" the waitress asked.

"What?"

She motioned to my suitcases sitting on the curb near my room. "I see you're all packed to go, so I figured you must be finished."

"Oh yeah," I said, thinking quickly, "at least for the most part. The rest I can finish at home."

"What's the title?"

"The what?"

"You know, the title."

"Oh, the title," I stalled. "Ah, *Crisfield Chronicles*."

She smiled appreciatively. "That's nice. Am I in it?"

"Afraid not. It's all technical stuff for the most part. Very dry."

I looked down the counter and the old guy was staring at me again. Maybe he was the FBI, I thought suddenly. Then I took a long pull on my tea. Get a grip, I told myself. You're going crazy.

"Well, good luck," the waitress said.

"Thanks a lot."

Above the counter, the television blared. It was the noon news. I recognized the reporter. Ted Barnett. I glanced out the window again, but she was nowhere in sight. So I listened to Ted:

". . . to a live remote with Attorney Ian Stanforth. Mr. Stanforth . . ."

"Yes, Ted."

"I'm sure by now you've heard the news that the search in the inner harbor has been terminated. The FBI has also been called off the American Rain case. The official word is both Henri Lafayette and his assistant, Donald Mallory, perished in Tuesday's auto accident. Your reaction?"

"Disappointment, Ted. This whole accident business seems just a bit . . . well, staged to me, but . . ."

"But Mr. Stanforth," Ted interrupted, "the FBI admits they have checked out every conceivable lead on the two and come up empty-handed. Isn't it possible this was simply the work of two men who had been driven to the brink. Did you not yourself file a one hundred billion dollar lawsuit against Mr. Lafayette?"

"Well, yes, Ted, I did but I . . ."

"And isn't it altogether possible that personal rather than professional motivations are fueling your drive against Mr. Lafayette and have been all along?"

Ian Stanforth started to fidget. Not much—but if you looked carefully, you could tell. "I am after all a human being, Ted," he said, trying to appear reasonable, "and I suppose . . ."

"Mr. Stanforth," Ted interrupted again, "I'm sure you are aware that the other key figure in the recent accusations against Dr. Lafayette, Agent Truman Spencer, was this morning dismissed from his position and placed on administrative leave. This coming on the heels of a preposterous report filed by him alleging that Dr. Lafayette had, in fact, kidnapped the noted physicist, Dr. Myron Wilmer, and through some hitherto unknown scientific process somehow "faxed" the doctor to another country for sinister purposes. Your comments?"

Ian Stanforth frowned noticeably. This was not going well for him at all and he knew it. "Well, Ted, it was my understanding that Agent Spencer secured that information from an alleged eyewitness by the name of Kiddo Kenny London who . . ."

"Who said he saw the doctor disappear in the lobby of a hotel in New Jersey." Ted Barnett struggled to subdue a laugh. "And who recently tossed away a half a million dollar a year job to fix fences and porch swings for free in a recently organized cult by the name of The Church of Good Works. Do you really consider this man to be a reliable source, Mr. Stanforth?"

"Well, no, Ted, I . . ."

"I'm sure you are aware Agent Spencer has been ordered to undergo psychiatric evaluations. He was pulled virtually kicking and screaming from his office shouting some outrageous pap about Dr. Lafayette now being a cowboy in Utah or some such place. Really, Mr. Stanforth, how long will these ridiculous, hysterical accusations continue?"

Ian Stanforth started to sweat. Trickles ran down his face. He pulled a handkerchief from his pocket and started dabbing. "Ted, I can only . . ."

"I'm sorry to interrupt again, Mr. Stanforth, but we have to break. I'll be right back to you."

A commercial came on for window cleaner. I glanced at my watch: 12:16—and still no sign of her. I rubbed my face nervously and called for another glass of tea,

In short order, Ted Barnett returned. The screen suddenly split, catching Ian Stanforth dabbing his forehead, then stuffing the handkerchief awkwardly back into his top pocket. He tried on a thin, humorless smile. "Yes, yes," he said, grabbing his earplug.

"Sorry to leave you hanging there, Mr. Stanforth" Ted said, shifting through his notes. "Now, last evening Dr. Lafayette's last will and testament was read publicly by Senator Clayton Crowntooth. I'm sure you heard it."

"Yes, Ted."

"Most considered it a moving and enormously conciliatory document, an earnest attempt at undoing whatever damage may have been done during the doctor's lifetime. In it, of course, he offered you the tidy sum of two million dollars in settlement for your law suit against him. Most independent observers considered that to be a very gracious offer, considering the fact that your law suit is dead in the water now with the good doctor's passing. Your reaction?"

Ian Stanforth fiddled with his earplug. "I'm currently studying the document, Ted, and I'm not presently in a position to comment . . ."

"Mister Stanforth, really! The will was only three paragraphs long. Are you trying to tell the television audience it takes an attorney of your reputation and skill days to read and understand three measly paragraphs? Or are you just hedging, Sir, waiting to step up the shrill invective that has so characterized the poor doctor's opposition?"

I smiled. Ian Stanforth was coming unglued. Sweat covered his face. He accidentally yanked the earplug from his ear and wrestled with it on camera, eyes bulging, as if it were a venomous snake. Finally, he was rescued by standby television personnel. At the counter where I sat, people shook their heads and laughed outright. Stanforth looked like a fool. Henri had done it to him again.

"I . . . I . . . I . . ." Stanforth stammered, "I would be only too happy, Ted, to put this matter to rest. If the document is what it seems to be . . ."

"Really, Mr. Stanforth, the man is dead. The document speaks for itself. This is not the courtroom, Sir. Please stop stalling and give the American people a clear answer. Will you accept the will and drop your lawsuit?"

Ian Stanforth took one giant gulp. "Yes."

"Thank you."

The picture of Stanforth faded. Ted smiled at us all. "And now to other news."

I looked down the road; still no sign of Marcy.

The waitress chuckled at the television. "Things got a way of working themselves out, don't they?"

"Yup."

I looked up at Ted Barnett. "And later on the news at noon a report from Lisa McDuffy on the continuing investigation into the bizarre disappearance of Dr. Myron Wilmer. Also, special reports from Brad Lucas with eyewitness to disaster, Bruno Diamond, on how witnessing the awful accident involving Dr. Lafayette has brought him closer to God. We will also get an inside look at Clayton Crowntooth and David Winthrop, two Senators whose stars are on the rise. Stay tuned."

It was then I saw her. I jumped from my stool and ran out into the parking lot. She leaped from the car and gave me a hug. "Sorry I'm late, but I stopped to close my bank account."

I hugged her again. "I didn't realize you were late," I lied. "It doesn't matter anyway." I was thrilled to see her.

She pulled out a copy of the morning paper. "You look pretty healthy for a dead man."

I looked in the obituary section, and there I was. I nodded. "Henri did a pretty good job. Anyone follow you?"

She shook her head no. "I don't think so. I was real careful."

I smiled. "Good. Well, let me get my luggage."

I piled my stuff into the trunk of her car. There wasn't much. "Where do you want to go?"

She shrugged. "Wherever we can be together."

I kissed her. "Sounds good."

She slid into the passenger's seat and threw me the keys. I stood at the door and took one last look around. It had been a year to remember. I had found love and discovered what destiny was all about; you couldn't ask much more from life than that. I had come seeking greatness and been reduced justifiably to nonexistence. But now it didn't matter.

I looked down the road. It stretched on forever. It would lead wherever I wanted it to go. On this June morning the slate had been wiped clean for me. I was no more, yet here I was. It was up to me to fill in the numbers and I was confident I could do it well. Wilmer had been right: the will is supreme. I patted the car door and smiled. For on this, the day of my obituary, I had never felt more alive.

Give a Gift of Provocative Reading to Your Colleagues and Friends!

ORDER FORM

YES, I want ___ copies of *American Rain* at $18.95 each, plus $3 shipping per book. (Maryland residents please include $.95 state sales tax.) Canadian orders must be accompanied by a postal money order in U.S. funds. Allow 30 days for delivery.

☐ Check/MO • Charge my ☐ VISA ☐ MC ☐ AmEx

Name _____

Phone _____

Address _____

City/State/Zip _____

Card # _____ Expires _____

Signature _____

Check your leading bookstore or call
your credit card order to:
1-301-898-0300

Please make your check payable and return to:

Monacacy River Press
9095 Bessie Clemson Road
Union Bridge, MD 21791